The Pract
Rational E
Behavior Therapy

Albert Ellis, PhD, holds MA and PhD degrees in clinical psychology from Columbia University, and is the founder and President of the Albert Ellis Institute for Rational Emotive Behavior Therapy in New York City. He sees many clients for individual and group psychotherapy each week at the Institute's clinic, supervises its therapy and counseling trainees, and each year gives scores of talks, workshops, intensives, and training sessions in New York, and in many cities and universities in the United States and throughout the world. He has published more than 60 books and monographs, over 700 articles, and more than 150 audio and video cassettes. His well-known books include *Sex Without Guilt, Reason and Emotion in Psychotherapy, A Guide to Rational Living, How to Stubbornly Refuse to Make Yourself Miserable About Anything—Yes, Anything!, Overcoming Resistance* (Springer Publishing Company), and *Better, Deeper and More Enduring Brief Therapy.* He has received many honors and awards, including awards for the highest professional and clinical contributions of the American Psychological Association, the American Counseling Association, and the Association for the Advancement of Behavior Therapy.

Windy Dryden, PhD, is Professor of Counseling at Goldsmiths' College, University of London. He authored and edited more than 100 books, numerous book chapters and articles, and he has edited 12 book series. Among those books published by Springer is the first edition of this book *The Practice of Rational-Emotive Therapy, The Essential Albert Ellis: Seminal Writings on Psychotherapy, Overcoming Resistance: Rational-Emotive Therapy With Difficult Clients,* and *Doing RET: Albert Ellis in Action.* He is a Fellow of the Albert Ellis Institute of Rational-Emotive Behavior Therapy, the British Psychological Society, the British Association for Counseling, and is Consulting Editor of the *Journal of Cognitive Psychotherapy: An International Quarterly* (Springer Publishing).

The Practice of Rational Emotive Behavior Therapy

SECOND EDITION

Albert Ellis, PhD
Windy Dryden, PhD

SPRINGER PUBLISHING COMPANY
New York

Springer Publishing Company, LLC
11 West 42nd Street
New York, NY 10036

www.springerpub.com

Production Editor: Pamela Ritzer
Cover design: Mimi Flow
Composition: International Graphic Services

07 08 09 10 / 5 4 3 2 1

13-digit ISBN: 978-0-8261-2216-2 © 2007 Springer Publishing
Company, LLC

Library of Congress Cataloging-in-Publication Data

Ellis, Albert.
    The practice of rational emotive behavior therapy / Albert Ellis,
Windy Dryden.
       p.   cm.
    Contains revised and updated articles previously published.
    ISBN 0-8261-5471-9 (HB)
    ISBN 0-8261-5472-7 (PB)
    1. Rational-emotive psychotherapy. I. Dryden, Windy. II. Title.
    [DNLM: 1. Psychotherapy, Rational-Emotive—collected works.
    WM 420.5.P8 E47P 1997]
RC489.R3E457   1997
616.89'142—dc20
DNLM/DLC
for Library of Congress   96-32061
                                        CIP

Printed in the United States of America by Berryville Graphics.

Contents

Foreword

Psychotherapy requires a great deal of intellectual knowledge. To become a successful therapist requires that one reads many books and articles, and listens to hundreds of hours of lectures and workshops. However, despite all this verbal intellectual activity, when you close the door and are alone with the client, you have to act. You have to decide quickly what to say, what to ask, or to remain inactive. Was that a choice, or did I act passively because I did not know what to do? After years of training psychotherapists, I have come to view the practice of psychotherapy more like a motor sport or skill than like an intellectual activity. However, psychotherapy is a motor skill that rests on a great deal of knowledge. How do clinicians learn to go from theory to practice? The title of this book by Ellis and Dryden reflects the action aspects of psychotherapy.

Systems of psychotherapy have a number of parts. First, they provide a theory of psychopathology that explains how human disturbance develops. Next, they have a theory of intervention that should follow from the theory of psychopathology. The strategies proposed from the theory of intervention should match the mechanisms that are thought to lead to the disturbance. The theory of interventions usually has two components. The first I will call *strategies* and the second *techniques*. Strategies are the verbal and logical statements that the clinician hypothesizes to mediate the structure of the disturbed behavior and emotion in the particular cases. On the basis of the theory and the individual case, clinicians develop what we call a case conceptualization. A theory must be fixable enough to explain many individual cases. Based on the case conceptualization, the strategy suggests a plan of intervention. It identifies what hypothetical constructs proposed by the theory and case conceptualization require change to achieve clinically significant improvement for the client. Many theories are good up to this point. However, they are short on technique. What specific things do the therapists do or say to implement the strategic plan? New trainees often get the theory of psychopathology; they struggle to get the case conceptualization and the strategic plan. Then they ask themselves: "What do I do now?" Going from the abstractions to the actions is not always clear.

The Practice of Rational Emotive Behavior Therapy represents a compilation of years of theoretical and clinical insights distilled into a specific theory of disturbance and therapy and deductions for specific clinical strategies and techniques. Albert Ellis has an immense list of scholarly publications. He is an impressive intellectual force who is well read in philosophy, anthropology, and psychology. However, he is first a master clinician. He has focused all of his incredible knowledge on how to help reduce human suffering one patient at a time. He has always exemplified the pragmatic scholar. He is one of those rare people with expansive knowledge who can use his knowledge with surgical precisions.

The world's greatest Albert Ellis scholar, Windy Dryden from London, joins Al in this volume. Not only has Windy spent several decades studying Al's writings, he has spent hundreds, maybe thousands, of hours watching Al do therapy. Like Al, Windy is most interested in the consistent implementation of the theory into practice.

The resulting collaboration here is not just a smartly written, clear presentation of one of the most philosophical theories of psychotherapy, but a very practical volume as well. They titled this book *The Practice of Rational Emotive Behavior Therapy* because both authors are not satisfied for therapists to have only an intellectual understanding of REBT. Will/can they do it with real clients?

The structure of this book focuses on an explication of the theory, a chapter on basic practice, and a chapter on an in-depth case study. A detailed chapter follows on the practice of individual psychotherapy. Although the book is not broken into sections, the next four chapters represent a real treasure. The authors focus on using REBT in couples, family, group, and marathons sessions. Doing REBT with one person is difficult to learn. Once the clinician adds more people to the room with different and sometimes competing agendas, things get more complicated. These chapters will help not only the novice clinician but also the experienced REBT therapists work better in these types of sessions.

So, consider yourself lucky for having picked up this book. Reading it will help many people (and hopefully yourself) get better.

Raymond DiGiuseppe, PhD, ScD
Director of Professional Education, Albert Ellis Institute
Professor and Chair
Department of Psychology
St. John's University

Preface

Many excellent books for professionals have been published on rational emotive behavior therapy (REBT), including several of our own (Bernard, 1991; Bernard & Wolfe, 1993; Dryden, 1994a, 1994b, 1995a, 1995b; Dryden & DiGiuseppe, 1990; Dryden & Hill, 1993; Dryden & Neenan, 1995; Ellis, 1985c, 1994c, 1996a; Ellis & Grieger, 1986; Walen, DiGiuseppe, & Dryden, 1992; Yankura & Dryden, 1990, 1994). None of these books, however, systematically considers the major way in which REBT is used clinically, such as its use in individual, group, couples, family, and intensives therapy. Consequently, there is still no volume that systematically reviews the regular practice of REBT.

We have previously written books and articles covering important aspects of the practice of REBT (Dryden, 1985b; Ellis, 1971a, 1985c, 1993b), but some of these are outdated and/or out of print. Therefore, in this book we have revised and updated this previous material, added several chapters on new REBT formulations, and attempted to produce a volume that will present a comprehensive picture of the practice of REBT that can be used effectively by any therapist who wants to employ its important clinical modalities.

Not that this book covers all of REBT. Some of the volumes mentioned above include applications of REBT that are only briefly mentioned here. And some of its psychoeducational practices—such as its use in workshops, courses, and rational emotive behavioral training intensives—are barely discussed here. But the professional who wants to use REBT in its most popular clinical modes will find them described in detail in this book. While we do not expect it to replace other REBT writings, we hope that it significantly and usefully supplements them.

ALBERT ELLIS, PhD
WINDY DRYDEN, PhD

1

The General Theory
of REBT

In this first chapter we discuss the general theory underpinning the practice of REBT. First, we put REBT in historical context and trace some of its major influences. Second, we outline REBT's major theoretical concepts. Third, we put forward an expanded version of REBT's well-known ABC framework. Fourth, we consider REBT's perspective on the nature of psychological disturbance and health. Fifth, we elaborate this theme by detailing REBT's viewpoint on how psychological disturbance is acquired and perpetuated. Finally, we outline the REBT general theory of therapeutic change.

THE HISTORICAL DEVELOPMENT OF REBT

I (AE) founded rational emotive behavior therapy (REBT) in 1955 when I was a New York clinical psychologist, having begun my career in the helping professions in the early 1940s. As a result of research I was doing at that time for a massive work to be entitled *The Case for Sexual Liberty*, I gained a local reputation for being an authority on sexual and marital relationships. I was consulted by my friends on their sexual and relationship problems and discovered that I could be successful in helping them with these problems in a short period of time. I decided to pursue formal training in clinical psychology after discovering that there were no formal training possibilities then offered in sex and marital counseling. After getting a PhD degree in clinical psychology, I chose to be trained in psychoanalysis, believing then that it was the deepest and most effective form of psychotherapy available. I decided on this course

Parts of this chapter were adapted from Dryden and Ellis (1986) and W. Dryden and A. Ellis, "Rational-Emotive Therapy," in K. S. Dobson (Ed.), *Handbook of Cognitive-Behavioral Therapies;* New York: Guilford, 1987 (used by permission) and have been previously published in *The Nurse Practitioner: The American Journal of Primary Health Care, 12(7),* July 1987.

of action because my experiences as an informal sex-marital counselor had taught me that disturbed relationships were really a product of disturbed persons "and that if people were truly to be helped to live happily with each other they first had better be shown how they could live peacefully with themselves" (Ellis, 1962, p. 3).

I initially enjoyed working as a psychoanalyst, partly because it allowed me to express both my helping and problem-solving interests. However, I became increasingly dissatisfied with psychoanalysis as an effective and efficient form of treatment. In the early 1950s, I began to experiment with different forms of therapy, including psychoanalytically oriented psychotherapy and eclectic-analytic therapy. But although I became more effective with my clients, I remained dissatisfied about the efficiency of these methods. During this period of experimentation I returned to my lifelong hobby of reading philosophy to help me with my search for an effective and efficient form of therapy. One of the major influences on my thought at that time was the work of the Greek and Roman Stoic philosophers (e.g., Epicurus, Epictetus, and Marcus Aurelius). They emphasized the primacy of philosophic causation of psychological disturbances—a viewpoint that was not popular in America in the 1950s—and deemphasized the part played by psychoanalytic psychodynamic factors. This view was also largely promoted by several ancient Asian philosophers, especially Confucius, Lao-Tsu, and Gautama Buddha. In essence, these ancient philosophies, which stated that people are disturbed not by things but by their view of things, became the foundation of REBT, and this perspective (following my pioneering formulations) remains at the heart of present-day cognitive-behavioral approaches to psychotherapy.

Major Philosophical Influences

Apart from ancient philosophy, present-day REBT owes a philosophical debt to a number of other sources that have influenced its development. Immanuel Kant's writings on the power (and limitations) of cognition and ideation strongly impressed me, and the work of Spinoza and Schopenhauer was also important in this respect. Philosophers of science, such as Popper (1959, 1963), Russell (1965), and Bartley (1984), were also influential in helping me see that all humans develop hypotheses about the nature of the world. Moreover, these philosophers stressed the importance of testing the usefulness of such hypotheses rather than assuming that they are necessarily helpful. The practice of REBT goes along in many respects with the logicoempirical methods of science (Ellis, 1962, 1979d). REBT also stresses the flexibility and anti-dogmatism of the scientific method and opposes all dogmas, just as science does, and it holds that rigid absolutism is one of the main cores of human disturbance (Ellis, 1983a). Also, REBT in some ways predated and in other ways endorses some of the views of postmodernism (Ellis, 1994c, 1996a, 1996b).

Although the philosophy of REBT is at variance with devout religiosity, in one respect Christian philosophy has been most influential. REBT's theory of human value (which will be discussed later) is similar to the Christian viewpoint of condemning the sin but forgiving the sinner (Ellis, 1991b, 1991c, 1994c; Hauck, 1991; Mills, 1993; Powell, 1976). Due to its stand on self-acceptance and its bias against all forms of human rating, REBT allies itself with the philosophy of ethical humanism (Russell, 1950, 1965), which opposes the deification and devil-ification of humans. Since REBT considers that humans are at the center of their universe (but not of *the* universe) and have the power of choice (but not of unlimited choice) with regard to their emotional realm, it has its roots in the existential philosophies of Heidegger (1949) and Tillich (1977). Indeed, REBT has a pronounced humanistic-existential outlook (Ellis, 1973, 1991c, 1994c, 1996a).

I was also influenced, particularly in the 1960s, by the work of the general semanticists (e.g., Korzybski, 1933). These theorists outlined the powerful effect that language has on thought and the fact that our emotional processes are heavily dependent on the way we, as humans, structure our thought by the language we employ.

Major Psychological Influences

In developing REBT, I (AE) have similarly been influenced by the work of a number of psychologists. I received a training analysis from an analyst of the Karen Horney school, and Horney's (1950) concept of the "tyranny of the shoulds" was certainly an early influence on my emphasis on the primacy of absolute, dogmatic evaluative thought in the creation and maintenance of much psychological disturbance.

The work of Adler was important to the development of REBT in several respects. Adler (1927) was the first great therapist to really emphasize inferiority feelings—while REBT similarly stresses self-rating and the ego anxiety to which it leads. Like Adler and his Individual Psychology, REBT also emphasizes people's goals, purposes, values and meanings. REBT follows Adler in regard to the use of active-directive teaching, the stress placed on social interest, the use of a holistic and humanistic outlook, and the employment of a highly cognitive-persuasive form of psychological treatment (Ellis, 1991b, 1991c, 1996a).

Although REBT was originally termed Rational Psychotherapy, it has always advocated the use of behavioral methods as well as cognitive and emotive techniques in the practice of therapy. Indeed, I (AE) utilized the methods advocated by some of the earliest pioneers in behavior therapy (Dunlap, 1932; M. C. Jones, 1924; Watson & Rayner, 1920), first, in overcoming my own early fears of speaking in public and approaching women, and second, in the active-directive form of sex therapy that I practiced in the 1940s and 1950s. This behavioral active-directive emphasis remains prominent in present-day REBT.

In its 40 years of existence, REBT has been practiced in various therapeutic modalities (individual, group, marital, and family), by many kinds of helping professionals (e.g., psychologists, psychiatrists, social workers), and with a variety of client populations (e.g., adults, children, the elderly) suffering from a wide range of psychological disorders. Apart from its use in counseling and psychotherapy, rational emotive behavioral principles have been applied in educational, industrial, and commercial settings. A recent development has been the application of REBT to public education in the form of 9-hour intensive workshops. In this respect it is playing a significant role in the field of preventive psychology. REBT is practiced throughout the world, and there are REBT institutes, or centers, in the United States, France, Italy, West Germany, Holland, Australia, England, Mexico, Israel, and India. It is thus a well-established form of cognitive-behavioral therapy.

MAJOR THEORETICAL CONCEPTS

REBT is based on a set of assumptions that stress the complexity and fluidity of human beings. Given this fundamental view of human nature, REBT uses the following theoretical concepts.

Goals, Purposes, and Rationality

According to REBT theory, humans are happiest when they establish important life goals and purposes and actively strive to attain these. It is argued that, in establishing and pursuing these goals and purposes, human beings had better mind the fact that they live in a social world and that a philosophy of self-interest, where a person places him or herself first, also implies putting others a close second. This is in contrast to a philosophy of selfishness, where the desires of others are neither respected nor regarded. Given that humans will tend to be goal-directed, *rational* in REBT theory means "that which helps people to achieve their basic goals and purposes, whereas 'irrational' means that which prevents them from achieving these goals and purposes" (Dryden, 1984c, p. 238). Thus, rationality is not defined in any absolute sense but is relative in nature.

Humanistic Emphasis

REBT does not pretend to be "purely" objective, scientific, or technique-centered but takes a definite humanistic-existential approach to human problems and their basic solutions. It primarily deals with disturbed human evaluations, emotions, and behaviors. It is rational and scientific but uses rationality and science to enable humans to live and be happy. It is hedonistic, but it espouses long-range instead of short-range hedonism so that people may achieve the pleasure of the moment *and* of the future and may arrive at maximum freedom *and* discipline. It hypothesizes that probably nothing superhuman exists and that devout belief in superhuman agencies tends to foster dependency and increase emotional disturbance. It assumes that no humans, whatever their antisocial or obnoxious behavior, are damnable nor subhuman. It particularly emphasizes the importance of will and choice in human affairs, even though it accepts the likelihood that some human behavior is partially determined by biological, social, and other forces (Bandura, 1986; Ellis, 1973, 1988, 1994c, 1996a).

The Interaction of Psychological Processes and the Place of Cognition

REBT theory has, from its inception, stressed an interactive view of human psychological processes. Cognitions, emotions, and behaviors are not experienced in isolation and often, particularly in the realm of psychological disturbance, overlap to a significant degree. Recently, REBT has stressed the inferential nature of activating events and has shown how events (or more correctly, how we perceive events) again interact with our cognitive evaluations, emotions, and behaviors (Ellis, 1994c, 1995a). This point will be amplified in the section titled "The Revised ABCs of REBT."

Given this interactional view, it is true, however, that REBT is most noted for the special place it has accorded cognition in human psychological processes, particularly the role that evaluative thought plays in psychological health and disturbance. One of REBT's unique contributions to the field of cognitive-behavior therapy lies in its distinction between rational, and irrational Beliefs. Rational Beliefs are evaluative cognitions of personal significance that are preferential (i.e., nonabsolute) in nature. They are expressed in the form of "desires," "preferences," "wishes," "likes," and "dislikes." People experience positive feelings of pleasure and satisfaction when they get what they desire and experience negative feelings of displeasure and dissatisfaction (e.g., sadness, concern, regret, annoyance) when they do not get what they desire. These negative feelings (the strength of which is closely related to the importance of the desire) are regarded as healthy responses to negative events and do not significantly interfere with the pursuit of established or new goals and purposes. These Beliefs, then, are "rational" in two respects. First, they are flexible, and second, they do not impede the attainment of basic goals and purposes.

Irrational Beliefs, on the other hand, differ in two respects from Rational Beliefs. First, they tend to be absolute (or dogmatic) and are expressed in the form of rigid "must's," "should's," "ought's," "have-to's," etc. Second, they lead to negative emotions that largely interfere with goal pursuit and attainment

(e.g., depression, anxiety, guilt, anger). Healthy Beliefs strongly tend to underlie functional behaviors, whereas unhealthy Beliefs underpin dysfunctional
behaviors such as withdrawal, procrastination, alcoholism, and substance abuse
(Ellis & Knaus, 1977; Ellis, McInerney, DiGiuseppe, & Yeager, 1988; Ellis &
Velten, 1992).

Two Basic Biological Tendencies

Unlike most other theories of therapy, which stress the impact of significant
life events on the development of psychological disturbance, REBT theory
hypothesizes that the biological tendency of humans to think irrationally and
dysfunctionally has a notable impact on such disturbance. Its view that irrational and dysfunctional thinking is heavily determined by biological factors
(always interacting with influential environmental conditions) rests on the
seeming ease with which humans think crookedly and the prevalence of such
thinking even among people who have been "rationally" raised (Ellis, 1976a).
While I (AE) have acknowledged that there are social influences operating
here, I have also noted that even if everybody had had the most rational
upbringing, virtually all humans would often irrationally change their individual and social preferences into absolutistic demands on (a) themselves, (b)
other people, and (c) the universe around them (Ellis, 1985a, 1988, 1994c).
    The following constitutes evidence in favor of REBT's hypothesis of the
biological basis of human irrationality:

1. Virtually all humans, including bright and competent people, show evidence of major human irrationalities and self-defeatism.
2. Virtually all the disturbance-creating irrationalities (absolutistic shoulds and
   musts) that are found in our society are also found in just about all social and
   cultural groups that have been studied historically and anthropologically.
3. Many of the self-destructive behaviors that we engage in, such as procrastination and lack of self-discipline, go counter to the teachings of parents, peers, and the mass media.
4. Humans—even bright and intelligent people—often adopt new irrationalities after giving up previous ones.
5. People who vigorously oppose various irrational behaviors often fall prey
   to these very irrationalities. Atheists and agnostics exhibit zealous and
   absolutistic philosophies, and highly religious individuals act immorally.
6. Insight into irrational thoughts, feelings, and behaviors helps only partially
   to change them. For example, people can acknowledge that drinking alcohol in large quantities is harmful, yet this knowledge does not necessarily
   help them abstain from heavy drinking.
7. Humans often fall back to self-defeating habits and behavioral patterns
   even though they have often worked hard to overcome them.

8. People often find it easier to learn self-defeating than self-enhancing behaviors. Thus, they very easily overeat but have great trouble following a sensible diet.
9. Psychotherapists who presumably should preferably be good role models of rationality often act irrationally in their personal and professional lives.
10. People frequently delude themselves into believing that certain bad experiences (e.g., divorce, stress, and other misfortunes) can never happen to them (Ellis, 1976a, 1979e, 1994c).

However, REBT holds that humans have a second constructivist biological tendency, namely, to exercise the power of human choice and to work toward changing their dysfunctional thinking and acting. Thus, they have (1) the ability to see that they make themselves disturbed by the irrational views they bring to situations, (2) the ability to see that they can change their thinking, and, most important, (3) the ability to actively and continually work toward changing this thinking and behaving by the application of cognitive, emotive, and behavioral methods. While REBT theory asserts that humans have a strong biological tendency to think dysfunctionally (as well as functionally), it holds that they are by no means slaves to this tendency and can transcend (although not fully) its effects. In the final analysis, then, the REBT image of the person is quite an optimistic one (Dryden, 1994a, 1995b, 1995c; Ellis, 1973, 1994c, 1996a; Ellis & Bernard, 1983, 1985; Kelly, 1955; Mahoney, 1991).

Two Fundamental Human Disturbances

According to REBT, humans easily make absolute demands on themselves, other people, and the world. However, if these demands are more closely investigated, they can be seen to fall into two major categories of psychological disturbance: ego disturbance and discomfort disturbance (Ellis, 1979a, 1980a, 1994c, 1996a).

In ego disturbance a person makes demands on self, others, and the world; and if these demands are not met in the past, present, or future, the person becomes disturbed by damning "self." As I (WD) have shown, self-damnation involves (1) the process of giving my "self" a global negative rating and (2) "devil-ifying" my "self" as being bad or less worthy (Dryden, 1984b). The rational and healthy alternative to self-damnation is unconditional self-acceptance (USA), which involves refusing to give one's "self" a single rating (because it is an impossible task due to one's complexity and fluidity and because it normally interferes with attaining one's basic goals and purposes) and acknowledging one's fallibility.

In discomfort disturbance or low frustration tolerance (LFT), the person again makes demands on self, others, and the world that are related to dogmatic commands that comfort and comfortable life conditions must exist.

When these demands are not met in the past, present, or future, the person feels disturbed and tends to *awfulize* and create *I-can't-stand-it-itis*. Tolerating discomfort in order to aid goal attainment and long-range happiness is the healthy and rational alternative to demands for immediate gratification.

Thus, as will be shown later, self-acceptance and a high level of frustration tolerance are two of the main cornerstones of the rational-emotive image of the psychologically healthy human being (Ellis, 1979e, 1994c, 1996a).

THE REVISED ABCS OF REBT

When REBT was originally established, I (AE) employed a simple ABC assessment framework to conceptualize clients' psychological problems (Ellis, 1962). In this schema, "A" stood for the Activating event, "B" represented a person's Belief about that event, and "C" denoted the person's emotional and behavioral responses, or Consequences, to holding the particular Beliefs at "B." The major advantage of the ABC framework lay in its simplicity. However, its simplicity was also a disadvantage in that important distinctions between different types of cognitive activity were glossed over (Wessler & Wessler, 1980). It is important to note that different REBT therapists use different expanded versions of the original ABC framework (cf. Ellis, 1985c; Wessler & Wessler, 1980). There is thus no absolutely correct way of conceptualizing clients' problems according to such an expanded schema. What is presented below is one version of the revised ABC framework (Ellis, 1985b, 1994c).

Activating Events or Activators (A's) of Cognitive, Emotional, and Behavioral Consequences (C's)

The REBT theory of personality and personality disturbances begins with people trying to fulfill their Goals (G's) in some kind of environment and encountering a set of Activating events or Activators (A's) that tend to help them achieve or block these Goals. The A's they encounter usually are present or current events or their own thoughts, feelings, or behaviors about these events, but they may be embedded in memories or thoughts (conscious or unconscious) about past experiences. People are prone to seek out and respond to these A's because of (1) their biological or genetic predispositions, (2) their constitutional history, (3) their prior interpersonal and social learning, and (4) their innately predisposed and acquired habit patterns (Ellis, 1976a, 1979e, 1983b, 1994c).

A's (Activating events) virtually never exist in a pure or monolithic state; they almost always interact with and partly include B's and C's. People bring themselves (their goals, thoughts, desires, and physiological propensities) to A's.

Beliefs about Activating Events

According to REBT theory, people have almost innumerable Beliefs (B's)—cognitions, thoughts, or ideas—about their Activating events (A's); and these B's importantly exert strong influences on their cognitive, emotional, and behavioral Consequences (C's). Although A's often seem to directly "cause" or contribute to C's, this is rarely true, because B's normally serve as important mediators between A's and C's and therefore more directly "cause" or "create" C's (Bard, 1980; Ellis, 1962, 1994c; Goldfried & Davison, 1994; Grieger & Boyd, 1980; Wessler & Wessler, 1980). People largely bring their Beliefs to A; and they prejudicially view or experience A's in the light of these biased Beliefs (expectations, evaluations) and also in the light of their emotional Consequences (C's). Therefore, humans virtually never experience A without B and C, but they also rarely experience B and C without A.

B's take many different forms because people have many kinds of cognitions. In REBT, however, we are mainly interested in their rational Beliefs (RBs), which, we hypothesize, lead to their self-helping behaviors, and in their irrational Beliefs (IBs), which, we theorize, lead to their self-defeating (and societal-defeating) behaviors. We can list some of the main (but not the only) kinds of B's as follows:

Nonevaluative Observations Example: "(I see) . . . the man is walking." Such observations do not go beyond the available data. They are nonevaluative because they are not relevant to our goals. When such observations are relevant to our goals, they become evaluative; for example, when the man walking is my father, who has just recovered from a car accident. The evaluative aspects of such "evaluative observations" are often implicit—for example, "(I am pleased that) . . . the man is walking."

Nonevaluative Inferences Example: "The man who is walking is going to the post office." Such cognitions are called "inferences" because they go beyond the available data. All we are able to observe in this example is a man walking in a certain direction. Although he is proceeding in the direction of the post office, he may or may not be "going to the post office." As such, inferences may be viewed as hypotheses about our observations that may or may not be correct. These inferences are nonevaluative when they are not relevant to our goals. When such inferences are relevant to our goals, they become evaluative—for example, when the man who may be going to the post office will bring us back our birthday parcels (if indeed he does make such a visit). The evaluative aspects of such "evaluative inferences" are again often implicit—for example, "(it is good that) . . . the man who is walking is going to the post office."

It is helpful to realize, for assessment purposes, that inferences are frequently chained together (Moore, 1983) and that it is often important to find the most relevant inference in the chain, that is, the one that overlaps with the person's "musturbatory" evaluations (i.e., events that are dogmatic in nature and couched in the form of must's, should's, ought's, and have-to's, etc.) Thus, if a client reports experiencing anger at his wife for forgetting the shopping, shopping may not actually be the "event" that triggers his anger-producing evaluations. The inference chain may be revealed thus: wife forgets shopping → I will mention this to her → she will nag me → I won't be able to watch the football game on TV in peace. Any of these inferences may trigger anger-creating evaluations, and it is often important to involve clients as fully as possible in the assessment process by asking questions to help them provide reliable information concerning their most relevant inferences in particular chains.

Positive Preferential Evaluations Example: "I prefer people to approve of me" or "I like people to approve of me . . . (but they do not have to)." These cognitions are termed "positive preferential evaluations" because (1) they are flexible and nonabsolute (statements like "but they do not have to" are rarely stated but are implicit in such cognitions), and (2) they refer to what the person evaluates as positive—"people approving of me." They are often termed "rational" in REBT theory because they tend to aid and abet a person's basic goals and purposes.

Let us assume that a man who holds the Belief "I prefer people to approve of me" observes a group of people laughing and infers that they are laughing *with* him. This person may conclude the following based on the positive preferential evaluation that he likes approval and the inference that they are laughing with him:

"(I presume) . . . they think I am funny."
"(I presume) . . . they like me."
"(I presume) . . . their liking me has real advantages."

These cognitions are all positive, nonabsolute inferences because (1) they go beyond the available data, (2) they are relevant to the person's goal (he is getting what he values), and (3) they are not held with absolute conviction.

"My ability to make them laugh is good."
"It's pleasant to hear them enjoy themselves."

The latter are both positive, nonabsolute evaluations because this man is appraising his ability to make them laugh and their pleasure at laughing in a positive but relative manner.

Positive Musturbatory Evaluations Example: "I must have people approve of me." Such cognitions are termed "positive musturbatory evaluations" because they are absolute and dogmatic and they refer to what the person evaluates as positive in a devout manner. They are often termed "irrational" in REBT theory in that they tend to impede and inhibit a person from achieving his or her other basic goals and purposes.

Let us again assume that a group of people are laughing with a man and presumably like him. He may conclude the following based on his positive musturbatory evaluations. Thinking errors are categorized in parentheses:

"I am a great, noble person!" (overgeneralization)
"My life will be completely wonderful!" (overgeneralization)
"I deserve to have only fine and wonderful things happen to me!" (demandingness and deification)

These are all positive, absolute evaluations. The evaluations of "I" and the world are positive and grossly exaggerated.

"I am sure they will always like me." (delusions of certainty)
"I am convinced that I will always please them." (delusions of certainty)

The latter are both positive, absolute inferences because (1) they go beyond the data at hand, (2) they are positively relevant to the person's goal, and (3) they are held with absolute conviction.

Negative Preferential Evaluations Example: "I prefer people not to disapprove of me . . ." or "I dislike people disapproving of me . . . (but there's no reason why they must not disapprove of me)." These cognitions are termed "negative preferential evaluations" because, once again, (1) they are flexible and nonabsolute (statements like "but there's no reason why they must not . . ." are also rarely stated but are again implicit in such Beliefs); and (2) they refer to what the person evaluates as negative—"people disapproving of me." They are also termed "rational" in REBT theory because they tend to aid and abet a person's basic goals and purposes.

This time let us assume that a man who holds the Belief "I prefer people not to disapprove of me" observes a group of people laughing but infers that they are laughing *at* him. This man may conclude the following based on the negative preferential evaluations:

"(I presume) . . . they think I am stupid."
"(I presume) . . . they don't like me."
"(I presume) . . . that their not liking me has real disadvantages."

These are all negative nonabsolute inferences because (1) they go beyond the data at hand, (2) they are relevant to the person's goal (he is getting what he dislikes), and (3) they are not held with absolute conviction.

This man may further conclude:

"It's unfortunate that they are laughing at me."
"It would be bad if I have some unfortunate trait."

These are both negative, nonabsolute evaluations. The evaluations of his "situation" and of his "unfortunate trait" are negative and nondevout (i.e., not absolutistic).

Negative Musturbatory Evaluations Example: "I must not have people disapprove of me." Such cognitions are termed "negative musturbatory evaluations" because (1) they are absolute and dogmatic and (2) they refer to what the person evaluates as negative in a devout manner. They are further examples of irrational Beliefs in that they tend to impede the achievement of a person's basic goals and purposes.

If we assume again that a group of people are laughing at a man and presumably disapprove of him, he may conclude the following based on the above negative musturbatory evaluations. Again, the categories of thinking errors are listed in brackets.

"I am an incompetent, rotten person!" (overgeneralization, self-downing)
"My life will be completely miserable!" (overgeneralization, awfulizing)
"The world is a totally crummy place!" (overgeneralization, awfulizing)
"I deserve to have only bad or good things happen to me!" (demandingness and damnation)
"This is awful, horrible, and terrible!" (awfulizing)
"I can't bear it!" (I-can't-stand-it-itis)

These are all examples of negative absolute evaluations. The people and things appraised are all evaluated in a negative and grossly exaggerated manner.

"I will always act incompetently and have significant people disapprove of me." (overgeneralization)
"They know that I am no good and will always be incompetent." (non sequitur, jumping to conclusions, mind reading)
"They will keep laughing at me and will always despise me." (non sequitur, jumping to conclusions, fortune-telling)
"They only despise me and see nothing good in me." (focusing on the negative, overgeneralization)
"When they laugh with me and see me favorably, that is only because they are in a good mood and do not see that I am fooling them." (disqualifying the positive, non sequitur, phonyism)
"Their laughing at me and disliking me will definitely make me lose my job and lose all my friends." (catastrophizing, magnification)

"They could only be laughing because of some foolish thing I have done
and could not possible be laughing for any other reason." (personalizing, non sequitur, overgeneralization)

The above seven are all examples of negative absolute inferences because
(1) they go beyond the data at hand, (2) they tend to sabotage the person's goal,
and (3) they are held with absolute conviction.

Consequences (C's) of Activating Events (A's) and Beliefs (B's) about A's

C's (cognitive, affective, and behavioral Consequences) follow from the interaction of A's and B's. We can say, mathematically, that A × B=C, but this for-
mula may actually be too simple, and we may require a more complex one
to express the relationship adequately. C is almost always significantly
affected or influenced but not exactly "caused" by A, because humans naturally react to some degree to stimuli in their environments. Moreover, when
A is powerful (e.g., a set of starvation conditions or an earthquake), it tends
to affect C profoundly.

When C consists of emotional disturbance (e.g., severe feelings of anxiety,
depression, hostility, self-deprecation, and self-pity), B usually (but not always)
mainly or more directly creates or "causes" C. Emotional disturbance, however, may at times stem from powerful A's—for example, from environmental
disasters such as floods or wars. Emotional disturbance may also follow from
factors in the organism—for example, hormonal, disease, or biochemical factors—that are somewhat independent of, yet may actually "cause" C's.

When strong or unusual A's significantly contribute to or "cause" C's or
when physiological factors "create" C's, they are usually accompanied by con-
tributory B's too. Thus, if people are caught in an earthquake or if they experience powerful biological changes and they "therefore" become depressed,
their A's and their physiological processes probably are strongly influencing
them to create irrational Beliefs (IB's), such as, "This earthquake shouldn't have
occurred! Isn't it awful! I can't stand it!" These IB's, in turn, add to or help create their feelings of depression at C.

C's usually consist of feelings and behaviors but may also consist of thoughts
(e.g., obsessions). C's (Consequences) that follow from A's and B's are virtually
never pure or monolithic but also partially include and inevitably interact with
A and B. Thus if A is an obnoxious event (e.g., a job refusal) and B is, first, a
rational Belief (e.g., "I hope I don't get rejected for this job!") as well as, second, an irrational Belief (e.g., "I must have this job! I'm no good if I don't get
it"), C tends to be, first, healthy feelings of frustration and disappointment and,
second, unhealthy feelings of severe anxiety, inadequacy, and depression.

So A × B=C. But people also *bring* feelings (as well as hopes, goals, and
purposes) to A. They would not keep a job unless they desired or favorably

evaluated it or unless they enjoyed some aspect of it. Their A therefore partially includes their B and C. The three, from the beginning, are related rather than completely disparate.

At the same time, people's Beliefs (B's) also partly or intrinsically relate to and include their A's and their C's. Thus, if they tell themselves, at B, "I want to get a good job," they partly create the Activating event at A (going for a job interview), and they partly create their emotional and behavioral Consequences at C (feeling disappointed when they encounter a job rejection). Without their evaluating a job as good they would not try for it nor have any particular feeling about being rejected.

A, B, and C, then, are all closely related, and none of them tends to exist without the other.

THE NATURE OF PSYCHOLOGICAL DISTURBANCE AND HEALTH

Psychological Disturbance

Rational emotive behavioral theory, then, posits that at the heart of neurotic disturbance lies the tendency of humans to make devout, absolutistic evaluations of the perceived events in their lives. As has been shown, these evaluations are couched in the form of dogmatic "must's," "should's," "have to's," "got to's," and "ought's." We hypothesize that these absolutistic cognitions are at the core of a philosophy of devout Beliefs that is a central feature of much human emotional and behavioral disturbance (cf. Ellis, 1991b, 1991c, 1995a). These Beliefs are deemed to be irrational in REBT theory in that they usually (but not invariably) impede and obstruct people in the pursuit of their basic goals and purposes. Absolutist must's do not invariably lead to psychological disturbance because it is possible for a person to devoutly believe "I must succeed at all important projects," have confidence that he or she will be successful in these respects, and actually succeed in them and thereby not experience psychological disturbance. However, the person remains vulnerable in this respect because there is always the possibility that he or she may fail in the future. So although on probabilistic grounds REBT theory argues that an absolutistic philosophy will frequently lead to such disturbance, it does not claim that this is absolutely so. Thus, even with respect to its view of the nature of human disturbance REBT adopts an antiabsolutistic position

REBT theory goes on to posit that if humans adhere to a philosophy of "musturbation" they will strongly tend to make a number of core irrational conclusions that are deemed to be derivatives of these "must's." These major derivatives are viewed as irrational because they too tend to sabotage a person's basic goals and purposes.

The first major derivative is known as "awfulizing." This occurs when a perceived event is rated as being more than 100% bad—a truly exaggerated and magical conclusion that stems from the Belief: "This must not be as bad as it is."

The second major derivative is known as "I-can't-stand-it-itis." This means believing that one cannot experience virtually any happiness at all, under any conditions, if an event that "must" not happen actually occurs or threatens to occur.

The third major derivative, known as "damnation," represents a tendency for humans to rate themselves and other people as "subhuman" or "undeserving" if self or other does something that they "must" not do or fails to do something that they "must" do. "Damnation" can also be applied to world or life conditions that are rated as being "rotten" for failing to give the person what he or she "must" have.

Although REBT holds that "awfulizing," "I-can't-stand-it-itis," and "damnation" are secondary irrational processes in that they tend to stem from the philosophy of "must's," these processes can sometimes be primary (Ellis, 1983b, 1994c, 1995a). Indeed, Wessler (1984) has argued that they are more likely to be primary and that "must's" are derived from them. However, the philosophy of "must's," on the one hand, and those of "awfulizing," "I-can't-stand-it-itis," and "damnation," on the other, are in all probability interdependent processes and often seem to be different sides of the same "cognitive" coin (Ellis, 1994c).

REBT notes that humans also make numerous kinds of illogicalities when they are disturbed (Ellis, 1985c, 1994c). In this respect, REBT agrees with cognitive therapists (Beck, Rush, Shaw, & Emery, 1979; Burns, 1980) that such cognitive distortions are a feature of psychological disturbance. However, REBT theory holds that such distortions almost always stem from the "must's." Some of the most frequent of them are

1. *All-or-none thinking:* "If I fail at any important task, as I *must* not, I'm a *total* failure and *completely* unlovable!"
2. *Jumping to conclusions and negative non sequiturs:* "Since they have seen me dismally fail, as I *absolutely should* not have done, they will view me as an incompetent worm."
3. *Fortune-telling:* "Because they are laughing at me for failing, as I *absolutely should* not have done, they will despise me forever."
4. *Focusing on the negative:* "Because I *can't stand* things going wrong, as they *must* not, I can't see any good that is happening in my life."
5. *Disqualifying the positive:* "When they compliment me on the good things I have done, they are only being kind to me and forgetting the foolish things that I *absolutely should* not have done."
6. *Allness and neverness:* "Because conditions of living ought to be good and actually are so bad and so intolerable, they'll *always* be this way and I'll *never* have any happiness."

7. *Minimization:* "My good shots in this game were lucky and unimportant. But my bad shots, which I *absolutely should* never have made, were as bad as could be and were totally unforgivable."

8. *Emotional reasoning:* "Because I have performed so poorly, as I *absolutely should* not have done, I feel like a total nincompoop, and my strong feeling proves that I *am* no damned good!"

9. *Labeling and overgeneralization:* "Because I *must* not fail at important work and have done so, I am a complete loser and failure!"

10. *Personalizing:* "Since I am acting far worse than I *absolutely should* act and they are laughing, I am sure they are only laughing at me, and that is *awful!*"

11. *Phonyism:* "When I don't do as well as I *ought* to do and they still praise and accept me, I am a real phony and will soon fall on my face and show them how despicable I am!"

12. *Perfectionism:* "I realize that I did fairly well, but I *absolutely should* have done perfectly well on a task like this and am therefore really an incompetent person!"

Although REBT clinicians at times discover all the unrealistic and illogical Beliefs just listed—and a number of others that are less frequently found with clients—they particularly focus on the unconditional "should's," "ought's," and "must's," that seem to constitute the philosophic core of irrational beliefs that lead to emotional disturbance. They hold that if they do not get to and help clients surrender these core Beliefs or underlying schemas, the clients will most probably keep holding them and create new irrational derivatives from them.

REBT practitioners also particularly look for "awfulizing," "I-can't-stand-it-itis," and "damnation," and they show clients how these almost invariably stem from their "must's" and can be surrendered if they give up their absolutistic demands on themselves, on other people, and on the universe. At the same time, rational emotive behavior therapists usually encourage their clients to have strong and persistent desires, wishes, and preferences, and to avoid feelings of detachment, withdrawal, and lack of involvement (Ellis, 1972a, 1973, 1985c, 1991c, 1994c, 1996a).

More important, REBT holds that unrealistic and illogical beliefs do not *in themselves* create emotional disturbance. Why? Because it is quite possible for people to unrealistically believe, "Because I frequently fail, I always do"; and it is possible for them also to believe illogically, "Because I have frequently failed, I always will." But they can, in both instances, rationally conclude, "Too bad! Even though I always fail, there is no reason why I *must* succeed. I would *prefer to*, but I never *have to* do well. So I'll manage to be as happy as I can be even *with* my constantly failing." They would then rarely be emotionally disturbed.

To reiterate, the essence of human emotional disturbance, according to REBT, consists of the absolutistic "must's" and "must not's" that people think *about* their failure, *about* their rejections, *about* their poor treatment by others, and *about* life's frustrations and losses. REBT therefore differs from other cognitive-behavioral therapies—such as those of Bandura (1986), Beck (1976), Goldfried & Davison (1994), Janis (1983), Lazarus (1989), Mahoney (1991), Maultsby (1984), and Meichenbaum (1992)—in that it particularly stresses therapists looking for clients' dogmatic, unconditional "must's," differentiating them from their preferences, and teaching them how to surrender the former and retain the latter (Bernard, 1991; Dryden, 1994a, 1995b, 1995c; Ellis, 1962, 1985c, 1994; Ellis & Becker, 1982; Ellis & Harper, 1975; Grieger & Woods, 1993; Phadke, 1982; Walen, DiGiuseppe, & Dryden, 1992).

Psychological Health

If the philosophy of musturbation is at the core of much psychological disturbance, then what philosophy is characteristic of psychological health? REBT theory argues that a philosophy of relativism or "desiring" is a central feature of psychologically healthy humans. This philosophy acknowledges that humans have a large variety of desires, wishes, wants, preferences, and so forth; but if they refuse to escalate these nonabsolute values into grandiose dogmas and demands, they will become less psychologically disturbed. They will, however, experience healthy negative emotions (e.g., sadness, regret, disappointment, annoyance) when their desires are not fulfilled. These emotions are considered to have constructive motivational properties in that they both help people to remove obstacles to goal attainment and help them to make constructive adjustments when their desires cannot be met.

Three major derivatives of the philosophy of desiring are postulated by rational emotive behavioral theory. They are deemed to be rational in that they tend to help people reach their goals or formulate new goals if their old ones cannot be realized.

The first major derivative of desiring, *rating or evaluating badness* (or anti-awfulizing), is the rational alternative to "awfulizing." Here, if a person does not get what she wants, she acknowledges that this is bad. However, because she does not believe "I *have to* get what I want," she contains her evaluation along a 0%–100% continuum of badness and therefore does not rate this situation as "awful"—a rating that is placed on an exaggerated level. In general, when the person adheres to the desiring philosophy, the stronger her desire, the greater her rating of badness will be when she does not get what she wants.

The second major derivative of desiring is known as *tolerance* and is the rational alternative to "I-can't-stand-it-itis." Here the person (1) acknowledges that an undesirable event has happened (or may happen), (2) believes that the event should empirically occur if it does, (3) rates the event along the badness continuum, (4) attempts to change the undesired event or accepts the "grim" reality if it cannot be modified, and (5) actively pursues other goals even though the situation cannot be altered.

The third major derivative, known as *acceptance*, is the rational alternative to "damnation." Here the person accepts herself and others as fallible humans who do not have to act other than they do and as too complex and fluid to be given any legitimate or global rating. In addition, life conditions are accepted as they exist. People who have the philosophy of acceptance fully acknowledge that the world is highly complex and exists according to laws that are often outside their personal control. It is important to emphasize that acceptance does not imply resignation. A rational philosophy of acceptance means that the person acknowledges that whatever exists empirically should exist but does not absolutely have to exist forever. This prompts the person to make active attempts to change reality. The person who is resigned to a situation usually does not attempt to modify it.

REBT theory also puts forward a number of criteria of psychological health. These include the following:

1. *Self-interest:* Sensible and emotionally healthy people tend to be primarily interested in themselves and to put their own interests at least a little above the interests of others. They sacrifice themselves to some degree for those for whom they care but not overwhelmingly or completely.

2. *Social interest:* Social interest is usually rational and self-helping because most people choose to live and enjoy themselves in a social group or community. If they do not act morally, protect the rights of others, and abet social survival, it is unlikely that they will create the kind of world in which they themselves can live comfortably and happily.

3. *Self-direction:* Healthy people tend mainly to assume responsibility for their own lives while simultaneously preferring to cooperate with others. They do not *need* or *demand* considerable support or succoring from others, though they may prefer and work for this.

4. *High frustration tolerance:* Rational individuals give both themselves and others the right to be wrong. Even when they intensely dislike their own and others' behavior, they refrain from damning themselves or others, as persons, for unacceptable or obnoxious behavior. People who are not plagued with debilitating emotional distress tend to go along with St. Francis and Reinhold Niebuhr by changing obnoxious conditions they can change, accepting those they cannot, and having the wisdom to know the difference between the two.

5. *Flexibility:* Healthy and mature individuals tend to be flexible in their thinking, open to change, and unbigoted and pluralistic in their view of other people. They do not make rigid, invariant rules for themselves and others.

6. *Acceptance of uncertainty:* Healthy men and women tend to acknowledge and accept the idea that we seem to live in a world of probability and chance where absolute certainties do not and probably never will exist. They realize that it is often fascinating and exciting and definitely not horrible to live in this kind of probabilistic and uncertain world. They enjoy a good degree of order

but do not demand to know exactly what the future will bring or what will happen to them.

7. *Commitment to creative pursuits:* Most people tend to be healthier and happier when they are vitally absorbed in something outside themselves and preferably have at least one powerful creative interest, as well as some major human involvement, that they consider so important that they structure a good part of their life around it.

8. *Scientific thinking:* Nondisturbed individuals tend to be more objective, realistic, and scientific than more disturbed ones. They are able to feel deeply and act concertedly, but they tend to regulate their emotions and actions by reflecting on them and evaluating their consequences in terms of the extent to which they lead to the attainment of short-term and long-term goals.

9. *Self-acceptance:* Healthy people are usually glad to be alive and accept themselves just because they are alive and have some capacity to enjoy themselves. They refuse to measure their intrinsic worth by their extrinsic achievements or by what others think of them. They frankly choose to have unconditional self-acceptance (USA), and they try to avoid rating themselves— their totality or their being. They attempt to enjoy rather than to prove themselves (Ellis, 1973, 1995a; Ellis & Harper, 1975; Hauck, 1991; Mills, 1993).

10. *Risk-taking:* Emotionally healthy people tend to take a fair amount of risk and to try to do what they want to do, even when there is a good chance that they may fail. They tend to be adventurous but not foolhardy.

11. *Long-range hedonism:* Well-adjusted people tend to seek both the pleasures of the moment *and* those of the future and do not often court future pain for present gain. They are hedonistic, that is, happiness-seeking and pain-avoidant, but they assume that they will probably live for quite a few years and that they had therefore better think of both today and tomorrow and not be obsessed with immediate gratification.

12. *Nonutopianism:* Healthy people accept the fact that utopias are probably unachievable and that they are never likely to get everything they want and to avoid all pain. They refuse to strive unrealistically for total joy, happiness, or perfection or for total lack of anxiety, depression, self-downing, and hostility.

13. *Self-responsibility for own emotional disturbance:* Healthy individuals tend to accept a great deal of responsibility for their own disturbance rather than defensively blame others or social conditions for their self-defeating thoughts, feelings, and behaviors.

Distinction between Healthy and Unhealthy Negative Emotions

Rational emotive behavioral theory argues that people can hold rational and irrational Beliefs at the same time. They can easily transmute their desires into demands. Thus, I may rationally believe "I want you to love me" and simultaneously believe that "since I strongly *want* you to love me, you *must* do so." Thus, it is important for therapists to discriminate between their clients' rational and irrational Beliefs. When such distinctions are made, it is easier to distinguish between helpful and unhelpful negative emotions. Healthy negative emotions are deemed to be associated with rational Beliefs and unhealthy negative emotions with irrational Beliefs. In the following, the healthy negative emotion is listed first.

    1. *Concern versus anxiety.* Concern is an emotion that is associated with the Belief, "I hope that this threat does not happen, but if it does, it would be unfortunate," whereas anxiety occurs when the person believes, "This threat *absolutely must not* happen, and it would be *awful* if it does."

    2. *Sadness versus depression.* Sadness is deemed to occur when the person believes, "It is very unfortunate that I have experienced this loss, but there is no reason why it should not have happened." Depression, on the other hand, is associated with the Belief "This loss *should not* have occurred and it is *terrible* that it did." Here, when the person feels responsible for the loss, he will tend to damn himself: "*I* am no good," whereas if the loss is outside the person's control, he or she will tend to damn the world/life conditions: "*It* is terrible." As shown earlier, REBT theory holds that it is the philosophy of musturbation implicit in such evaluations that leads the person to consider that he will never get what he wants, an inference that leads to feelings of hopelessness. Example: "Because I *must always* get the things I really want and did not get it this time, I'll *never* get it at all. It's hopeless!"

    3. *Regret versus guilt.* Feelings of regret or remorse occur when a person acknowledges that he has done something bad in public or private but accepts himself as a fallible human being for doing so. The person feels badly about the act or deed but not about himself because he holds the belief, "I prefer not to act badly, but if I do, too bad!" Guilt occurs when the person damns himself as bad, wicked, or rotten for acting badly. Here, the person feels badly about both the act and his "self" because he holds the belief, "I *must* not act badly, and if I do it's *awful* and I am a *rotten* person!"

    4. *Disappointment versus shame/embarrassment.* Feelings of disappointment occur when a person acts "stupidly" in public and acknowledges the stupid act but accepts herself in the process. The person feels disappointed about her *action* but not with *herself* because she prefers but does not demand that she act well. Shame and embarrassment occur when the person recognizes that she has acted "stupidly" in public and then condemns herself for acting in a way that she *absolutely should not* have done. People who experience shame and embarrassment often predict that the watching audience will think badly of them, in which case they tend to agree with these perceived judgments. Thus, they often believe that they absolutely *need* the approval of these others. Shame can sometimes be distinguished from embarrassment in that the public "prat-

fall" is regarded by the person as more serious when she feels shame. However, both emotions involve self-denigration.

5. *Annoyance versus anger.* Annoyance occurs when another person disregards an individual's rule of living. The annoyed person does not like what the other has done but does not damn him or her for doing it. Such a person tends to believe, "I wish the other person did not do that, and I don't like what he/she did, but it does not follow that he/she must not break my rule." In anger, however, the person does believe that the other absolutely must not break the rule and thus damns the other for doing so. REBT holds that it is healthy to be angry at another's *acts* but not at the *person* for acting badly.

It should be noted that rational emotive behavioral therapists do not generally target healthy negative emotions for change during therapy because they are deemed to be Consequences of rational thinking (Crawford & Ellis, 1989; Ellis, 1994c, 1996a).

ACQUISITION AND PERPETUATION OF PSYCHOLOGICAL DISTURBANCE

Rational emotive behavioral theory does not put forward an elaborate view concerning the acquisition of psychological disturbance. This partly follows from the hypothesis that humans have a distinct biological tendency to think and act irrationally but it also reflects the REBT viewpoint that theories of acquisition do not necessarily suggest therapeutic interventions. REBT holds that humans' tendencies toward irrational thinking are biologically rooted, but it also acknowledges that environmental variables do contribute to psychological disturbance and thus encourage people to make their biologically influenced demands (Ellis, 1976a, 1979e, 1994c). Thus, parents and culture usually teach children *which* superstitions, taboos, and prejudices to abide by, but they do not originate their basic tendency toward superstitiousness, ritualism, and bigotry (Ellis, 1991b, 1994c, 1995a).

Rational emotive behavioral theory also posits that humans vary in their disturbability. Some people emerge relatively unscathed psychologically from being raised by uncaring or overprotective parents; others emerge emotionally damaged from "healthier" child-rearing regimens. In this respect, REBT claims that individuals with serious aberrations are more innately predisposed to have rigid and crooked thinking than are those with lesser aberrations and that consequently they are likely to make lesser advances. Thus, the REBT theory of acquisition can be summed up in the view that as humans we are not disturbed simply by our experiences; rather, we bring our ability to disturb ourselves to our experiences (Ellis, 1976a, 1994c, 1995a).

Although rational emotive behavioral theory does not posit an elaborate view to explain the acquisition of psychological disturbance, it does deal more extensively with how such disturbance is perpetuated. First, people tend to maintain their psychological problems by their own naive theories concerning the nature of these problems and to what they can be attributed. They lack what REBT calls REBT Insight No. 1: that psychological disturbance is often primarily determined by the absolutistic Beliefs that people hold about negative life events (B determines C). Rather, they consider that their disturbances are mainly caused by these situations (A causes C). Because people make incorrect hypotheses about some of the major determinants of their problems, they consequently attempt to change A rather than B. Second, people may have Insight No. 1 but lack REBT Insight No. 2: that people remain disturbed by reindoctrinating themselves *in the present* with their absolutistic Beliefs. Although they may see that their problems are largely determined by their Beliefs, they may distract themselves and thus perpetuate their problems by searching for the historical antecedents of these Beliefs instead of directing themselves to change them as currently held. Third, people may have Insights No. 1 and No. 2 but still sustain their disturbance because they lack REBT Insight No. 3: that only if they diligently work and practice in the present as well as in the future to think, feel, and act against their irrational beliefs are they likely to change them and make themselves significantly less disturbed. People who have all three insights clearly see that they had better persistently and strongly challenge their destructive beliefs cognitively, emotively, and behaviorally to break the perpetuation of the disturbance cycle. Merely acknowledging that a Belief is irrational is usually insufficient to effect change (Ellis, 1962, 1979e, 1994c, 1996a).

REBT contends that a major reason that people perpetuate their psychological problems is that they adhere to a *philosophy of low frustration tolerance* (LFT) (Ellis, 1979a, 1980a). Such people believe that they *must* be comfortable and thus do not work to effect change because such work involves experiencing discomfort. They are short-range hedonists in that they are motivated to avoid short-term discomfort, even though accepting and working against their temporary uncomfortable feelings would probably help them to reach their long-range goals. Such people rate cognitive and behavioral therapeutic tasks as too painful, even more painful than the psychological disturbance to which they have achieved some measure of habituation. They prefer to remain with their "comfortable" discomfort rather than face the change-related discomfort that they believe they must not experience. Maultsby (1984) has argued that people often back away from change because they are afraid that they will not feel right about it. He calls this the "neurotic fear of feeling a phony" and actively shows clients that these feelings of "unnaturalness" are natural concomitants of relearning. Another prevalent form of LFT is "anxiety about anxiety." Here, individuals believe that they *must not* be anxious and thus do not expose themselves to anxiety-provoking situations because they might become anxious if they did so—an experience they would rate as "awful." As such, they perpetuate their problems and overly restrict their lives to avoid experiencing anxiety.

Anxiety about anxiety constitutes an example of the clinical fact that people often make themselves *disturbed about their disturbances*. Having created secondary (and sometimes tertiary) disturbances about their original disturbance, they become preoccupied with these "problems about problems" and thus find it difficult to get back to solving the original problem. Humans are often very inventive in this respect. They can make themselves depressed about their depression, guilty about being angry (as well as anxious about their anxiety), and so on. Consequently, people often had better tackle their disturbances about their disturbances before they can successfully solve their original problems (Ellis, 1979a, 1980a, 1993, 1994c, 1996).

REBT theory endorses the Freudian view of human defensiveness in explaining how people perpetuate their psychological problems (A. Freud, 1937). Thus, people maintain their problems by employing various defense mechanisms (e.g., rationalization, avoidance) that are designed to help deny the existence of these problems or to minimize their severity. The REBT view is that these defenses are often used to ward off self-damnation tendencies and that under such circumstances, if these people were to honestly take responsibility for their problems, they would tend to severely denigrate themselves for having them. In addition, these defense mechanisms are also employed to ward off discomfort anxiety, because if such people admitted their problems, they would rate them as "too hard to bear" or "too difficult to overcome."

I (AE) have noted that people sometimes experience a form of perceived payoff for their psychological problems other than avoidance of discomfort (Ellis, 1979e). The existence of such payoffs serves to perpetuate these problems. Thus, a woman who claims to want to overcome her procrastination may avoid tackling the problem because she is afraid that should she become successful she might then be criticized by others as being "too masculine," a situation she would evaluate as "awful." Her procrastination serves to protect her (in her mind) from this "terrible" state of affairs. I (WD) have noted that "rational emotive behavior therapists stress the phenomenological nature of these payoffs, i.e., it is the person's view of the payoff that is important in determining its impact, not the events delineated in the person's description" (Dryden, 1984c, p. 244).

Finally, the well-documented "self-fulfilling prophecy" phenomenon helps to explain why people perpetuate their psychological problems. Here, people act according to their evaluations and consequent predictions and thus often elicit from themselves or from others responses that they then interpret in a manner that confirms their initial hypotheses. Thus, a socially anxious man may believe that other people would not want to get to know "a worthless individual such as I truly am." He then attends a social function and acts as if he were worthless, avoiding eye contact and keeping away from others. Unsurprisingly, such social behavior does not invite approaches from others, a lack of response that he interprets and evaluates thus: "You see, I was right. Other people don't want to know me. I really am no good."

In conclusion, REBT theory holds that people "naturally tend to perpetuate their problems and have a strong innate tendency to cling to self-defeating, habitual patterns and thereby resist basic change. Helping clients change, then, poses quite a challenge for REBT practitioners" (Dryden, 1984c, pp. 244–245).

THE THEORY OF THERAPEUTIC CHANGE

We have argued that the rational emotive behavioral view of the person is basically an optimistic one: although it posits that humans have a distinct biological tendency to think irrationally, it also holds that they have the constructive capacity to *choose* to work toward changing this irrational thinking and its self-defeating effects.

There are various levels of change. REBT theory holds that the most elegant and long-lasting changes that humans can effect are ones that involve philosophic restructuring of irrational Beliefs. Change at this level can be specific or general. Specific philosophic change means that individuals change their absolutistic demands ("must's," "should's") about *given* situations to rational relative preferences. General philosophic change involves people adopting a nondevout attitude toward life events in general.

To effect a philosophic change at either the specific or general level, people are advised to

1. First, realize that they create, to a large degree, their own psychological disturbances and that although environmental conditions can significantly contribute to their problems they are usually of secondary consideration in the change process.
2. Fully recognize that they do have the ability to significantly change their own disturbances.
3. Understand that emotional and behavioral disturbances stem largely from irrational, absolutistic, dogmatic Beliefs.
4. Detect their irrational beliefs and discriminate them from their rational alternatives.
5. Dispute these irrational beliefs, using realistic, logical, and heuristic methods and by feeling and acting against them.
6. Work toward the internalization of their new, effective Beliefs by employing a number of cognitive, emotive, and behavioral methods of change.
7. Continue this process of challenging irrational Beliefs and using multimodal methods of change for the rest of their lives.

When people effect a philosophic change at B in the ABC model of REBT, they often are able to spontaneously correct their distorted inferences of reality (overgeneralizations, faulty attributions, etc.). However, they can often benefit from challenging these distorted inferences more directly, as REBT has always emphasized (Ellis, 1962, 1971a, 1973, 1994c, 1996a; Ellis & Harper, 1961a, 1961b) and as Beck (Beck et al., 1979) and other cognitive therapists have also stressed (Maultsby, 1984; Meichenbaum, 1992).

Although rational emotive behavioral theory argues that irrational beliefs are the breeding ground for the development and maintenance of inferential distortions, it is possible for people to effect inferentially based changes without making a profound philosophic change. Thus, they may regard their inferences or "automatic thoughts" as hunches about reality rather than facts, may generate alternative hypotheses, and may seek evidence and/or carry out experiments that test each hypothesis, They may then accept the hypothesis that represents the "best bet" of those available.

Consider a man who thinks that his co-workers view him as a fool. To test this hypothesis he might first specify their negative reactions to him. These constitute the data from which he too quickly draws the conclusion, "They think I'm a fool." He might then realize that what he has interpreted to be negative responses to him might not be negative. If they seem to be negative, he might then carry out an experiment to test the meaning he attributes to his co-workers' responses. Thus, he might enlist the help of a colleague whom he trusts to carry out a "secret ballot" of others' opinions of him. Or he could test his hunch more explicitly by directly asking them for their view of him.

As a result of these strategies this person may conclude that his co-workers find some of his actions foolish rather than considering him to be a complete fool. His mood may lift because his inference about the situation has changed, but he may still believe, "If others think I'm a fool, they're right, I *am* a fool and that would be *awful*." Thus, he has made an inferential change but not a philosophic one. If this person were to attempt to make a philosophic change, he would *first* assume that his inference was true, *then* address himself to his evaluations about this inference and hence challenge these if they were discovered to be irrational (i.e., musturbatory evaluations). Thus, he might conclude, "Even if I act foolishly, that makes me a *person with* foolish behavior, not a *foolish person*. And even if they deem me a total idiot, that is simply *their* view, with which I can choose to disagree." REBT therapists hypothesize that people are more likely to make a profound philosophic change if they first assume that their inferences are true and then challenge their irrational Beliefs, rather than if they first correct their inferential distortions and then challenge their underlying irrational Beliefs. However, this hypothesis awaits full empirical inquiry.

People can also make direct changes of the situation at A (Activating event). Thus, in the example quoted above, the man could leave his job or distract himself from the reactions of his colleagues by taking on extra work and devoting himself to that. Or he might carry out relaxation exercises whenever he comes in contact with his co-workers and thus distract himself once again from their perceived reactions. Additionally, the man might have a word with his supervisor, who might then instruct the other workers to change their behavior toward the man.

When we use the REBT model to consider behavioral change, it is apparent that a person can change his or her behavior to effect inferential and/or philosophic change. Thus, again using the above example, a man whose co-workers view him as a fool might change his own behavior toward them and thus elicit a different set of responses from them that would lead him to reinterpret his previous inference (behavior change to effect inferential change). However, if it could be determined that they did indeed consider him to be a fool, then the man could actively seek them out and show himself that he could stand their disapproval and that just because they *think* him a fool does not make him one. He would thus learn to accept himself in the face of people's views while exposing himself to their negative reactions (behavior change to help effect philosophic change).

While REBT therapists prefer to help their clients make profound philosophic changes at B, they do not dogmatically insist that their clients make such changes. If it becomes apparent that clients cannot or will not, at any given time, change their irrational Beliefs, then REBT therapists endeavor to help them either to change A directly (by avoiding the troublesome situation or by behaving differently) or to change their distorted inferences about the situation.

In the next chapter we build upon these theoretical underpinnings and consider the basic practice of REBT.

2

The Basic Practice of REBT

In this chapter we outline the basic practice of REBT. First, we consider aspects of the therapeutic relationship between clients and therapists in REBT. Second, we deal with issues pertaining to inducting clients into REBT and assessing their problems in REBT terms. Third, we specify basic treatment strategies in REBT. Fourth, we specify the major treatment techniques that are employed during REBT. Fifth, we note a number of obstacles that emerge in the process of REBT and how they might be overcome. Finally, we distinguish between preferential and general REBT (or cognitive-behavior therapy [CBT]) and specify their differences.

THE THERAPEUTIC RELATIONSHIP

REBT is an active-directive form of psychotherapy in that therapists are active in directing their clients to identify the philosophical source of their psychological problems and in showing them they can challenge and change their irrational musturbatory evaluations. As such, REBT is an educational form of therapy. I (AE) have sometimes conceptualized the role of the effective REBT therapist as that of an authoritative (but not authoritarian!) and encouraging teacher who strives to teach his or her clients how to be their own therapists once formal therapy sessions have ended (Ellis, 1979c, 1994d, 1995a, 1996a).

Therapeutic Conditions

Given the above role, REBT therapists strive to *unconditionally accept* their clients as fallible human beings who often act self-defeatingly but are never

Parts of this chapter were adapted from Dryden and Ellis (1986) and W. Dryden and A. Ellis, "Rational-Emotive Therapy," in K. S. Dobson (Ed.), *Handbook of Cognitive-Behavioral Therapies;* New York: Guilford, 1987 (used by permission), and have been previously published in *The Nurse Practitioner: The American Journal of Primary Health Care, 12*(7), July 1987.

essentially bad (or good). No matter how badly clients behave in therapy, the REBT therapist attempts to accept them as people but will frequently, if appropriate, let them know his or her reactions to the client's negative behavior (Ellis, 1973, 1994c, 1996a, 1996b; Woods & Ellis, 1996).

In our role as therapists we strive to be as open as therapeutically feasible and will not hesitate to give highly personal information about ourselves should our clients ask for it, except when we judge that clients would use such information against themselves. REBT therapists often disclose examples from their own lives concerning how they experienced similar problems and, more important, how they have gone about solving these problems. Thus, they strive to be *therapeutically genuine* in conducting sessions.

REBT therapists tend to be *appropriately humorous* with most of their clients because they think that much emotional disturbance stems from the fact that clients take themselves and their problems, other people, and the world too seriously. They thus strive to model for their clients the therapeutic advantages of taking a serious but humorously ironic attitude to life. They endeavor, however, not to poke fun at the clients themselves but at their self-defeating thoughts, feelings, and actions (Ellis, 1977b, 1977c, 1981, 1987b). In the same vein, and for similar purposes, REBT therapists tend to be informal and easygoing with most of their clients. However, REBT opposes therapists unethically indulging themselves in order to enjoy therapy sessions at their clients' expense (Ellis, 1985c, 1996a, 1996b).

REBT therapists show their clients a special kind of empathy. They not only offer them "affective" empathy (i.e., communicating that they understand how their clients feel) but also offer them *philosophic empathy* (i.e., showing them that they understand the philosophies that underlie these feelings).

Thus, with certain modifications, they agree with Rogers's (1961) views concerning therapist empathy, genuineness, and unconditional positive regard. However, REBT therapists are wary of showing the vast majority of their clients undue warmth. If REBT practitioners get really close to their clients and give them considerable warmth, attention, caring, and support, as well as unconditional acceptance, then these therapists run two major risks (Ellis, 1982a, 1985a).

The first major risk is that therapists may unwittingly reinforce their clients' dire "needs" for love and approval—two irrational ideas that are at the core of much human disturbance. When this happens, clients appear to improve because their therapists are indeed giving them what they believe they must have. They begin to "feel better" but do not necessarily "get better" (Ellis, 1972a, 1991a, 1994c, 1996a, 1996b). Their "improvement" is illusory because their irrational philosophies are being reinforced. Because they seem to improve, their therapists have restricted opportunities to identify these ideas, to show them how they relate to their problems, and to help them challenge and change them. Consequently, although such clients are helped by their therapists, they are now shown how they can help themselves and are thus vulnerable to future upset.

The second major risk is that therapists may unwittingly reinforce their clients' philosophy of low frustration tolerance (LFT) or discomfort disturbance. Clients with LFT problems "almost always try to seek interminable help from others instead of coping with life's difficulties themselves. Any kind of therapy that does not specifically persuade them to stop their whining and to accept responsibility for their own happiness tends to confirm their belief that others *must* help them. Close relationship therapy is frequently the worst offender in this respect and thereby may do considerable harm" (Ellis, 1982a, p. 206).

However, since REBT is flexible and is against the formulation of absolute, dogmatic therapeutic rules, it does recognize that under certain conditions (e.g., where a client is extremely depressed, accompanied by powerful suicidal ideation), distinct therapist warmth may be positively indicated for a period of time (Ellis, 1985a).

Therapeutic Style

I (AE) recommend that REBT therapists adopt an active-directive style with most clients and a particularly forceful version of that style with some very disturbed and resistant clients (Ellis, 1979, 1985c, 1996a, 1996b). However, not all REBT therapists concur with this view. Some recommend a more passive, gentle approach under specific or most conditions with clients (e.g., Young, 1984). Eschenroeder (1979) notes that it is important to ask in REBT, "Which therapeutic style is most effective with which kind of client?" (p. 5). In the same vein, recent proponents of eclectic forms of therapy argue that style of therapeutic interaction had better be varied to meet the special situations of individual clients (Beutler, 1983; Lazarus, 1989). This is a scantily researched area in REBT, but it may be best for REBT therapists to avoid (1) an overly friendly, emotionally charged style of interaction with "hysterical" clients, (2) an overly intellectual style with "obsessive-compulsive" clients, (3) an overly directive style with clients whose sense of autonomy is easily threatened, and (4) an overly active style with clients who easily retreat into passivity. This line of reasoning fits well with the notion of flexibility that REBT therapists advocate as a desirable therapeutic quality. Varying one's therapeutic style in REBT does not mean departing from the theoretical principles on which the content of therapy is based. As Eschenroeder (1979) points out, in REBT, "there is no one-to-one relationship between theory and practice" (p. 3).

Personal Qualities of Effective Rational Emotive Behavioral Therapists

Unfortunately, no research studies have been carried out to determine the personal qualities of effective REBT therapists. REBT theory, however, does put forward a number of hypotheses concerning this topic (Ellis, 1978a, 1995c,

1996a, 1996b), but it is important to regard these as both tentative and await-ing empirical study.

1. Because REBT is a fairly structured form of therapy, its effective practi-tioners are usually comfortable with structure but flexible enough to work in a less structured manner when the need arises.

2. REBT practitioners tend to be intellectually, cognitively, or philosoph-ically inclined and become attracted to REBT because the approach provides them with opportunities to fully express this tendency.

3. Because REBT is often to be conducted in an active-directive manner, effective REBT practitioners are usually comfortable operating in this mode. Nevertheless, they have the flexibility to modify their interpersonal style with clients so that they provide the optimum conditions to facilitate client change.

4. REBT emphasizes that it is important for clients to put their therapy-derived insights into practice in their everyday lives. As a result, effective prac-titioners of REBT are usually comfortable with behavioral instruction and teaching and with providing the active prompting that clients often require if they are to follow through on homework assignments.

5. Effective REBT therapists tend to have little fear of failure themselves. Their personal worth is not invested in their clients' improvement. They do not need their clients' love and/or approval and are thus not afraid of taking calculated risks if therapeutic impasses occur. They tend to accept both them-selves and their clients as fallible humans and are therefore tolerant of their own mistakes and the irresponsible acts of their clients. They tend to have, or persistently work toward acquiring, a philosophy of high frustration tolerance, and they do not get discouraged when clients improve at a slower rate than they desire. Thus, effective practitioners tend to score highly on most of the criteria of positive mental health outlined in chapter 1, and they serve as healthy role models for their clients.

6. REBT strives to be scientific, empirical, antiabsolutistic, and undevout in its approach to people's selecting and achieving their own goals (Ellis, 1978a, 1994c, 1995a, 1996a, 1996b). Thus, effective practitioners of REBT tend to show similar traits and are definitely not mystical, antiintellectual, or magical in their beliefs.

7. REBT advocates the use of techniques in a number of different modali-ties (cognitive, imagery, emotive, behavioral, and interpersonal). Its effective practitioners are thus comfortable with a multimodal approach to treatment and tend not be people who like to stick rigidly to any one modality.

Finally, I (AE) note that some REBT therapists often modify the preferred practice of REBT according to their own natural personality characteristics (Ellis, 1978b). Thus, for example, some therapists practice REBT in a slow-moving, passive manner, do little disputing, and focus therapy on the relation-

ship between them and their clients. Whether such modification of the preferred practice of REBT is effective is a question awaiting empirical enquiry.

INDUCTING CLIENTS INTO REBT

When clients seek help from REBT therapists, they vary concerning how
much they already know about the type of therapeutic process they are likely
to encounter. Some may approach the therapist because they know he or she is
a practitioner of REBT; others may know nothing about this therapeutic
method. In any event it is often beneficial to explore clients' expectations for
therapy at the outset of the process. Duckro, Beal, and George (1979) have
argued that it is important to distinguish between preferences and anticipations when expectations are assessed. Clients' preferences for therapy concern
what kind of experience they want, whereas anticipations concern what service they think they will receive. Clients who have realistic anticipations for
the REBT therapeutic process and have a preference for this process require,
in general, far less induction into this process than clients who have unrealistic anticipations of the process and/or preferences for a different type of therapeutic experience.

Induction procedures, in general, involve showing clients that REBT is an
active-directive structured therapy oriented to discussing clients' present and
future problems and one that asks clients to play an active role in the change
process. Induction can take a number of different forms. First, therapists may
develop and use a number of pretherapy role induction procedures, in which a
typical course of REBT is outlined and productive client behaviors demonstrated (Macaskill & Macaskill, 1983). Second, therapists may give a short lecture at the outset of therapy concerning the nature and process of REBT. Third,
therapists may employ induction-related explanations in the initial therapy sessions, using client problem material to illustrate how these problems may be
tackled in REBT and to outline the respective roles of client and therapist.

ASSESSMENT OF CLIENTS' PROBLEMS

The next stage of therapy concerns assessment. Assessment of the kind and
degree of emotional disturbance of clients is held to be important in REBT
for several reasons:

- To determine how seriously disturbed clients are, so that therapists can
  see how likely they are to benefit from any form of therapy, including
  REBT and so that they can also decide which REBT techniques (of the
  many possible ones that are available) may be most suitably employed

(and which techniques avoided) with each particular client under the conditions in which he or she may be expected to live.

- To determine—or at least guess with a fair degree of accuracy—how difficult clients are likely to be, how they will probably take to the main REBT procedures, and how long psychotherapy with each of them is likely to be required.

- To discover which type of therapist involvement (e.g., a more or less active or a more or less passive and supportive kind) is likely to help the individual client.

- To discover what types of skill deficiencies clients have and what kinds of training (either in the course of REBT or outside therapy) they might best undertake to remedy some of their skill deficiencies. Thus, on the basis of this assessment, certain kinds of skill training, such as assertiveness, social skills, communication, or vocational training, may be recommended for specific clients.

REBT practitioners are at liberty to use all kinds of assessment procedures but generally favor the type of cognitive-behavioral interventions described in Kendall and Hollon (1980). They tend to take a dimmer view of diagnostic procedures such as the Rorschach and other projective techniques than they do of more objective personality questionnaires and behavioral tests, largely because the former often have dubious validity, incorporate questionable psychoanalytic and psychodynamic interpretations, and usually are not particularly applicable to effective treatment processes.

Together with many other REBT practitioners, we take the view that although assessment interviews and some standard diagnostic tests may at times be useful in exploring clients' disturbances, perhaps the best form of assessment consists of having several REBT sessions with the client. Some of the advantages of this kind of therapy-oriented assessment are as follows:

1. In the course of such an assessment procedure, clients can get to work almost immediately on their problems, can gain therapeutically while being assessed, and can be helped to suffer less pain, hardship, and expense while undergoing treatment.

2. The preferable techniques to be used with different clients are often best determined mainly through experimenting with some of these techniques in the course of the therapeutic process. Although the use of standard personality tests, such as the Minnesota Multiphasic Personality Inventory (MMPI), may help the therapist start off with some REBT methods rather than other methods with a given client, only by actually experimenting with certain specific methods is the therapist likely to see how the client reacts to them and consequently how they had better be continued or discontinued.

3. Assessment procedures divorced from ongoing psychotherapy (such as giving a whole battery of tests prior to beginning therapy) may be iatrogenic for a number of clients. During this testing process, especially if the assessment procedures are long-winded and take some time to complete, clients may imagine "horrors" about themselves that lead them astray and make it more difficult for them to benefit from therapy.

4. Certain conventional assessment procedures—for example, the Rorschach and Thematic Apperception Test (TAT)—may wrongly predict problems, symptoms, and dynamics that many clients do not really have and may help lead their therapists up the garden path and away from more scientifically based evaluations.

5. Clients sometimes take diagnoses obtained from complicated assessment procedures as the gospel truth, feel that they have thereby received a valid "explanation" of what ails them, and wrongly conclude that they have been helped by this "explanation." REBT assessment procedures, including using therapy itself as an integral part of the assessment process, primarily focus on what clients had better do to change rather than emphasize clever diagnostic "explanations" of what ails them.

Because REBT is strongly cognitive, emotive, and behavioral, it assesses not only clients' irrational Beliefs but also their inappropriate feelings and their self-defeating behaviors. The usual REBT assessment process almost always includes the following:

> Clients are helped to acknowledge and describe their unhealthy negative feelings (e.g., anxiety, depression, anger, and self-hatred), and these are clearly differentiated from their healthy negative feelings (e.g., disappointment, sadness, frustration, and displeasure).
>
> They are led to acknowledge and delineate their self-defeating behaviors (e.g., compulsions, addictions, phobias, and procrastination) rather than to overemphasize idiosyncratic but nondeleterious behaviors (e.g., unusual devotion to socializing, sex, study, or work).
>
> They are asked to point out specific Activating events in their lives that tend to occur just prior to their experienced disturbed feelings and behaviors.
>
> Their Rational Beliefs that accompany their Activating events and that lead to undisturbed Consequences are assessed and discussed.
>
> Their Irrational Beliefs that accompany their Activating events and that lead to disturbed Consequences are assessed and discussed.
>
> Their Irrational Beliefs that involve absolutistic "must's" and grandiose demands on themselves, others, and the universe are particularly determined.

Their second-level Irrational Beliefs that tend to be derived from their
absolutistic "should's" and "must's"—that is, their "awfulizing," their
"I-can't-stand-it-itis," their "damning" of themselves and others, and
their unrealistic overgeneralizations—are also revealed.

Their Irrational Beliefs that lead to their disturbance about their disturbances—that is, their anxiety about their anxiety and their depression
about being depressed—are particularly revealed and discussed.

As these specialized REBT assessment and diagnostic procedures are instituted, specific treatment plans are made, normally in close collaboration with
the clients, to work first on the most important and self-sabotaging emotional
and behavioral symptoms that they present and later on related and possibly
less important symptoms. REBT practitioners, however, always try to maintain an exceptionally open-minded, skeptical, and experimental attitude
toward the clients and their problems so that what at first seem to be their
crucial and most debilitating ideas, feelings, and actions may later be seen in
a different light and emphasis may be changed to working on other equally
or more pernicious disturbances that might not be evident during the clients'
early sessions.

REBT therapists may spend relatively little time gathering background
information on their clients, although they may ask them to fill out forms
designed to assess which irrational ideas they spontaneously endorse at the
outset of therapy (see Figure 2.1). Rather, they are likely to ask clients for a
description of their major problems(s). As clients describe their problems,
REBT therapists intervene fairly early to break these down into their ABC
components. If clients begin by describing A (the Activating event), then their
therapists ask for C (their emotional and/or behavioral reactions). However,
if clients begin by outlining C, therapists ask for a brief description of A.

Background information on their own and their close relatives' lives may be
briefly obtained, especially if it is suspected that clients have endogenous or
biologically based disturbances—such as endogenous depression. This kind of
information may be particularly useful in assessing whether they are run-of-
the-mill neurotics or also suffer from severe personality disorders or organic
and neurological problems.

In REBT, A and C are normally assessed before B and are usually assessed
in the order that clients report them. C refers to both disturbed emotional and
behavioral consequences of the preferential or musturbatory evaluations made
at B. Careful assessment of emotional C's is advocated in REBT because they
serve as a major indicator of what type of evaluations are probably to be found
at B. In this regard, it is important to reiterate that healthy negative emotions
are different from "unhealthy" negative emotions. Emotions such as sadness,
regret, annoyance, and concern are termed "healthy" in REBT in that they
are deemed to accompany rational, preferential evaluations at B and encour-

age people to attempt to change, for the better, obnoxious situations at A. The "unhealthy" versions of emotional states are depression, guilt, anger, and anxiety. These are deemed to stem largely from irrational, musturbatory evaluations at B and tend to interfere with people's constructive attempts to change undesirable situations. In some cases, however, disturbed C's may directly result from innate biological defects, as when endogenous depression stems from serotonic deficiency.

When emotional C's are being assessed, it is important to realize three important points. First, clients do not necessarily use affective terminology in the same way that REBT therapists do. It is often helpful to inform them about the nature of the unique discriminations made between "healthy" and "unhealthy" negative emotional states so that therapist and client can come to use a shared emotional language. Second, disturbed emotional C's are often chained together. For example, anger is frequently chained to anxiety in that one can experience anger to cover up feelings of inadequacy. And one can feel depressed after a threat to one's self-esteem emerges (Wessler, 1981). Finally, REBT therapists had better realize that clients do not always want to change every "unhealthy" negative emotion as defined by REBT theory; that is, they may not see a particular unhealthy emotion (e.g., anger) as being truly unhealthy or self-defeating. Thus, a good deal of flexibility and clinical acumen is called for in the assessment of disturbed emotional C's to be targeted for change.

C is assessed mainly by the client's verbal report, but occasionally clients experience difficulty in accurately reporting their emotional and behavioral problems. When this occurs, REBT therapists may use a number of methods to facilitate this part of the assessment process. Thus, a variety of emotive (e.g., Gestalt two-chair dialogue, psychodrama), imagery, and other techniques (e.g., keeping an emotion/behavior diary) can be used in this respect (Dryden, 1984b).

Although we have chosen to highlight the assessment of disturbed emotional C's, similar points can be made about the assessment of dysfunctional behavioral C's. As noted earlier, withdrawal, procrastination, alcoholism, and substance abuse are generally regarded as dysfunctional behaviors related to irrational, musturbatory evaluations at B (Ellis, 1979a, 1980a; Ellis & Knaus, 1977; Ellis & Lange, 1994; Ellis et al., 1988; Ellis & Velten, 1992).

When B is assessed, some REBT therapists prefer to fully assess the client's inferences in search of the most relevant inference that is linked to the client's musturbatory evaluations, given that C is self-defeating. This is known as *inference chaining* (Moore, 1983). An example of this procedure is described below:

THERAPIST: So what was your major feeling here?
    CLIENT: I guess I was angry.
THERAPIST: Angry about what? (Here the therapist has obtained C and is probing for A.)

FIGURE 2.1 Personality data form.

Name _____

(last)   (first)   (middle)

Consultation Center

Albert Ellis Institute for Rational Emotive Behavior Therapy
45 East 65th Street, New York, N.Y. 10021

Personality Data Form—Part 1

Instructions: Please answer all the following items as honestly as you can, so that we will be able to help you most with your problems. Read each of the items and circle after each one the word OFTEN, SOMETIMES, or SELDOM, to indicate how often you have the feeling that is described in the item. Thus, if you frequently feel quite foolish or embarrassed when you make a mistake when other people are watching, circle the word OFTEN in item 1; and if you seldom or rarely feel ashamed to do the things you really want to do if you think others will disapprove of you for doing them, circle SELDOM in item 2. Please make sure that you circle one, and only one, word in every item. DO NOT SKIP ANY ITEMS. And again, for your own good, be as honest as you can possibly be.

Acceptance

1. I feel quite foolish or embarrassed when I make a mistake and other people are watching   OFTEN   SOMETIMES   SELDOM.

2. I feel ashamed to do the things I really want to do if I think others will disapprove of me for doing them   OFTEN   SOMETIMES   SELDOM.

3. I feel humiliated when people discover undesirable things about my family or my background   OFTEN   SOMETIMES   SELDOM.

4. I feel put down if my house, car, finances, or other possessions are not as good as are those of others   OFTEN   SOMETIMES   SELDOM.

5. I feel quite uncomfortable when I am the center of people's attention   OFTEN   SOMETIMES   SELDOM.

6. I feel quite hurt when a person I respect criticizes me negatively   OFTEN   SOMETIMES   SELDOM.

36

7. I feel uneasy about my looks or about the way I am dressed when I am out in public   OFTEN   SOMETIMES   SELDOM.

8. I feel that if people get to know me well they will discover how rotten I really am   OFTEN   SOMETIMES   SELDOM.

9. I feel terribly lonely   OFTEN   SOMETIMES   SELDOM.

10. I feel that I simply must have the approval or love of certain people who are important to me   OFTEN   SOMETIMES   SELDOM.

11. I feel dependent on others and am miserable if I cannot get their help   OFTEN   SOMETIMES   SELDOM.

Frustration

12. I feel upset when things proceed slowly and can't be settled quickly   OFTEN   SOMETIMES   SELDOM.

13. I feel like putting off things I know it would be better for me to do'   OFTEN   SOMETIMES   SELDOM.

14. I feel upset about life's inconveniences or frustrations   OFTEN   SOMETIMES   SELDOM.

15. I feel quite angry when someone keeps me waiting   OFTEN   SOMETIMES   SELDOM.

16. I feel jealous of people who have better traits than I   OFTEN   SOMETIMES   SELDOM.

17. I feel terribly resentful when other people do not do my bidding or give me what I want   OFTEN   SOMETIMES   SELDOM.

18. I feel I can't stand and must change people who act stupidly or nastily   OFTEN   SOMETIMES   SELDOM.

19. I feel that I can't handle serious responsibility   OFTEN   SOMETIMES   SELDOM.

20. I resent my having to make a real effort to get what I want   OFTEN   SOMETIMES   SELDOM.

21. I feel very sorry for myself when things are rough   OFTEN   SOMETIMES   SELDOM.

22. I feel unable to persist at things I start, especially when the going gets hard   OFTEN   SOMETIMES   SELDOM.

23. I feel unexcited and bored about most things   OFTEN   SOMETIMES   SELDOM.

24. I feel that I cannot discipline myself   OFTEN   SOMETIMES   SELDOM.

(continued)

FIGURE 2.1 *(continued)*

Injustice

25. I feel revengeful toward others for the wrongs they have done	OFTEN SOMETIMES SELDOM.
26. I strongly feel like telling off wrongdoers and immoral people	OFTEN SOMETIMES SELDOM.
27. I get upset about the injustices of the world and feel that their perpetrators should be severely punished	OFTEN SOMETIMES SELDOM.

Achievement

28. I blame myself severely for my poor performances	OFTEN SOMETIMES SELDOM.
29. I feel very ashamed when I fail at important things	OFTEN SOMETIMES SELDOM.
30. I feel anxious when I have to make important decisions	OFTEN SOMETIMES SELDOM.
31. I feel afraid to take risks or to try new things	OFTEN SOMETIMES SELDOM.

Worth

32. I feel guilty about my thoughts or actions	OFTEN SOMETIMES SELDOM.
33. I feel that I am pretty worthless as a person	OFTEN SOMETIMES SELDOM.
34. I feel suicidal	OFTEN SOMETIMES SELDOM.
35. I feel like crying	OFTEN SOMETIMES SELDOM.
36. I feel that I give in too easily to others	OFTEN SOMETIMES SELDOM.
37. I feel hopeless about my being able to change my personality for the better	OFTEN SOMETIMES SELDOM.
38. I feel that I am quite stupid	OFTEN SOMETIMES SELDOM.
39. I feel that my life is meaningless or without purpose	OFTEN SOMETIMES SELDOM.

Control

40. I feel I cannot enjoy myself today because of my poor early life	OFTEN	SOMETIMES	SELDOM.
41. I feel that because I have failed at important things in the past I must inevitably keep failing in the future	OFTEN	SOMETIMES	SELDOM.
42. I resent my parents for treating me the way they did and for causing so many of my present problems	OFTEN	SOMETIMES	SELDOM.
43. I feel that I cannot control my strong emotions, such as anxiety or rage	OFTEN	SOMETIMES	SELDOM.

Certainty

44. I feel lost without some higher being or purpose on which to rely	OFTEN	SOMETIMES	SELDOM.
45. I feel that I should keep doing certain things over and over, even though I don't want to do them, because something bad will happen if I stop	OFTEN	SOMETIMES	SELDOM.
46. I feel quite uncomfortable when things are not well ordered	OFTEN	SOMETIMES	SELDOM.

Catastrophizing

47. I worry about what's going to happen to me in the future	OFTEN	SOMETIMES	SELDOM.
48. I worry about my having some accident or illness	OFTEN	SOMETIMES	SELDOM.
49. I am terrified at the idea of going to new places or meeting a new group of people	OFTEN	SOMETIMES	SELDOM.
50. I am terrified at the thought of my dying	OFTEN	SOMETIMES	SELDOM.

CLIENT: I was angry that he did not send me a birthday card. (Client provides inference about A.)

THERAPIST: And what was anger-provoking about that? (Probing to see whether this is the most relevant inference in the chain)

CLIENT: Well . . . he promised me he would remember. (Inference 2)

THERAPIST: And because he broke his promise? (Probing for relevance of inference 2)

CLIENT: I felt that he didn't care enough about me. (Inference 3)

THERAPIST: But let's assume that for a moment. What would be distressing about that? (Probing for relevance of inference 3)

CLIENT: Well, he might leave me. (Inference 4)

THERAPIST: And if he did? (Probing for relevance of inference 4)

CLIENT: I'd be left alone. (Inference 5)

THERAPIST: And if you were alone? (Probing for relevance of inference 5)

CLIENT: I couldn't stand that. (disturbed, unhealthy Belief)

THERAPIST: OK, so let's back up a minute. what would be most distressing for you, the birthday card incident, the broken promise, the fact that he doesn't care, being left by your husband, or being alone? (Therapist checks to see which inference is most relevant in the chain)

CLIENT: Definitely being alone.

This example shows that not only are inferences chained together but, as mentioned earlier, disturbed emotions are too. Here anger was chained with anxiety about being alone. Although this therapist chose then to dispute the client's irrational Belief underlying her anxiety, he still has to deal with her anger-creating Belief. Other REBT therapists might have chosen to take the first element in the chain (anger about the missing birthday card) and disputed the irrational Belief related to anger. Skillful REBT therapists do succeed in discovering the hidden issues underlying the "presenting problem" during the Disputing process. It is often important for REBT therapists to assess correctly *all* relevant issues related to a presenting problem. How they do this depends on personal style and how particular clients react to different assessment procedures.

When irrational musturbatory Beliefs are assessed, clients are helped to see the link between these irrational Beliefs and their unhealthy affective and behavioral Consequences at C. Some REBT therapists like to give a short lecture at this point on the role of the "must's" in emotional disturbance and how they can be distinguished from preferences. I (AE), for example, often use the following teaching dialogue:

ELLIS: Imagine that you prefer to have a minimum of $11 in your pocket at all times and you discover you only have $10. How will you feel?

CLIENT: Frustrated.

ELLIS: Right. Or you'd feel concerned or sad, but you wouldn't kill yourself. Right?

CLIENT: Right.

ELLIS: OK. Now this time imagine that you absolutely *have to* have a minimum of $11 in your pocket at all times. You *must* have it, it is a *necessity*. You *must*, you *must*, you *must*, have a minimum of $11, and again you look and you find you only have $10. How will you feel?

CLIENT: Very anxious.

ELLIS: Right, or depressed. Right. Now remember it's the same $11 but a different Belief. OK, now this time you still have the same belief. You *have to* have a minimum of $11 at all times, you *must*. It's absolutely *essential*. But this time you look in your pocket and find that you've got $15. How will you feel?

CLIENT: Relieved, content.

ELLIS: Right. But with that same Belief, you *have to* have a minimum of $11 at all times—something will soon occur to you to scare you shitless. What do you think that would be?

CLIENT: What if I lose $5?

ELLIS: Right. What if I lose $5, what if I spend $5, what if I get robbed? That's right. Now the moral of this model—which applies to just about all humans, rich or poor, black or white, male or female, young or old, in the past or in the future, assuming that humans are still human—is, people *make themselves* miserable if they don't get what they think they *must*, but they are also panicked when they do—because of the *must*. For even if they have what they think they *must*, they could always lose it.

CLIENT: So I have no chance to be happy when I don't have what I think I *must*—and little chance of remaining unanxious when I do have it?

ELLIS: Right! Your *must*urbation will get you nowhere—except depressed or panicked!

An important goal of the assessment stage of REBT is to help clients distinguish between their primary problems (e.g., depression, anxiety, withdrawal, addiction) and their secondary problems, that is, their problems about their primary problems (e.g., depression about depression, anxiety about anxiety, shame about withdrawal, and guilt about addiction). REBT therapists often assess secondary problems before primary problems because these often require prior therapeutic attention because, for example, clients frequently find it difficult to focus on their original problem of anxiety when they are severely blaming themselves for being anxious. Secondary problems are assessed in the same manner as primary problems.

When particular problems have been adequately assessed according to the ABC model and clients clearly see the link between their irrational Beliefs and their dysfunctional emotional and behavioral Consequences, then therapists can proceed to the disputing stage. One purpose of Disputing is to help clients gain *intellectual insight* into the fact that there is no evidence in support of the existence of their absolutistic demands or the irrational derivatives of these demands ("awfulizing," "I-can't-stand-it-itis," and "damnation"). There exists only evidence that, if they stay with their nonabsolutistic preferences and if these are not fulfilled, they will get unfortunate or "bad" results; whereas if they are fulfilled, they will get desirable or "good" results. Intellectual insight in REBT is defined as an acknowledgment that an irrational Belief frequently leads to emotional disturbance and dysfunctional behavior and that a rational Belief almost always abets emotional health. But when people see and hold rational Beliefs only *weakly* and *occasionally*, they have intellectual insight that may not help them change (Ellis, 1963, 1985c, 1994c, 1996a). So REBT does not stop with intellectual insight but uses it as a springboard for the working-through phase of therapy. In this phase clients are encouraged to use a large variety of cognitive, emotive, and behavioral techniques designed to help them achieve emotional and behavioral insight. Emotional insight in REBT is defined as a very strong and frequently held belief that an irrational idea is dysfunctional and that a rational idea is helpful (Ellis, 1963). When a person has achieved emotional insight, he or she will tend to think-feel-behave according to the rational Belief.

Two other points relevant to the assessment stage of REBT bear mention. First, therapists had better be alert to problems in *both* areas, ego and discomfort disturbance. In particular, ego and discomfort disturbance often interact, and careful assessment is required to disentangle one from the other. Second, REBT practitioners pay particular attention to other ways that humans perpetuate their psychological problems and attempt to assess these carefully in therapy. Thus, humans often seek to defend themselves from threats to their ego and to their sense of comfort. Therapists are often aware that much dysfunctional behavior is defensive and help their clients to identify the irrational Beliefs that underlie such defensive dysfunctional behavior. In addition, psychological problems are sometimes perpetuated because the person *defines* their consequences as payoffs, and ignores their disadvantages. These payoffs also require careful assessment if productive therapeutic strategies are to be implemented.

TREATMENT STRATEGIES IN REBT

There are two forms of REBT—preferential and general (Ellis, 1980b). General REBT is synonymous with cognitive behavior therapy (CBT), whereas preferential REBT is unique in a number of important respects. Because a major aim of this book is to present the distinctive features of REBT, the emphasis here will be on preferential REBT (although it should be noted that REBT therapists routinely use strategies derived from both forms of REBT). The major goal of preferential REBT is an ambitious one: to encourage clients to make a profound philosophic change in the two main areas of ego disturbance and discomfort disturbance. This involves helping clients, as far as is humanly possible, to give up their irrational musturbatory thinking processes and to replace them with rational nonabsolute thinking, as discussed in chapter 1.

In preferential REBT, the major goals are to help clients pursue their long-range basic goals and purposes and to help them do so as effectively as possible by fully accepting themselves and tolerating unchangeable uncomfortable life conditions. Practitioners of preferential REBT further strive to help clients obtain the skills they can use to prevent the development of future disturbance. In encouraging clients to achieve and maintain this profound philosophic change, REBT therapists implement the following strategies. They help their clients see that

1. Emotional and behavioral disturbances have cognitive accompaniments, and these cognitions normally take the form of absolutistic devout evaluations. REBT practitioners train their clients to observe their own psychological disturbances and trace these back to their ideological, emotional, and behavioral roots.
2. People have a distinct measure of self-determination and can thus *choose* to work at undisturbing themselves. Thus, clients are shown that they are not slaves to their biologically based and learned dysfunctional thinking processes.
3. People can implement their choices and maximize their freedom by actively working at changing their destructive musturbatory beliefs. This is best achieved by employing cognitive, emotive, and behavioral methods—often in quite a forceful and vigorous manner (Ellis, 1979c, 1994c, 1996a).

With the majority of clients, from the first session onward REBT therapists are likely to use strategies designed to effect profound philosophic change. The therapist begins therapy with the hypothesis that this particular client may be able to achieve such change and thus begins preferential REBT, which he or she will abandon after collecting sufficient data to reject the initial hypothesis. We regularly implement this viewpoint, which is based on the notion that the client's response to therapy is the best indicator of his or her prognosis. It is not known what proportion of REBT therapists share and regularly implement this position.

When it is clear that the client is not able to achieve philosophic change, whether on a particular issue or in general, the therapist often switches to general REBT and uses methods to effect inferential and behaviorally based change. A good example of this change in strategy is one reported by a therapist of our acquaintance. He was working with a middle-aged married woman who reported feeling furious every time her aging father telephoned her and inquired "Noo, what's doing?" She inferred that this was a gross invasion of her privacy and absolutistically insisted that he had no right to do this. The therapist initially intervened with a preferential REBT strategy by attempting to Dispute this client's dogmatic Belief and tried to help her see that there was no law in the universe that stated that her father *must not* act as he did.

Meeting initial resistance, the therapist persisted with different variations of this theme, all to no avail. Changing tack, he began to implement a general REBT strategy designed to help the client question her inference that her father was actually invading her privacy. Given her father's age, the therapist inquired, was it not more likely that his question represented his usual manner of beginning telephone conversations rather than an intense desire to pry into her affairs? This inquiry proved successful in that the client's rage subsided because she began to reinterpret her father's motives. Interestingly enough, although he returned to the specialized strategy later, the therapist never succeeded in helping this client to give up her irrational musturbatory Belief! However, some clients are more amenable to reevaluating their irrational musturbatory Beliefs *after* they have been helped to correct distorted inferences. We had better do research on this topic if we are to answer the question "Which strategy is most appropriate for which clients at which stage in therapy?" Meanwhile, it is important to note that REBT therapists, if they follow our lead, are unique in that they are more likely to challenge musturbatory cognitions and to dispute these self-defeating Beliefs of their clients much earlier in the therapeutic process than do other cognitive-behavioral therapists. Further differences between preferential REBT and general REBT (or cognitive-behavior therapy) will be discussed at the end of this chapter.

MAJOR TREATMENT TECHNIQUES IN REBT

REBT represents a major form of eclecticism known as "theoretically consistent eclecticism" (Dryden, 1987) in that techniques are liberally borrowed from other therapeutic systems but employed for purposes usually consistent with REBT's underlying theory. In particular, REBT therapists are mindful of the short-term and long-term effects of particular therapeutic techniques and will rarely employ a technique that has beneficial immediate but harmful long-range consequences. Although a large number of cognitive, emotive, and behavioral techniques are employed, only the major ones will be discussed here. It should be noted at the outset that probably all the following techniques have cognitive, emotive, and behavioral elements to them and that "pure" techniques (e.g., purely cognitive) probably do not exist. Techniques are grouped below to show which psychological process predominates.

Cognitive Techniques

Probably the most common technique employed by REBT therapists with the majority of their clients is the *disputing of irrational beliefs*. There are three subcategories of Disputing (Phadke, 1982). *Detecting* consists of looking for dysfunctional beliefs—particularly "must's," "should's," "ought's," and "have to's"—that lead to self-defeating emotions and behaviors. *Debating* consists of the therapist asking a number of questions that are designed to help the client give up irrational Beliefs. Questions such as "Where is the evidence . . .?" "In what way is this Belief accurate or inaccurate?" and "What makes it so?" are frequently employed. The therapist proceeds with such questioning until the client acknowledges the inaccuracy of his or her irrational Belief and, in addition, acknowledges the accuracy of its rational alternative. As will be shown in the next section when examples of Albert Ellis's use of disputing are analyzed, REBT therapists use three major arguments when debating or disputing their client's irrational beliefs. These arguments are empirical, logical, and pragmatic. *Discriminating* involves the therapist's helping the client to distinguish clearly between his nonabsolute values (his wants, preferences, likes, and desires) and his absolutistic values (his needs, demands, and imperatives). REBT therapists are often very creative in their use of Disputing sequences (e.g., Young, 1984) and sometimes employ such methods in a highly dramatic fashion (Dryden, 1984b). A formal version of Disputing that includes some of its main components is known as DIBS (Disputing Irrational Beliefs). I (AE) have outlined its form thus:

QUESTION 1: What unhealthy Belief do I want to dispute and surrender?
ANSWER: I must be as effective and sexually fulfilled as most other women.
QUESTION 2: Can I empirically, logically, and pragmatically support this Belief?
ANSWER: No. It is unrealistic because I don't *have to* be effective sexually. It is illogical because it doesn't follow that if I strongly *want* to be fulfilled sexually, I therefore must be. It is impractical because if I think I *have to* be good sexually, I will probably *interfere with* my good sex relations.
QUESTION 3: What evidence exists of the accuracy of this Belief?
ANSWER: None, only evidence that it would be preferable for me to do well sexually but not that it would be necessary.
QUESTION 4: What evidence exists of the inaccuracy of my Belief that I must be as orgasmic as other women are?
ANSWER: The fact that I am and easily can remain less orgasmic than other women are.
QUESTION 5: What are the worst possible things that could actually happen to me if I never achieved the orgasm that I think I must achieve?
ANSWER: I will lose some degree of pleasure and may lose some partners who demand that I be more effective sexually—and who obviously are not for me!
QUESTION 6: What good things could happen or could I make happen if I never achieved the heights of orgasm that I think I must achieve?
ANSWER: I could devote myself to other pleasurable things, could find a partner who would accept me as I am, could unfrantically explore other sex possibilities, and so on (Ellis, 1974a; Ellis & Harper, 1975).

DIBS is one example of *cognitive homework* that is frequently given to clients to do between sessions after the client has been trained to use them. Other examples appear in Figures 2.2 (page 48) and 2.3 (page 52). The purpose of these forms is to provide a clear framework for clients to do Disputing for themselves.

Clients can also use audiocassettes as an aid to the Disputing process. They can listen to audiotapes of therapy sessions and also Dispute their own irrational Beliefs on tape (*Disputing on tape*). Here they initiate and sustain a dialogue between the rational and irrational parts of themselves (Ellis, 1988; Ellis & Abrams, 1994; Ellis & Velten, 1992).

Clients who do not have the intellectual skills necessary to perform cognitive disputing are usually helped to develop *rational self-statements* that they can memorize or write out on 3" × 5" cards and repeat at various times between sessions. An example developed by one of us (WD) with a client was "Just because my being overweight is bad doesn't mean that I am bad. My overeating makes me too heavy and is therefore wrong, but I can correct it and get better results."

Three cognitive methods that therapists often suggest to their clients to help them reinforce that new rational philosophy are (1) *bibliotherapy*, where clients are given self-help books and materials to read (e.g., Ellis, 1988; Ellis & Becker, 1982; Ellis & Harper, 1975; Young, 1974); (2) listening to *audiocassettes of REBT lectures* on various themes (e.g., Ellis, 1971b, 1976b, 1989, 1990); and (3) *using REBT with others*, where clients use REBT to help their friends and relatives with their problems. In doing so they gain practice at using rational arguments (Ellis & Abrahms, 1978).

A number of semantic methods are also employed in REBT. *Defining* techniques are sometimes employed, the purpose of which is to help clients use language in a less self-defeating manner. Thus, instead of "I can't . . ." clients are urged to use "I haven't yet. . . ." *Referenting* techniques are also employed (Danysh, 1974). Here, clients are encouraged to list both the negative and positive referents of a particular concept such as "smoking." This method is employed to counteract clients' tendencies to focus on the positive aspects of a harmful habit and to neglect its negative aspects.

REBT therapists also employ a number of imagery techniques. Thus, *rational-emotive imagery* (Ellis, 1993; Maultsby, 1971) is often employed. Clients thereby gain practice at changing their "unhealthy" negative emotions to "healthy" ones (C) while maintaining a vivid image of the negative event at A. Here they are in fact learning to change their self-defeating emotions by changing their underlying Beliefs at B. *Time projection* imagery methods are also employed in REBT (Lazarus, 1989). Thus, a client may say that a particular event would be "awful" if it occurred. Rather than directly challenging this dysfunctional belief at this stage, the therapist may temporarily go along with this but help the client to picture what life might be like at regular intervals after the "awful" event has occurred. In this way clients are indirectly helped to change their irrational Belief because they come to "see" that life goes on after the "awful" event, that they will usually recover from it, and that they can continue to pursue their original goals or develop new ones. Such realizations encourage the person to reevaluate his or her irrational Belief. Finally, a number of therapists have successfully employed REBT in a *hypnosis* paradigm (e.g., Ellis, 1993; Golden, Dowd, & Friedberg, 1987; Tosi & Murphy, 1995); see also chapter 11.

Examples of Albert Ellis's Disputing Work

In this segment I (WD) will provide and comment on therapeutic work carried out by Albert Ellis disputing the irrational beliefs of three of his clients. Each sequence focuses on a particular argument.

Using Empirical Arguments In this sequence, Ellis, using primarily empirical arguments, is disputing the irrational belief of a client who insists that she absolutely must succeed in her career.

> ELLIS: Why MUST you have a great career?
> CLIENT: Because I very much want to have it.
> ELLIS: Where is the evidence that you *must* fulfill this strong desire?
> CLIENT: I'll feel much better if I do.
> ELLIS: Yes, you probably will. But how does your feeling better prove that you must succeed?

[So far, Ellis has been using Socratic-type questions. Note how he takes the client's answers that represent evidence in support of her rational belief (i.e., "I want to have a great career, but I don't have to have one") and asks whether or not such evidence supports her irrational belief.]

> CLIENT: But that's what I want more than anything else in the world.
> ELLIS: I'm sure you do. But if we take 100 people like you, all of whom want a great career, want it more than anything else in the world, and would feel much better if they achieved it, do they all *have* to succeed at it?

[Here Ellis probably realizes that he has to use a different type of argument with this client. So he asks whether or not it is empirically true that 100 people who have the same strong preference as the client would all change this into a must.]

> CLIENT: If they are to have any joy in life, they have to do so.

[The client still does not get the point that Ellis is implying through his Socratic-type questions.]

> ELLIS: Really? Can't they have *any* pleasure if they fail to get a great career?

(continued on page 58)

FIGURE 2.2 REBT self-help form.

REBT SELF-HELP FORM

Albert Ellis Institute for Rational Emotive Behavior Therapy
45 East 65th Street, New York, N.Y. 10021
(212) 535-0822

(A) ACTIVATING EVENTS, thoughts, or feelings that happened just before I felt emotionally disturbed or acted self-defeatingly: _____

(C) CONSEQUENCE or CONDITION—disturbed feeling or self-defeating behavior—that I produced and would like to change: _____

(B) BELIEFS—Irrational BELIEFS (IBs) leading to my CONSEQUENCE (emotional disturbance or self-defeating behavior). Circle all that apply to these ACTIVATING EVENTS (A).	(D) DISPUTES for each circled IRRATIONAL BELIEF. Examples: "Why MUST I do very well?" "Where is it written that I am a BAD PERSON?" "Where is the evidence that I MUST be approved or accepted?"	(E) EFFECTIVE RATIONAL BELIEFS (RBs) to replace my IRRATIONAL BELIEFS (IBs) Example: "I'd PREFER to do very well but I don't HAVE TO." "I am a PERSON WHO acted badly, not a BAD PERSON." "There is no evidence that I HAVE TO be approved, though I would LIKE to be."
1. I MUST do well or very well!		
2. I am a BAD OR WORTHLESS PERSON when I act weakly or stupidly.		

48

3. I MUST be approved or accepted by people I find important!

4. I am a BAD, UNLOVABLE PERSON if I get rejected.

5. People MUST treat me fairly and give me what I NEED!

6. People who act immorally are undeserving, ROTTEN PEOPLE!

7. People MUST live up to my expectations or it is TERRIBLE!

8. My life MUST have few major hassles or troubles.

9. I CAN'T STAND really bad things or very difficult people!

10. It's AWFUL or HORRIBLE when major things don't go my way!

49

(continued)

Figure 2.2 (continued)

11. I CAN'T STAND IT when life is really unfair!

12. I NEED to be loved by someone who matters to me a lot!

13. I NEED a good deal of immediate gratification and HAVE TO feel miserable when I don't get it!

Additional Irrational Beliefs:

14.

15.

16.

17.

18.

(F) FEELINGS and BEHAVIORS I experienced after arriving at my **EFFECTIVE RATIONAL BELIEFS:** _____

I WILL WORK HARD TO REPEAT MY EFFECTIVE RATIONAL BELIEFS FORCEFULLY TO MYSELF ON MANY OCCASIONS SO THAT I CAN MAKE MYSELF LESS DISTURBED NOW AND ACT LESS SELF-DEFEATINGLY IN THE FUTURE.

Joyce Sichel, Ph.D. and Albert Ellis, Ph.D.
Copyright © 1984 by Albert Ellis Institute for Rational Emotive Behavior Therapy.

100 forms $10.00
1000 forms $80.00

ABC

OF

EMOTIONAL AND BEHAVIOURAL PROBLEMS

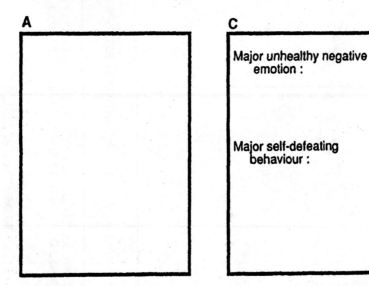

A

C

Major unhealthy negative
emotion :

Major self-defeating
behaviour :

A = ACTIVATING EVENT

- Describe the aspect of the
  situation you were most
  disturbed about

- Assume temporarily that *A* is
  true

- An *A* can be *internal* or
  external

- An *A* can refer to an event in
  the *past, present or future*

- An *A* can be an *interpretation*

C = CONSEQUENCE

Unhealthy Negative Emotions :

- Anxiety

- Depression

- Anger

- Guilt

- Shame & Embarrassment

- Hurt

- Jealousy

FIGURE 2.3 ABC of emotional and behavioral problems.

iBs

DOGMATIC DEMAND :
AWFULISING :
LOW FRUSTRATION TOLERANCE :
SELF/ OTHER DOWNING :

D

Is it true ? Is it logical ? Is it helpful ?
Is it true ? Is it logical ? Is it helpful ?
Is it true ? Is it logical ? Is it helpful ?
Is it true ? Is it logical ? Is it helpful ?

iBs = IRRATIONAL BELIEFS

Look for :

- DOGMATIC DEMANDS
(musts, absolute shoulds, oughts)

- AWFULISING
(It's awful, terrible, horrible)

- LOW FRUSTRATION TOLERANCE
(I can't stand it, I can't bear it)

- SELF/OTHER DOWNING
(bad, worthless, less worthy)

D = DISPUTING

- Where is the evidence to support the existence of my irrational belief ? Is it *consistent with reality* ?

- Is my belief *logical* ? Does it logically follow from my rational belief ?

- Where is holding this belief getting me ? Is it *helpful* ?

(continued)

rBs

NON-DOGMATIC PREFERENCE :
EVALUATING BADNESS :
HIGH FRUSTRATION TOLERANCE:
SELF/ OTHER ACCEPTANCE :

E

New healthy negative emotion :

New constructive behaviour :

rBs = RATIONAL BELIEFS

Strive for :

- NON-DOGMATIC PREFERENCES
  (wishes, wants, desires)

- EVALUATING BADNESS
  (It's bad, unfortunate)

- HIGH FRUSTRATION TOLERANCE
  (I can stand it, I can bear it)

- SELF/OTHER ACCEPTANCE
  ("Fallible human being" concept)

E = NEW EFFECT

Healthy Negative Emotions :

- Concern

- Sadness

- Annoyance

- Remorse

- Disappointment

- Regret

- Concern about my relationship

FIGURE 2.3, continued

HOMEWORK :

(continued)

Sheet Explaining the Use of Dryden & Walker's
(1992) Written Self-Help Form

When using this form it is very important that you select a specific example of your problem. The more specific you can be, the better. Then complete the form in the following order.

First, Complete 'C'

(i)   Choose one unhealthy negative emotion from those listed (which could be the main one) and write down the self-defeating behavior associated with it.
(ii) Use one form for each emotion if you experienced more than one unhealthy negative emotion in the episode under consideration.
(iii) If your problem is associated only with self-defeating behavior leave the "emotion" section blank.

Second, Complete 'A'

(i)   Here, it is very important that you focus on the aspect about which you were most disturbed.
(ii) As it says on the form, it is most important that you assume temporarily that 'A' is true. You will have an opportunity later to check on its accuracy.

Third, Write Down your iBs and 'A'

(i)   Work from the top of the form to the bottom and complete the relevant sections.
(ii) Leave blank any section that does not apply.

FIGURE 2.3, continued

Fourth, Complete the 'D' Section
(i)   Answer each of the three questions.
(ii) Don't give a "parrot" answer. Think through each of your responses and prove to yourself why the correct answer is "no."

Fifth, Complete the rBs Section
(i)   Again, work from the top of the form to the bottom and complete the relevant sections.
(ii) Make sure that you assert the rational belief and negate the irrational belief in each completed section.

Sixth, Complete the 'E' Section
(i)   Provide a healthy negative emotion from those listed, making sure that it is a constructive alternative to the unhealthy negative emotion listed under 'C.'
(ii) Write down your constructive negative behavior associated with the new emotion.
(iii) If your problem was associated only with self-defeating behavior, just complete the "New constructive behavior" part of the form, leaving the "emotion" section blank.

Seventh, Reconsider 'A'
(i)   While holding the new rational beliefs, go back to 'A' and correct any distorted inferences that you find there.

Finally, Homework
(i)   Discuss a suitable homework assignment with your therapist to strengthen your conviction in your rational beliefs.

[Taking the lead form the client's last response, Ellis changes the focus of his argument again. If 100 people all must have a great career, none of them will have any pleasure if they don't achieve it. Ellis then questions whether this is empirically the case.]

CLIENT: Well, yes. I guess they can have *some* pleasure.

[This is the first time that the client shows any sign that she can think rationally about the issue at hand. Note how Ellis capitalizes on this.]

ELLIS: And could some of them have a great deal of pleasure?
CLIENT: Um. Probably, yes.
ELLIS: Probably?
CLIENT: Well, highly probably.
ELLIS: Right. So no matter how much people greatly want success and would feel better about gaining it, they don't have to get it. Right?

[Here Ellis summarizes the rational point and asks for agreement. I might have asked, "What do you think of this idea?" in order to encourage the client to be more independent in her thinking.]

CLIENT: Well, yes.
ELLIS: Social reality is that way—isn't it?
CLIENT: It seems so.
ELLIS: Back to you. Does *your* great desire for a successful career mean that you *absolutely must* achieve it—that the world *has to* fulfill this desire?

[Having got the rational point over in an abstract way, Ellis then seeks to apply it to the client's own specific set of personal circumstances.]

CLIENT: I see what you mean. Social reality is the way it is, no matter how unpleasant I find it to be.

[The client shows signs of really understanding Ellis's point.]

ELLIS: Exactly. Make a note of that Effective New Philosophy you just arrived at and keep thinking that way until you thoroughly believe it!

Using Logical Arguments In this segment Ellis is disputing the irrational beliefs of a client who insists that because he treated his friend very nicely and fairly, this friend *absolutely should* treat him the same way. He does so using primarily logical arguments.

ELLIS: Let's suppose that you're describing the situation with your friend accurately and that he treats you shabbily and unfairly after you consistently

treat him well. How does it follow that because of your good behavior he
has to respond in kind?

CLIENT: But he's unfair if he doesn't!

ELLIS: Yes, we're agreeing on that. He *is* unfair, and you are fair. Can you jump
from "Because I'm very fair to him, he *has to be* fair to me?"

CLIENT: But he's wrong if he isn't fair when I am.

[At this point Ellis and the client appear to be at cross-purposes. Ellis keeps
asking the client why his friend *must* be fair to him, and the client keeps reply-
ing that his friend is wrong and unfair, which Ellis is not questioning.]

ELLIS: Agreed. But because you are fair, and presumably right, and because he
takes advantage of your unfairness, does it *still* follow that he has to be right
and to treat you fairly?

CLIENT: It logically follows.

ELLIS: Does it? It looks like a complete nonsequitur to me.

CLIENT: How so?

[This is a typical Ellis change of emphasis. He asserts that the client's belief is
illogical and waits for the latter to ask why before expanding on his theme. He
wants to get his client into an inquiring, "Why do you say that?" mode.]

ELLIS: Well, it's logical or consistent that he preferably should treat you fairly
when you treat him well. But aren't you making an illogical—or "magical"—jump from "Because he *preferably* should treat me fairly he *absolutely
has to* do so?' What "logical" law of the universe leads to your "He
absolutely has to do so?"

CLIENT: No law, I guess.

ELLIS: No, in logic we get necessitous conclusions, such as "If all men are human
and John is a man, John must be human." But your "logic" says, 'People
who get treated fairly, often treat others fairly; I treat my friend fairly;
therefore it is absolutely *necessary* that he treat me similarly." Is that a logical conclusion?

[This is another typical Ellis strategy. He begins by making a point in didactic fashion. As occurs here, this point illustrates a rational idea (in this case a
logical idea). He then contrasts this with the client's irrational idea (in this case
an illogical idea) but does not tell the client that his idea is illogical. Rather he
encourages the client to think for himself by asking, "Is that a logical conclusion?" It is worth studying this sequence in detail because it is so typical of
Ellis's effective disputing work.]

CLIENT: I guess not.

ELLIS: Moreover, you seem to be claiming that because you act fairly and your
friend behaves unfairly, his *acts* make him a *rotten person*. Is that logical
thinking?

[Ellis infers other-downing from his client's *must*. He is probably correct; however, my practice is to check my hunch with the client before proceeding.]

CLIENT: Why not?

[As you will see, Ellis immediately answers the client's question. I would have encouraged the client to make a stab at answering his own question before going into didactic mode.]

ELLIS: It's illogical because you're overgeneralizing. You're jumping from one of his rotten *behaviors*—or even one of his *traits*—to categorizing *him*, his totality as "rotten." How does that overgeneralization follow from a few of his behaviors?

[Here Ellis states the logical error that the client is making, shows him in what way the error is present in his belief about his friend, and finally questions him about the logicality of that belief.]

CLIENT: I can see now that it doesn't.
ELLIS: So what could you more logically conclude instead?

[Here, Ellis encourages the client to be active in his thinking.]

CLIENT: Well, I could think that he isn't one of his main behaviors. He is a person who often, but not always, acts rottenly.
ELLIS: Good! Alfred Korzybski and his followers in General Semantics would approve of your new conclusion!

Using Pragmatic Arguments In the following piece of work, the client insists that if she believes that she must do well, she will succeed better at school and win others' approval. Ellis shows her that her irrational belief will in all probability produce poor results.

CLIENT: If I am anxious about doing poorly at school because, as you say, I think that I must do well, won't my must and my anxiety motivate me to do better?
ELLIS: Yes, in part. But won't they also defeat you?

[Here Ellis gives a straight answer to the client's straight question. But he then follows up by asking a question to encourage the client to think about the issue for herself. This is another typical Ellis disputing strategy.]

CLIENT: How so?
ELLIS: If you keep making yourself very anxious with "I must do well! I must perform perfectly!" won't you preoccupy yourself so much that you *detract* from the time and energy you can give to studying?

[Yet another typical Ellis intervention. Here Ellis is really making a statement in the guise of a question. The question format is to encourage the client's active participation, but the rational point that Ellis is making is clear.]

    CLIENT: Maybe. But I'll still feel quite motivated.
    ELLIS: Mainly motivated to obsess! You'll be *driven* to study. And while you drive yourself, you'll keep thinking, "But suppose I fail! Wouldn't that be *awful?*" You'll worry about what your texts will be like, how you will handle them, how you will subsequently perform, and so on. How will keeping the future so much in mind help you focus on the *present* studying?

[This intervention comprises a number of didactically made points with the question twist at the end.]

    CLIENT: It may not help.
    ELLIS: No, it's much more likely to sabotage. Moreover, even if you somehow succeed in your courses, do you want to be miserably anxious and depressed, *while* you are succeeding?
    CLIENT: Frankly, no.
    ELLIS: And do you want to be *so* absorbed in worrying about school that you have little time for relationships, sports, music, and other enjoyments?

[Having succeeded in getting the point across to the client that her irrational belief will do her more harm than good, Ellis spends time (cf. his last two interventions and much of his following responses) underscoring this important point.]

    CLIENT: I don't think so. I passed my courses last term but was able to do little else.
    ELLIS: See! And what about the physical results of your constant worry and perfectionism?
    CLIENT: My physician thinks they are making my digestive tract hyperactive.
    ELLIS: I'm not surprised. And when you constantly worry, how do you feel about *you* for being such a worrier?
    CLIENT: Pretty shitty.
    ELLIS: Is *that* feeling worth it? But even if you felt bad about your anxiety and didn't put *yourself* down for having it, you would still bring on endless frustration and disappointment by indulging in it.
    CLIENT: You may be right.
    ELLIS: Don't take my word for it. Look for yourself at the results you get from your perfectionistic demands and figure out what you could say to yourself to replace them.

[Ellis often urges his clients not to take his word for it. However, his didactic style does encourage clients not used to thinking for themselves to do just that. Greater extended use of Socratic disputing might achieve this result more effectively.]

CLIENT: Well, I could tell myself, "It's great to do well at school, but I *don't have to be perfect*. Even if my anxiety sometimes helps me to get good marks, it, too, has too many disadvantages and it isn't worth it."

ELLIS: Good! That's a much better way to think.

Emotive Techniques

REBT has often been falsely criticized for neglecting emotive aspects of psychotherapy. However, this is far from the truth, and REBT therapists frequently employ a number of emotive techniques. As has already been shown, they offer their clients the emotional attitude of *unconditional acceptance*. No matter how badly clients behave, their therapists strive to accept them as fallible humans but do not go along with their bad behavior. REBT therapists use a variety of emotive techniques that are designed to help clients challenge their dysfunctional Beliefs. First, a number of *humorous* methods are employed to encourage clients to think rationally by not taking themselves too seriously (Ellis, 1977b, 1977d, 1987). Second, REBT therapists do not hesitate to model a rational philosophy through *self-disclosure*. They honestly admit that they have had similar problems and show that they overcame them by using REBT. Thus, I (WD) frequently tell clients that I used to feel ashamed of my stammer. I then relate how I accepted myself with my speech impediment and how I forced myself to tolerate the discomfort of speaking in public whenever the opportunity arose. Third, REBT therapists frequently use a number of *stories, mottoes, parables, witticisms, poems,* and *aphorisms* as adjuncts to cognitive Disputing techniques (Ellis & Abrams, 1994; Wessler & Wessler, 1980). Fourth, we have written a number of humorous songs that are designed to present rational philosophies in an amusing and memorable format (Ellis, 1977b, 1977d, 1981c, 1987). The following is a humorous song written by one of us (WD) to the tune of "God Save the Queen":

> God save my precious spleen
> Send me a life serene
> God save my spleen!
> Protect me from things odious
> Give me a life melodious
> And if things get too onerous
> I'll whine, bawl, and scream!

In an important paper, I (AE) first advocated the use of force and energy in the practice of psychotherapy (Ellis, 1979a). REBT is unique among the cognitive-behavioral therapies in emphasizing the employment of such interventions that fully involve clients' emotions. Thus, REBT therapists suggest that clients can help themselves go from intellectual to emotional insight by *vigorously Disputing* their irrational Beliefs (Ellis, 1993g). Vigor is often employed by clients in *role reversal*, where they forcefully and dramatically adopt the role of their rational "self," whose goal is to successfully Dispute self-defeating Beliefs as articulated by their irrational "self." Force and energy also play a significant part in REBT's now famous *shame-attacking exercises* (Ellis, 1969, 1971b; Ellis & Becker, 1982). Here clients deliberately seek to act "shamefully" in public in order to accept themselves and to tolerate the ensuing discomfort. Because clients should not harm themselves nor other people, minor infractions of social rules often serve as appropriate shame-attacking exercises (e.g., calling out the time in a crowded department store, wearing bizarre clothes designed to attract public attention, and going into a hardware store and asking if they sell tobacco). *Risk-taking exercises* come into the same category. Here clients deliberately force themselves to take calcu-lated risks in areas where they wish to make changes. While disputing rele-vant irrational beliefs, I (AE) overcame my anxiety about approaching women by deliberately forcing myself to speak to 100 women in the Bronx Botanical Gardens. I (WD) pushed myself to speak on national and local radio as part of a campaign to overcome my public-speaking anxiety. Both of us took these risks while showing ourselves that nothing "awful" would result from such experiences. *Repeating rational self-statements in a passionate and forceful man-ner* is often used in conjunction with such exercises (Ellis, 1985c, 1988; Ellis & Abrams, 1994; Ellis & Velten, 1992).

Behavioral Techniques

REBT has advocated the use of behavioral techniques (particularly *homework assignments*) from its inception in 1955 because it is realized that cognitive change is very often facilitated by behavioral change (Emmelkamp, Kuipers, & Eggeraat, 1978). Because REBT therapists are concerned to help clients raise their level of frustration tolerance, they encourage them to carry out homework assignments based on *in vivo desensitization*, and *flooding* paradigms rather than those that are based on the gradual desensitization paradigm (Ellis, 1979d; Ellis & Abrahms, 1978; Ellis & Becker, 1982; Ellis & Grieger, 1977). However, prag-matic considerations do have to be considered, and some clients refuse to carry out such assignments. When this occurs, REBT therapists would negotiate a compromise encouraging such clients to undertake tasks that are sufficiently challenging for them but that are not overwhelming, given their present status (Dryden, 1985a).

Other behavioral methods frequently employed in REBT include (1) *"stay in there" activities* (Grieger & Boyd, 1980), which present clients with oppor-tunities to tolerate chronic discomfort while remaining in *uncomfortable* situa-tions for a long period of time; (2) *antiprocrastination exercises*, where clients are encouraged to push themselves to start tasks sooner rather than later while again tolerating the discomfort of breaking the *mañana* habit (Ellis & Knaus,

1977); (3) the use of *rewards and penalties*, which are employed to encourage clients to undertake uncomfortable assignments in the pursuit of their long-range goals (Ellis, 1979d) (stiff penalties are found to be particularly helpful with chronically resistant clients [Ellis, 1985c]); and (4) Kelly's *fixed role therapy*, sometimes employed in REBT, where clients are encouraged to act "as if" they already think rationally, to enable them to get the experience that change is possible.

A number of other behavioral methods are employed in both preferential and general REBT (e.g., various forms of *skills training methods*). When these are used in preferential REBT, they are done to encourage philosophic change, whereas in general REBT they are employed to teach clients skills that are absent from their repertory. When skill training is the goal in preferential REBT, it is employed *along with* Disputing of irrational Beliefs and while some measure of philosophic change is being sought (Ellis, 1988; Ellis & Abrams, 1994; Ellis & Velten, 1992).

Techniques That Are Avoided in REBT

By now it will be clear that REBT is a multimodal form of therapy that advocates the employment of techniques in the cognitive, emotive, and behavioral modalities. However, because the choice of therapeutic techniques is inspired by REBT theory, the following available therapeutic techniques are avoided or used sparingly in the practice of REBT (Ellis, 1979d, 1983b, 1994c, 1995a, 1996a, 1996b).

- Techniques that help people become more dependent (e.g., undue therapist warmth as a strong reinforcement and the creation and analysis of a transference neurosis).
- Techniques that encourage people to become more gullible and suggestible (e.g., pollyanna-ish positive thinking).
- Techniques that are long-winded and inefficient (e.g., psychoanalytic methods in general and free association in particular; encouraging clients to give lengthy descriptions of Activating experiences at A).
- Methods that help people feel better in the short term rather than get better in the long term (Ellis, 1972a) (e.g., some experiential techniques like fully expressing one's feelings in a dramatic, cathartic, and abreactive manner (i.e., some Gestalt methods and primal techniques). The danger here is that such methods may encourage people to practice dysfunctional philosophies underlying such emotions as anger).
- Techniques that distract clients from working on their dysfunctional philosophies (e.g., relaxation methods, Yoga, and other cognitive distrac-

tion methods). These methods may be employed, however, *along with* cognitive Disputing designed to yield some philosophic change.

- Methods that may unwittingly reinforce clients' philosophy of low frustration tolerance (e.g., gradual desensitization).
- Techniques that include an antiscientific philosophy (e.g., faith healing and mysticism).
- Techniques that attempt to change Activating events (A) before or without showing clients how to change their irrational Beliefs (B) (e.g., some strategic family systems techniques).
- Techniques that have little empirical support (e.g., neurolinguistic programming), nondirective therapy, and rebirthing therapy.

Finally, to reiterate, REBT therapists do not absolutistically avoid using the above methods. They may on certain occasions with certain clients utilize such techniques, particularly for pragmatic purposes. For example, if faith healing is the only method that will prevent some clients from harming themselves, then REBT therapists might either employ it themselves or, more probably, refer such clients to a faith healer (Ellis, 1985c, 1994a, 1994c, 1996a).

OVERCOMING OBSTACLES TO CLIENT PROGRESS

When REBT is practiced efficiently and effectively and when clients understand and are prepared to continually implement its basic concepts, then it can achieve remarkable results. However, frequently (and perhaps more frequently than most therapists are prepared to admit!), various obstacles to client progress are encountered in the practice of REBT (and indeed all other forms of therapy). Three major forms of obstacles may occur in REBT: (1) relationship obstacles, (2) therapist obstacles, and (3) client obstacles (Ellis, 1985c).

Relationship Obstacles to Client Progress

These can be first attributed to poor therapist–client matching. Such mismatching may occur for many reasons. Thus, clients "may have a therapist who, according to their diosyncratic tastes or preferences, is too young or too old, too liberal or too conservative, too active or too passive" (Ellis, 1983c, p. 29). If these "relationship match" obstacles persist, then it is preferable for that client to be transferred to a therapist with more suitable traits. Other relationship obstacles may occur because the therapist and client may get on "too well" and get distracted form the more mundane tasks of therapy. In such cases, the paradox is that if the client improves, the "life" of the satisfactory relationship is

:hreatened. As a result, collusion may occur between therapist and client to ıvoid making therapy as effective an endeavor as it might otherwise be. This ɔroblem can be largely overcome if the therapist helps first himself or herself ınd then the client to overcome the philosophy of low frustration tolerance .mplicit in this collusive short-range hedonism.

Therapist Obstacles to Client Progress

There are two major types of therapist obstacles: skill-oriented obstacles and disturbance-oriented obstacles. When obstacles to client progress can be mainly attributed to therapist skill deficits, these may appear in a variety of forms, but most commonly therapists may impede client progress by

1. Improperly inducting clients into therapy and failing to correct unrealistic expectations such as "my therapist will solve my problems for me."
2. Incorrectly assessing clients' problems and thus working on "problems" that clients do not have.
3. Failing to show clients that their problems have ideological roots and that C is largely (but not exclusively) determined by B and not by A. Inexpert therapists often fail to persist with this strategy or persist with an ineffective strategy.
4. Failing to show clients that the ideological roots of their problems are most frequently expressed in the form of devout, absolutistic "must's" or one of the three main derivatives of musturbation. Instead, inexpert REBT therapists frequently dwell too long on their clients' antiempirical or inferentially distorted thinking.
5. Assuming that clients will automatically change their absolute thinking once they have identified it. Inexpert REBT therapists either fail to dispute such thinking at all or use Disputing methods sparingly and/or with insufficient vigor. In addition, inexpert therapists routinely fail to (1) give their clients homework assignments, which provide them with opportunities to practice Disputing their irrational Beliefs; (2) check on their clients' progress on these assignments; and (3) help their clients to identify and change their philosophic obstacles to continually working at self-change.
6. Failing to realize that clients often have problems about their problems and thus working only on a primary problem when the client is preoccupied with a secondary problem.
7. Frequently switching from ego to discomfort disturbance issues within a given session so that clients get confused and thus distracted from working on either issue.
8. Working at a pace and a level inappropriate to the learning abilities of clients so that these clients are insufficiently involved in the therapeutic process due to confusion or boredom.

For these reasons it is highly desirable for REBT therapists to strive to continually improve their skills by involving themselves in ongoing supervision and training activities (Dryden, 1983; Woods & Ellis, 1996).

Client progress can also be hindered because therapists may bring their own disturbance to the therapeutic process. I (AE) have outlined five major irrational beliefs that lead to therapeutic inefficiency (Ellis, 1985c):

> "I *have* to be successful with all my clients practically all of the time."
> "I *must* be an outstanding therapist, clearly better than other therapists I know or hear about."
> "I *have* to be greatly respected and loved by all my clients."
> "Since I am doing my best and working so hard as a therapist, my clients *should* be equally hardworking and responsible, *should* listen to me carefully, and *should* always push themselves to change."
> "Because I am a person in my own right, I *must* be able to enjoy myself during therapy sessions and to use these sessions to solve my personal problems as much as to help clients with their difficulties."

In such cases, it is recommended that REBT therapists apply REBT principles and methods to search for and Dispute their own self- and client-defeating Beliefs, which may (1) impede them from confronting their clients, (2) distract them and their clients from getting the therapeutic job done, (3) foster undue therapist anxiety and anger, and (4) encourage inappropriate behavior that is anathema to the practice of effective and ethical therapy.

Client Obstacles to Client Progress

In order to really benefit from REBT, clients had better achieve the following three forms of insight: (1) Psychological disturbance is mainly determined by the absolutistic Beliefs that they hold about themselves, others, and the world; (2) even when people acquired and created their irrational Beliefs in their early lives, they perpetuate their disturbance by reindoctrinating themselves in the present with these beliefs; (3) only if they constantly work and practice in the present and future to think, feel, and act against these irrational Beliefs are clients likely to surrender their irrationalities and make themselves significantly less disturbed.

In a study by one of us (AE) of the characteristics of clients who "failed" in REBT, the following findings emerged: (1) Clients who did poorly failed to do consistent *cognitive* self-Disputation. They were characterized, among other factors, by extreme disturbance, grandiosity, lack of organization, and plain refusal to do these cognitive assignments; (2) "failure" clients, who refused to accept responsibility for their unhealthy emotions and refused to forcefully and *emotively* change their beliefs and actions, were more clingy, more severely depressed and inactive, more often grandiose, and more frequently stubbornly rebellious than clients who benefited from REBT; (3) "failure" clients who did poorly in the *behavioral* aspects of REBT showed "abysmally low frustration tolerance, had serious behavioral addictions, led disorganized lives, refrained from doing their activity homework assignments, were more frequently psychotic and generally refused to work at therapy" (Ellis, 1983a, p. 165).

Thus, clients' own extreme level of disturbance is a significant obstacle to their own progress. Although a full discussion of what "special" therapeutic methods and techniques to employ with such clients is outside the scope of this chapter (see Ellis, 1985c), therapists can adopt a number of strategies to enhance therapeutic effectiveness with these DCs ("difficult customers"). Among other tactics, therapists, first, are advised to be consistently and forcefully encouraging in their therapeutic interactions with these clients, showing them that they can do better if they try. Second, therapists would be wise to keep vigorously showing these resistant clients that they, the therapists, do, in fact, unconditionally accept them with all their psychological difficulties and that they can indeed accept themselves in the same way. Third, therapists can often be successful with such clients by consistently showing them that their refusal to work on their problems will generally lead to bad consequences and needless suffering. Fourth, therapists are advised to be flexible in experimenting with a wide range of therapeutic techniques (including some unusual ones!) in their persistent efforts to help their "difficult" clients. Above all, REBT therapists should preferably be good representatives of their therapeutic system and accept themselves and tolerate the discomfort of working with difficult clients while sticking to the therapeutic task!

Termination preferably takes place in REBT when clients have made some significant progress and when they have become proficient in REBT's self-change techniques. Thus, terminating clients should preferably be able to (1) acknowledge that they experience "unhealthy" negative emotions and act dysfunctionally when they do, (2) detect the irrational and dysfunctional beliefs that underpin these experiences, (3) discriminate their Irrational Beliefs from their rational alternatives, (4) challenge these dysfunctional Beliefs, and (5) counteract them by using cognitive, emotive, and behavioral self-change methods. In addition, it is often helpful for therapists to arrange for their clients to attend a series of follow-up sessions after termination to monitor their progress and deal with any remaining obstacles to sustained improvement.

PREFERENTIAL REBT VERSUS GENERAL REBT (CEBT)

We have already alluded to the differences between preferential REBT and general REBT which, I [AE] have argued, is synonymous with broad-based cognitive-behavior therapy [CBT] (Ellis, 1979c, 1980b). Let us close this chapter by noting these differences in greater detail. Preferential REBT

1. Has a distinct philosophic emphasis that is one of its central features and that other forms of CBT often omit. Thus, it stresses that humans appraise themselves, others, and the world in terms of (1) rational, preferential, flexible, and tolerant philosophies and in terms of (2) irrational, musturbatory, rigid, intolerant, and absolutistic philosophies.

2. Has an existential-humanistic outlook that is intrinsic to it and that is omitted by most other CBT approaches. Thus, it sees people "as holistic, goal-directed individuals who have importance in the world just because they are human and alive; it unconditionally accepts them with their limitations, and it particularly focuses upon their experiences and values, including their self-actualizing potentialities" (Ellis, 1980b, p. 327). It also shares the views of ethical humanism by encouraging people to emphasize human interest (self and social) over the interests of deities and material objects.

3. Favors striving for pervasive and long-lasting (philosophically based) rather than symptomatic change (Ellis, 1996a).

4. Attempts to help humans eliminate all self-ratings and views self-esteem as a self-defeating concept that encourages them to make conditional evaluations of self. Instead, it teaches people *un*conditional self-acceptance (Ellis, 1972a, 1976c, 1985c, 1994c, 1996a, 1996b; Hauck, 1991; Mills, 1993).

5. Considers psychological disturbance to reflect an attitude to taking life "too" seriously and thus advocates the appropriate use of various humorous therapeutic methods (Ellis, 1977b, 1977c, 1981, 1987a).

6. Stresses the use of antimusturbatory rather than antiempirical Disputing methods. Because it considers that inferential distortions often stem from dogmatic "must's," "should's," and the like, preferential REBT favors going to the philosophic core of emotional disturbance and Disputing the irrational beliefs at this core rather than merely disputing antiempirical inferences, which are more peripheral. Also, preferential REBT favors the use of forceful logicoempirical and pragmatic Disputing of Irrational Beliefs whenever possible rather than the employment of functionally oriented, coping self-statements. When feasible, preferential REBT teaches clients how to become their own scientists instead of parroting therapist-inculcated Rational Beliefs.

7. Employs but only mildly encourages the use of palliative cognitive methods that serve to distract people from their disturbed philosophies (e.g., relaxation methods). Preferential REBT holds that such techniques may help clients better in the short term but do not encourage them to identify challenge and change in the long term the devout philosophies that underpin their psychological problems. Indeed, these palliative methods may make it harder for people to engage in philosophic Disputing because they may be less likely to do this when they are calm and relaxed than when they are motivated by their

emotional distress. For these reasons, preferential REBT also employs problem-solving and skill training methods, along with, but not instead of, teaching people to work at understanding and changing their dysfunctional Beliefs.

8. Gives a more central explanatory role to the concept of discomfort anxiety in psychological disturbance than do other cognitive-behavioral therapies. Discomfort anxiety is defined as "emotional hypertension that arises when people feel (1) that their life or comfort is threatened, (2) that they *must* not feel uncomfortable and *have to* feel at ease, and (3) that it is awful (rather than merely inconvenient or disadvantageous) when they don't get what they supposedly must" (Ellis, 1980a, p. 331). Although other cognitive-behavioral therapies recognize specific instances of discomfort anxieties (e.g., "fear of fear" [Mackay, 1984]), they tend not to regard discomfort disturbance to be as centrally implicated in psychological problems as does preferential REBT.

9. Emphasizes, more than some other approaches to CBT, that humans frequently make themselves disturbed about their original disturbances. Thus, in preferential REBT therapists actively look for secondary and tertiary symptoms of disturbances and encourage clients to work on overcoming these before addressing themselves to the primary disturbance.

10. Has clear-cut theories of disturbance and its treatment but is eclectic or multimodal in its techniques. However, it favors some techniques (e.g., active Disputing) over others (e.g., cognitive distraction) and strives for profound or elegant philosophic change where feasible. If nothing else works with certain clients, it is flexible enough to sometimes use "irrational" or "antiscientific" methods (Ellis, 1994c, 1996a).

11. Discriminates between "healthy" and "unhealthy" negative emotions. Preferential REBT considers such negative emotions as sadness, annoyance, concern, regret, and disappointment as "healthy" affective responses to thwarted desires, based on a nondevout philosophy of desire, and views them as healthy when they do not needlessly interfere with people's goals and purposes. However, it sees depression, anger, anxiety, guilt, shame/embarrassment, self-pity, and feelings of inadequacy usually as "unhealthy" emotions based on absolutistic demands about thwarted desires. Preferential REBT considers these latter feelings as symptoms of disturbance because they very frequently (but not always) sabotage people and keep them from constructively pursuing their goals and purposes. Other CBT approaches do not make such fine discriminations between "healthy" and "unhealthy" negative emotions.

12. Advocates therapists giving unconditional acceptance rather than giving warmth or approval to clients. Other cognitive-behavioral therapies tend not to make this distinction. Preferential REBT holds that therapist warmth and approval have their distinct dangers in that they may unwittingly encourage clients to strengthen their dire needs for love and approval. When REBT therapists unconditionally accept their clients they also serve as good role models, in that they also help clients to to unconditionally accept themselves.

13. Stresses the importance of the use of vigor and force in counteracting irrational philosophies and behaviors (Dryden, 1984b; Ellis, 1979c, 1993g, 1994c, 1995a, 1996a). Preferential REBT is one of the few cognitive-behavioral therapies that stresses that humans are, for the most part, biologically predisposed to originate and perpetuate their disturbances and often experience great difficulty in changing the ideological roots of these problems. Because it holds this view, it urges both therapists and clients to use considerable force and vigor in interrupting clients' irrational beliefs.

14. Is more selective than most other cognitive-behavioral therapies in choosing behavioral change methods. Thus, it favors the use of penalization in encouraging resistant clients to change. Often these clients will not change to obtain positive reinforcements but may be encouraged to change to avoid stiff penalties. Furthermore, preferential REBT has reservations concerning the use of social reinforcement in therapy. It considers that humans are too reinforceable and that they often do the right thing for the wrong reason. Thus, they may change to please their socially reinforcing therapists, but in doing so they have not been encouraged to think and act for their own sake. Preferential REBT therapists aim to help many clients become more self-reliant and self-directed and therefore may use social reinforcement techniques sparingly. Finally, preferential REBT often favors the use of in vivo desensitization and flooding methods instead of the use of gradual desensitization techniques; it argues that the former procedures best help clients to raise their level of frustration tolerance (Ellis, 1962, 1983b, 1985c, 1994c, 1995a, 1996a).

Although REBT therapists *prefer* to use preferential REBT wherever feasible, they do not dogmatically insist that it be employed. When, on pragmatic grounds, they employ general REBT, their therapeutic practice is frequently indistinguishable from that of other cognitive-behavioral therapists.

In the remaining chapters we show how REBT is practiced in its various therapeutic and educational modalities, but first, in the next chapter we present a case study of REBT.

3

A Case Illustration of the Basic Practice of REBT: The Case of Jane

REBT, as shown in this book, is used in a variety of settings and ways. Often, clients only have individual sessions of psychotherapy, or they have a few individual sessions and then mainly participate in a regular, once-a-week therapy group. Some clients have individual and group sessions at the same time, and some have several months or more of individual therapy and then switch to group therapy, which they then largely continue with few or no subsequent individual sessions.

To give an illustration of the basic clinical practice of REBT, we include in this chapter a case illustration of a 27-year-old woman afflicted with severe social and work anxiety. I (AE) saw this client, Jane, once a week for 3 months and then mainly in group therapy on a once-a-week basis. She decided to switch to group therapy because she felt that she was beginning to understand the basic principles of REBT and to use them fairly consistently, but that she found individual therapy with me "too safe" and wanted to risk speaking up about her problems in the group, trying to relate to the other group members, and learning to practice REBT by helping to talk them out of their irrational beliefs and behaviors. If she had not volunteered to join one of my groups, I would have probably urged her to do so anyway, because I frequently encourage my shy and socially anxious clients to join a group, to help them learn to cope more successfully with social situations, and to get them to undertake more risk-taking experiences.

When she joined one of my regular therapy groups, Jane continued to learn and practice REBT along the same lines that she had begun during her first

Parts of this chapter were adapted from Albert Ellis, "Rational-Emotive Therapy," in I. L. Kutash and A. Wolf (Eds.), *Psychotherapist's Casebook* (pp. 277–287); San Francisco: Jossey-Bass, 1986. Used by permission.

few months of individual sessions, so that her group participation added to and went beyond some of the new kinds of thinking, feeling, and behaving on which she had already embarked. She was at first hesitant to say very much to the other group members about their problems, although she freely spoke up about her own. But when I helped her to look at this hesitance and to see how she was defining ineffective group behavior as "awful" and "self-deprecating," and when I persisted in drawing her out to talk about other members' problems, she soon overcame her shyness and developed into one of the most active group participants.

When I initially saw Jane she was (as all the members of her therapy group later agreed and kept pointing out to her) unusually attractive. Hardly a day passed when some man (or some lesbian) did not try to pick her up at her office, on the subway, on the street, or in the stores where she shopped. In spite of all this attention, she was extremely shy with men, especially the ones she found most desirable, and reported that her mind went absolutely blank when she was about to talk to one. She was so self-conscious that she could hardly face storekeepers and often had her mother do her shopping. When men persisted in trying to date her—which they often did—she would first avoid them because of her shyness. Then she would desperately latch onto one who was most persistent and who just would not take no for an answer. When he proved (as he always did) to be an unsuitable mate, she would stay with him much longer than she wanted to, being deathly afraid to return to the mating "rat race."

Jane, who had quite a good sense of humor in spite of her conversational ineptness, referred to herself as a "basket case" in her vocational as well as her social life. She had been trained as a high school teacher but could not bear facing a classroom of kids and therefore had taken a Civil Service job as an administrative assistant—a job she easily got by scoring high on an examination. She would have liked to get any number of better jobs for which she was qualified, but she was terrified of job interviews and therefore never applied. She hated herself for sticking at her present low-level position, but this self-hatred only made her more convinced that she was incapable of adequate interpersonal relations.

Before my seeing her, Jane had had 1 year of Rogerian therapy with a college counselor when she was 19. She felt that it had helped her feel a little better but had not made inroads against her shyness. She had had 2 years of psychoanalytically oriented therapy by the time she was 23 but felt that it had only made her very dependent on her analyst and more than ever afraid to face the world on her own. She was disillusioned with therapy and was prepared to give up all hope of ever changing when her twin sister, who had very similar problems and who had had a year of REBT, which resulted in considerable improvement, virtually insisted that she come to the Institute for Rational Emotive Behavior Therapy and even volunteered to pay for her first 2 months of treatment. Still reluctant to go into therapy again but not assertive enough to resist her sister's entreaties, Jane agreed to give REBT a chance.

As is typical in my practice of REBT, I used a number of cognitive, emotive, and behavioral methods with Jane, the most important of which I shall now describe.

COGNITIVE METHODS OF REBT

The main cognitive techniques of REBT that I used with Jane were the following:

Teaching the ABCs of REBT

Because of her previous therapy, Jane held the common psychoanalytical belief that people become disturbed because of the traumatic events of their childhood. I used the first few sessions to modify this notion and to show her that we all strongly tend to bring ourselves—and especially our innate and unique proclivities to desire and to demand—to our parents and teachers in early life and they impart to us preferences and standards that we tend to adopt. Thereafter, as Pogo has aptly stated, we have met the enemy and it is us! Consequently, we take many of our preferences and standards from our early caretakers (and from TV!), but we add absolutistic "musts" to them and make those preferences into dire "needs" (Ellis, 1957, 1962, 1994c; Ellis & Becker, 1982; Ellis & Harper, 1975). Moreover, I showed Jane that no matter how and where she originally acquired her dysfunctional "shoulds," "oughts," and "musts," she still had them today, and she had better acknowledge their power to upset her and work at understanding and changing them.

Although Jane at first resisted taking responsibility for her Irrational Beliefs (IBs) because she found it more acceptable to blame her "dominating" mother for "making" her shy, she soon changed her tune when I showed her that her younger sister, who was even more dominated by her mother (because she was the baby of the family), had always refused to give into this domination and turned out to be unusually outgoing and assertive—as, indeed, the mother herself was. Jane and her twin sister, in contrast, seemed to take after their shy and unassertive father, who was divorced from their mother when they were 5 years old and who thereafter had little to do with any of his three daughters. When, after our third session, Jane decided that she really had largely created her own IBs (for example, "I must never be disapproved by people I find significant") and that these Beliefs (and not her dominating mother) had made her pathologically shy, she "bought" much of the REBT theory and started to look actively for her self-defeating philosophies.

Detecting Irrational Beliefs

In rational emotive behavioral therapy, D stands for disputing irrational beliefs (IBs) (Phadke, 1982). But D can be subdivided into there main processes: *detecting IBs, discriminating* them from rational healthy beliefs (RBs), and *debating* them. I first showed Jane how to detect her IBs and particularly how to look for her absolutistic "should's," "ought's," and "must's." She soon came up with some basic dysfunctional Beliefs: (1) "I *must* speak well to people I find attractive," (2) "I *must* be interesting and clever," (3) "I *must* speak easily and spontaneously without too much effort," (4) "When I don't speak well and impress people as I *should*, I'm a stupid, inadequate person!"

These IBs, Jane was able to see, were the main and most direct contributors to, or "causes" of, her gut feelings of anxiety. But as is commonly the case and as REBT always investigates, she also had some IBs about her anxiety. Whenever she experienced (or thought she might experience) anxiety, she almost immediately thought, first, "I must not be anxious! It's terrible if I am!" and then "I especially must not show others how anxious I am. If I do, they will surely reject me—and that would be awful!" These IBs about her nervousness led Jane to take her primary symptom (anxiety) and turn it into a deadly secondary symptom (anxiety about anxiety); and once she developed this secondary anxiety, she was so upset by it that her original nervousness escalated. She then went on to a tertiary feeling of panic and hopelessness, motivated by her tertiary IB: "Now that I'm so panicked and can't get myself out of feeling this way, I'll never be able to overcome my anxiety. I can't stand this intense panic—and I can't change!"

Discriminating Irrational Beliefs from Rational Beliefs

I showed Jane that she had not only IBs (musts) but a number of RBs (preferences) and that the latter were legitimate and self-helping. For example, on the secondary and tertiary level, some of her RBs were "I don't like being anxious and showing it to others, but I can accept these feelings and work at getting rid of them" and "If people do reject me for showing them how anxious I am, that will be most unfortunate, but I can stand it." With the help of REBT, Jane was able to see that these rational Beliefs (preferences) were quite different from her irrational beliefs (unrealistic demands) and that she had the option of choosing to hold the former rather than the latter.

Debating Irrational Beliefs

I asked, and taught Jane how to ask herself, several logical and empirical questions to debate and Dispute (at point D) her secondary and tertiary IBs. For example: (1) "Even though my panic (and panic about my panic) is so intense and handicapping, where is the evidence that I *can't stand* it and that I *can't* overcome it?" (2) "Granted that my anxiety will turn some people off, will everyone boycott me for displaying it? And if some people do despise me for showing panic, will that really be terrible, and do I truly need their approval?"

As she Disputed these secondary and tertiary IBs that led to her anxiety about her anxiety, Jane also went back, under my guidance, to her primary IBs and actively and persistently began to debate them in this vein: (1) "*Why* must I speak well to people I find attractive?" (2) "*Where is it written* that I have to be interesting and clever?" (3) "Do I really *have to* speak easily and spontaneously, without too much effort?" (4) "When I don't speak well and impress people, how does that make a *a stupid, inadequate person?*" (5) "What kind of results will I get if I continue to strongly believe that I *absolutely have to* impress others or else am a thorough loser?" She answered these Disputes as follows: (1) "There is no reason I must speak well to people I find attractive, but it would be desirable if I do so, so I shall make an effort—but not kill myself—to do so." (2) "It is written *only in my head* that I *have to* be interesting and clever, but it would be nice if I were!" (3) "I can speak uneasily and unspontaneously and *still* get by with most people with whom I converse." (4) "When I speak poorly and fail to impress people, that only makes me a *person who* spoke unimpressively this time—not *a totally stupid or inadequate person.*" (5) "If I continue to believe strongly that I *absolutely have to* impress others, I will make myself very panicked and shy."

As she did this Disputing and questioned her own irrational Beliefs, Jane began to feel much better and was more willing to speak up with people she favored.

Coping Self-Statements

I used another of REBT's favorite methods with Jane: having her figure out, write down, and repeat to herself several times a day helpful coping statements (rational beliefs) that she would eventually internalize (Ellis, 1962, 1973; Ellis & Becker, 1982; Lazarus & Folkman, 1984; Meichenbaum, 1992). Some of those that she found most helpful were the following: "I *can* speak up to others, even when I feel uncomfortable doing so." "I would like to speak well, but I never *have to.*" "No one *dies* of social anxiety!" "When people I favor reject me, it often reveals more about them and their tastes than about me." "Even when I act stupidly and impress people badly, I can still learn a lot and enjoy myself with them."

Referenting

An REBT technique adopted from general semantics is referenting (Danysh, 1974; Korzybski, 1933). Using this method with Jane, I helped her to write down and regularly review the advantages of making herself uncomfortable and overcoming her low frustration tolerance when she forced herself to act unsuitably.

Normally she referented to herself only the disadvantages (e.g., her feelings of awkwardness) when she spoke up with desirable people. She now listed several benefits of doing so, especially these: (1) she would get practice in speaking and thereby become more fluent, (2) she would learn what it was best to say—and not to say—to others, (3) she would meet a larger sample of people from whom to choose friends or lovers, (4) she would see that many people were as shy and as conversationally backward as she was, (5) she could accept the challenge of doing badly and of then not putting herself down, (6) she would find her life more interesting, (7) her anxiety would be more intense but less prolonged. She also listed several of the disadvantages of her speaking up to people in spite of her discomfort in doing so. As she continued to do this kind of referenting, Jane found that she was able to carry out her homework assignments of encountering others with much more ease than she had ever had in doing similar things before.

Teaching REBT to Others

I used to warn my clients, when I practiced psychoanalysis, not to analyze their friends and relatives because they almost always did so badly and thereby harmed themselves and their clients. However, I now do the opposite and strongly encourage many clients to teach REBT to their associates and to try to talk these others out of their dysfunctional Beliefs, for as Bard (1980) has experimentally shown, teaching REBT to others frequently helps the teachers learn its Disputing and other methods and to use them themselves. Jane particularly used REBT with her mother, her younger sister, and her close women friends, and she reported that actively working with them to discover and surrender some of their Irrational Beliefs significantly helped her to observe and effectively debate several of her own.

Psychoeducational Methods

REBT has always promoted the use of books and audiotapes in teaching its principles to clients and members of the public. For example, REBT encourages clients to record their own therapy sessions and to listen to them several times to remember better and to zero in more effectively on the points made by both the therapist and the client during a session. Jane found recordings of her own sessions to be extremely valuable teaching tools and regularly listened to each one a few times between sessions.

Problem Solving

REBT sees people as having two kinds of problems: (1) practical problems, such as Jane's not having an interesting job or her winding up with unsuitable male partners, and (2) emotional problems, or problems about having practical problems. With Jane, as we usually do in REBT, I started with her emotional problems and showed her how to minimize or eliminate them. Then I worked with Jane on her practical problems. For example, I went over her job-seeking problems with her, showed her how she could write a good résumé, and discussed the difficulties of how to get interviews, how to handle these interviews, and how to turn down some jobs and wait for the better one she was actually seeking. We also discussed the practical issues of how she could look for a suitable male partner and how she could eliminate the poor prospects and do better with the good ones.

Use of Humor

According to REBT theory, the irrational Beliefs (IBs) that people adopt and create with which to upset themselves emotionally usually arise from their giving due meaning or consideration to their desires and preferences (which is rational) and then going far beyond this to give exaggerated significance to these wishes. They take things much *too* seriously. As one of its main techniques to combat this kind of exaggerated, or "awfulizing," thinking, REBT employs a good deal of humor. It reduces some clients' ideas to absurdity, shows them how contradictory and ridiculous these views are, and gets them to sing (and preferably internalize) some rational, humorous songs that they can use to overcome their overserious cognitions (Ellis, 1977b, 1977c, 1987).

Since Jane had a good sense of humor, I used many humorous sallies with her, and some of them proved quite effective. She particularly found benefit in singing to herself some of my humorous songs when she had fits of anxiety or depression. Two that she found especially useful were these:

Perfect Rationality
(to the tune *Funiculi, Funicula* by Luigi Denza)

Some think the world must have a right direction
And so do I! And so do I!
Some think that with the slightest imperfection
They can't get by—and so do I!

For I, I have to prove I'm superhuman,
And better far than people are!
To show I have miraculous acumen—
And always rate among the Great!

Perfect, perfect rationality
Is, of course, the only thing for me!
How can I ever think of being
If I must live fallibly?
Rationality must be a perfect thing for me!

I'm Depressed, Depressed!
(to the tune *The Band Played On* by Charles B. Ward)

When anything slightly goes wrong with my life,
I'm depressed, depressed!
Whenever I'm stricken with chickenshit strife,
I feel most distressed!
When life isn't fated to be consecrated
I can't tolerate it at all!
When anything slightly goes wrong with my life,
I just bawl, bawl, bawl!*

EMOTIVE METHODS OF REBT

As I have emphasized for many years (and as some writers on psychotherapy have nonetheless chosen to ignore), REBT is almost always a multimodal school of psychotherapy and rarely treats a client without using several emotive and behavioral, as well as cognitive, methods (Bard, 1980; Bernard, 1991; Dryden, 1994a, 1994b, 1995b, 1995c; Ellis, 1962, 1969, 1973, 1996a; Ellis & Becker, 1982; Ellis & Harper, 1975; Grieger & Boyd, 1980; Walen, DiGiuseppe, & Dryden, 1992; Wessler & Wessler, 1980; Yankura & Dryden, 1990, 1994). Some of the main emotive-evocative methods that I used with Jane will now be discussed.

Rational-Emotive Imagery

Using rational-emotive imagery (Ellis, 1993d; Maultsby, 1971), I showed Jane how to imagine some of the worst things she could think of, such as meeting a man she found very attractive, having him speak to her, and then being struck dumb and unable to talk intelligibly. Imagining this, she felt exceptionally depressed and self-hating. She then worked on making herself only feel healthily disappointed and sorry rather than unhealthily depressed and self-downing. She practiced this kind of rational-emotive imagery several times each day for 30 or more days in a row until the image of this kind of social failure (or actual in vivo failure) quickly and automatically brought on the healthy feelings of disappointment and regret—not unhealthy feelings of anxiety and inadequacy.

Shame-Attacking Exercises

Jane derived a good deal of benefit from the shame-attacking exercises I created in the 1960s that have since been used by REBT and several other forms of therapy (Ellis, 1969; Ellis & Abrahms, 1978; Ellis & Becker, 1982; Ellis &

---

*Lyrics by Albert Ellis. Copyright @ 1977 by the Albert Ellis Institute for Rational Emotive Behavior Therapy.

Grieger, 1977). She first picked several silly things—such as yelling aloud the stops in the New York subway and singing at the top of her voice on the street—and forced herself to do them, while working to make herself feel unashamed. When she could succeed at this, she then spoke to a number of strange (and attractive) men on buses, in elevators, in the supermarket, and in other public places; tried to get into conversations with them; and asked whether they would like to call her for lunch or a date. She was terrified to do this at first, but after she had it done about 20 times, she lost almost all her anxiety and shame and was able to meet several suitable men in this manner and to begin dating one steadily.

Role Playing

I role-played several job-interview and social-encounter situations with Jane. I discussed with her what she was telling herself to make herself anxious and shy in these situations and what she could tell herself instead, and I brought out some negative feelings of which she was not fully aware and helped her change them. I also critiqued her skills in these situations and got her to reconsider and revamp them. Even better, when the members of one of my therapy groups, which she attended for 6 months, did role-playing routines with her, they were able to get her to bring out more apprehensive feelings, to show her what she was telling herself to create these feelings, and to give her some excellent suggestions on how to deal with her feelings and how to improve her social skills. I often find it valuable for shy and inhibited people like Jane to join one of my REBT therapy groups for a while because they have more social learning opportunities in the group than they usually have in one-to-one therapy. In group she also learned to talk other members out of their Irrational Beliefs, which helped her to dispute her own dysfunctional beliefs (Ellis, 1982b, 1992c).

Group Socializing

In one of my groups, Jane also learned to relate better to several of the other members, to call on them for help in between therapy sessions, and to try social-izing activities with some of them that she might not have done by herself.

Forceful Self-Statements

REBT theorizes that people disturb themselves not only by ideas, thoughts, attitudes, and philosophies but also by holding onto their musturbatory beliefs strongly, forcefully, and vehemently. It therefore encourages clients like Jane to reindoctrinate themselves forcefully and vividly with dramatic impact (Dryden, 1984c; Ellis, 1979c, 1994c, 1995a, 1996a). Jane was shown how to devise rational self-statements and to powerfully repeat them to herself (and to others) many times until she solidly began to feel them and to be convinced of their truth. Thus, she often vigorously told herself, "It's a pain in the ass to get rejected socially or in a job interview, but it's not *awful*!" "I want very much to find a suitable mate, but I don't *have to*!" "If people see how anxious I am, they will hardly run away screaming. And if they do, tough shit!" "I *can* talk to attractive men, no matter *how* uncomfortable I feel!"

Forceful Self-Dialogue

Another REBT emotive technique Jane used was to have a forceful dialogue with herself and record it (Ellis & Becker, 1982). She would start with an Irrational Belief—such as that she *must* speak easily and spontaneously, without effort—and then rationally but with real vigor argue against this belief so that her rational voice finally won out over her dysfunctional one and her feelings changed appropriately. She would listen to these tapes herself or let friends or therapy group members listen to them and check with them to see whether her rational arguments were good and to see how powerfully she convinced herself of them.

Sometimes, doing role reversal, I or a member of her group would pretend to strongly hold Jane's self-defeating ideas. She would role-play her sensible Beliefs and try vigorously to argue us out of our dysfunctional thinking.

Unconditional Self-Acceptance

I always unconditionally accepted Jane, as this is an integral part of REBT, no matter how badly she behaved inside and outside therapy. Even when she came late to sessions or got behind in paying her bill to the Institute, I firmly showed her that her *behavior* was bad but that I never considered her a *bad person*. Going further, I taught her how to fully accept herself under all conditions and to rate only her acts and traits and never her totality, her being, or her self (Ellis, 1962, 1972b, 1973, 1976d, 1994c, 1996a, 1996b; Ellis & Becker, 1982; Ellis & Harper, 1975; Hauck, 1991; Miller, 1983; Mills, 1993). Of all the things she learned in REBT, unconditional self-acceptance, she thought, was the most useful.

BEHAVIORAL METHODS OF REBT

As with virtually all my clients, I used several behavioral methods of REBT with Jane, particularly the following.

Activity Homework

From the start of her therapy, Jane agreed to take activity homework assignments: to talk to men she found attractive, to go on job interviews, to make some public talks, and to tell her lovers she no longer wanted to see them once she was fairly sure they were not for her (Ellis, 1962, 1979d, 1994c, 1995a, 1996a). She did many of these assignments even though she felt uncomfortable doing them—and thereby learned the REBT maxim, "There's little gain without pain." Whenever she did them, she soon got over her discomfort and even started enjoying some of them, such as talking to and flirting with suitable males. By doing these assignments she also clearly observed how anxious and ashamed she was at first, and she was able to zero in on the dysfunctional Beliefs behind her anxiety.

Reinforcements and Penalties

Jane was shown how to reinforce herself—usually with reading or going to a concert—after she did her homework and to refrain from this kind of reinforcement if she did not do it. She found reinforcements especially useful for helping her do her REBT homework, because she would sometimes do it for several days in a row and then slack off and forget about it if she had no reinforcer.

REBT uses penalties as well as reinforcers for clients who do not do their homework (Ellis & Abrahms, 1978; Ellis & Becker, 1982; Ellis & Grieger, 1977; Ellis & Velten, 1992; Ellis & Whiteley, 1979). When Jane did not carry out her assignments, she chose to burn a $20 bill, and that quickly worked to help her do them.

Skill Training

Jane was given, in individual sessions, in group therapy, and in several workshops for the public that are regularly held at the New York Institute for Rational Emotive Behavior Therapy, instruction in assertion training, in social encountering, in writing a résumé, and in communication skills. Skill training helped her in various areas—such as communicating better with her mother—that she never directly brought up as serious psychological problems. And partly because of it, she said, toward the close of her sessions, "I am very happy that I started REBT for my social anxiety and other emotional difficulties. But the great bonus of these sessions has been my being able to actualize and better enjoy myself in several ways that I never even realized therapy could benefit me. But I am delighted to say that it really has!"

CONCLUSION

I saw Jane for 9 months, first once a week for individual sessions of REBT and then mainly in group therapy. By the time therapy ended, she was able to talk easily to the men she found attractive; she was preparing to take a teaching job, which she had always previously avoided; she had no trouble confronting sales-people when she shopped; she was able to change her unsuitable male part-ners after she had gone with them for only a few weeks or months; and she was in a public speaking group, Toastmasters, and did so well there that she was made an assistant.

I no longer see Jane for therapy, but she frequently attends my Friday night workshops on problems of daily living and often participates actively in them, asking questions of and giving rational suggestions to the volunteers with whom I have public demonstration session of REBT. She also stays for the cof-fee sessions we arrange for the workshop participants and easily socializes with people at these sessions. She is most grateful for her REBT experience and refers a number of her friends and associates to me and our other therapists at the Institute for Rational Emotive Behavior Therapy.

Jane's case is not entirely typical of clients suffering from social anxiety because she worked harder at REBT than many other clients do, and her improvement was therefore faster and more profound than it sometimes is in similar cases of overwhelming anxiety. But her progress does show that some of the most severely anxious people can help themselves considerably in a rela-tively short time if they accept and persistently use some of the main REBT formulations and techniques.

4

Individual Therapy

CONTEXTUAL CONSIDERATIONS

Prochaska and Norcross (1983) carried out a survey of the practices of 410 psychologists who belonged to Division 29 (Psychotherapy) of the American Psychological Association and reported on a similar survey (Norcross & Prochaska, 1982) on a representative sample of psychologists who were members of APA Division 12 (Clinical Psychology). The findings of these two surveys indicated that members of both divisions spent most of their therapy time practicing individual therapy (65.3%, Division 29 members; 63.5%, Division 12 members). Although there are no available data on the distribution of working time of therapists of different orientations, there is little reason to suggest that a different pattern would be found among REBT therapists. If this is so, the absence of data also makes it hard to explain the reasons for this pattern.

Dryden (1984d) has argued that there are various sources of influence that impinge upon the therapist and client as they seek to determine in which therapeutic modality to work. First, therapists are influenced by the settings in which they work. Such settings may impose practical limitations on the practice of therapy in modalities other than, for example, individual therapy and/or have different norms of practice that favor the practice of one particular modality over others. Therapists who work in private practice usually find that the exigencies of this mode of work means that individual therapy constitutes the major part of their workload. Second, therapists are influenced by the ways in which they account for their clients' disturbances. Because the REBT model of disturbance emphasizes the role played by the individual's Belief system in his or her psychological problems, this may influence its practitioners to work more frequently in the modality of individual therapy than in other modali-

Parts of this chapter were adapted from W. Dryden, "Therapeutic Arenas," in Dryden (1984a). Used by permission.

ties. Third, clients' preferences are very salient here, and these often exert a considerable influence on the choice of therapeutic modality.

In this regard, I (AE) have argued: "I am usually able to go along with the basic desire of any clients who want individual, marital, family or group psychotherapy. It is only in relatively few cases that I talk them into taking a form of therapy they are at first loathe to try" (Dryden, 1984a, p. 15). Information is needed concerning the impact of clients' pretherapy modality preferences on the working practice of REBT therapists. Given that we do not have any data concerning (1) how they distribute their working time among the various therapeutic modalities, (2) what factors determine such decisions, and (3) who is largely responsible for making these decisions, much of our thinking on the issue of when (and when not) to work in individual therapy is determined by our clinical experience.

Indications for Individual Therapy

1. Individual REBT, by its nature, provides clients with a situation of complete confidentiality. It is indicated, therefore, when it is important for clients to be able to disclose themselves in privacy without fear that others may use such information to their detriment. Some clients are particularly anxious concerning how others (e.g., in a group therapy context) would react to their disclosures, and such anxiety precludes their productive participation in that modality. Similarly, clients who otherwise would not disclose "secret" material are best suited to individual REBT. As in other situations, transfer to other modalities may be indicated later when such clients are more able and/or willing to disclose themselves to others.

2. Individual therapy, by its dyadic nature, provides an opportunity for a closer relationship to develop between therapist and client than may exist when other people (e.g., a co-therapist and other clients) are present. This factor may be particularly important for some clients who have not developed close relationships with significant people in their lives and for whom group therapy, for example, may prove initially too threatening.

3. In individual therapy, REBT can be conducted to best match the client's pace of learning. Thus, it is particularly suited for clients who, due to their present state of mind or speed of learning, require their therapist's full and undivided attention. This is especially important for clients who are quite confused and who would only be distracted by the complexity of interactions that can take place in other therapeutic modalities.

4. Individual REBT is particularly indicated when clients' major problems involve their relationship with themselves rather than their relationships with other people.

5. Individual therapy may be indicated for clients who wish to differentiate themselves from others (e.g., those who have decided to leave a relationship

and wish to deal with individual problems that this may involve). Here, how-ever, some conjoint sessions with the partner may also be helpful, particularly in matters of conciliation.

6. In chapter 2 we argued that it can be helpful for therapists to vary their therapeutic style with clients in order to minimize the risk of perpetuating the client's problems by providing an inappropriate interactive style. Individual REBT provides therapists with an opportunity to vary their interactive styles with clients free from the concern that such variation may adversely affect other clients present, as may occur in other therapeutic modalities.

7. Individual therapy is particularly indicated for clients who have profound difficulties sharing therapeutic time with other clients.

8. Individual therapy may also be indicated for negative reasons. Thus, clients may be seen in individual therapy who may not benefit from working in other therapeutic modalities. Clients who may monopolize a therapy group, who may be too withdrawn within it to benefit from the experience, or who are thought too vulnerable to benefit from family therapy are often seen in individual REBT.

Contraindications for Individual Therapy

1. Individual therapy is contraindicated for clients who are likely to become overly dependent on the therapist, particularly when such dependency becomes so intense as to lead to client deterioration. Such clients may be more appro-priately helped in group therapy, where such intense dependency is less likely to develop due to the fact that the therapist relates to other people.

2. Individual REBT, which does not in general advocate close interpersonal relationships between therapists and clients, can still be a close interpersonal encounter for the client and as such is less likely to be indicated for clients who may find such degree of intimacy or the prospect of such intimacy unduly threatening.

3. Individual therapy may be contraindicated for clients who find this modality too comfortable. Based on the idea that personal change is often best facilitated in situations where there is an optimal level of arousal, individual therapy may not provide enough challenge for such clients. Ravid (1969) found that it may be unproductive to offer individual therapy to clients who have had much previous individual therapy but still require further therapeutic help.

4. Individual therapy may not be appropriate for clients for whom other modalities are deemed to be more therapeutic. For example, clients who are particularly shy, retiring, and afraid to take risks are more likely to benefit from group therapy (if they can be induced to join) than from the less risky situation of individual therapy. Second, partners who can productively use the conjoint situation of couple therapy often benefit more from this modality than from working in individual REBT. This is particularly true when they have largely

overcome their disturbed feelings about their unproductive relationship and are dealing with issues devoted to enhancement of relationship satisfaction, a situation that particularly warrants their joint participation (see chapter 5).

Other Issues

Once therapists and clients have decided to work in a particular modality, it is important to stress that this decision is not irrevocable. Clients may move from modality to modality, and thus individual therapy, in this context, can be best viewed as part of a comprehensive treatment strategy. This can occur for both positive and negative reasons. Productive movement to and from individual therapy occurs when clients have made therapeutic gain in one modality but may benefit more from being transferred to a different one. Negative movement in and out of individual therapy occurs when the clients do not improve in a given therapeutic modality.

Although we have provided some indications and contraindications for the practice of individual therapy, we conclude by stressing that the state of the art concerning this issue is far from being well developed, and we would advise REBT therapists thus: Work with clients in the modality that seems to be most productive for them but regard such decisions as tentative and to a large degree experimental. Perhaps the best way of determining whether a client will benefit or not from individual therapy is in fact to work with him or her in that modality and to monitor his or her response to it.

THE PROCESS OF INDIVIDUAL REBT

In this section we will outline the initial, middle, and end phases of individual REBT.

The Initial Phase

When a client enters individual REBT, it is likely that that person will know little or nothing about the nature of this therapeutic approach. Thus, the basic task of the individual therapist is to induct the client into REBT, helping him or her to understand the nature of the approach and what it involves concerning the participation of client and therapist. As noted in chapter 2, some REBT therapists attempt to induct clients into REBT by involving them in pretherapy induction activities. Even when these methods are employed, it is important during the initial phase of REBT to check out the client's understanding of REBT and to correct any misconceptions that he or she may still have. Of course, when such pretherapy induction activities are not employed, this becomes a major task of the therapist in the initial phase of individual REBT.

(continued on page 96)

FIGURE 4.1 Biographical information form.

Date _____ _____ _____
        mo.   day   yr

Consultation Center.

Albert Ellis Institute for Rational Emotive Behavior Therapy
45 East 65th Street, New York, N.Y. 10021

Biographical Information Form

Name _____ _____ _____
        (last)   (first)   (middle)

Instructions To assist us in helping you, please fill out this form as frankly as you can. You will save much time and effort by giving us full information. You can be sure that, like everything you say at the Institute, the facts on this form will be held in the strictest confidence and that no outsider will be permitted to see your case record without your written permission. PLEASE TYPE OR PRINT YOUR ANSWERS.

1. Date of birth: _____ _____ _____   Age: _____   Sex: M _____ F _____
                     mo.   day   yr

2. Address: _____   _____   _____
              street   city   state   zip

3. Home phone: _____   Business phone: _____

4. Permanent address (if different from above) _____

_____

5. Who referred you to the Institute? (check one)

_____ (1) self   _____ (2) school or teacher   _____ (3) psychologist or psychiatrist   _____ (4) social agency

_____ (5) hospital or clinic   _____ (6) family doctor   _____ (7) friend   _____ (8) relative

_____ (9) other (explain) _____   Has this party been here?   _____ Yes   _____ No

6. Present marital status:

_____ (1) never married   _____ (2) married (living together) now for first time

_____ (3) married (living together) now for second (or more) time

_____ (4) separated   _____ (5) divorced and not remarried   _____ (6) widowed and not remarried

Number of years married to present spouse ....   Ages of male children ....   Ages of female children ....

7. Years of formal education completed (circle number of years):

1 2 3 4 5 6 7 8 9 10 11 12 13 14 15 16 17 18 19 20 more than 20

8. How religious are you? (circle number on scale that best approximates your degree of religiosity):

very   average   atheist
1   2   3   4   5   6   7   8   9

9. Mother's age: _____   If deceased, how old were you when she died? _____

10. Father's age: _____   If deceased, how old were you when he died? _____

(continued)

89

Figure 4.1 (continued)

11. If your mother and father separated, how old were you at the time? _____

12. If your mother and father divorced, how old were you at the time? _____

13. Total number of times mother divorced _____ Number of times father divorced _____

14. Number of living brothers _____ Number of living sisters _____

15. Ages of living brothers _____ Ages of living sisters _____

16. I was child number _____ in a family of _____ children.

17. Were you adopted? _____ Yes _____ No

18. What kind of treatment have you previously had for emotional problems?
_____ hours of individual therapy, spread over _____ years, ending _____ years ago.

19. Hours of group therapy _____ Months of psychiatric hospitalization _____

20. Are you undergoing treatment anywhere else now? _____ Yes _____ No

21. Number of times during past year you have taken antidepressants _____

22. Type of psychotherapy you have mainly had (briefly describe method of treatment—ex, dream analysis, free association, drugs, hypnosis, etc.)

_____

_____

23. Briefly list (PRINT) your present main complaints, symptoms, and problems:

_____

_____

_____

_____

24. Briefly list any additional past complaints, symptoms, and problems:

_____

_____

_____

25. Under what conditions are your problems worse?

_____

_____

_____

26. Under what conditions are they improved?

_____

_____

_____

(continued)

Figure 4.1 (*continued*)

27. List the things you like to do most, the kinds of things and persons that give you pleasure: ———

———

———

28. List your main assets and good points: ———

———

29. List your main bad points: ———

———

———

30. List your main social difficulties: ———

———

———

31. List your main love and sex difficulties: _____

_____

_____

_____

32. List your main school or work difficulties: _____

_____

_____

_____

33. List your main life goals: _____

_____

_____

34. List the things about yourself you would most like to change: _____

_____

_____

_____

35. List your chief physical ailments, diseases, complaints, or handicaps: _____

_____

_____

_____

(continued)

Figure 4.1 *(continued)*

36. What occupation(s) have you mainly been trained for? _____

   Present occupation _____ Full time _____ Part time _____

37. Spouse's occupation _____ Full time _____ Part time _____

38. Mother's occupation _____ Father's occupation _____

39. Mother's religion _____ Father's religion _____

40. If your mother and father did not raise you when you were young, who did? _____

41. Briefly describe the type of person your mother (or stepmother or person who substituted for your mother) was when you were a child
   and how you got along with her: _____
   _____
   _____

42. Briefly describe the type of person your father (or stepfather or father substitute) was when you were a child and how you got along
   with him: _____
   _____

43. If there were unusually disturbing features in your relationship to any of your brothers, briefly describe: _____

_____

_____

44. If there were unusually disturbing features in your relationship to any of your sisters, briefly describe: _____

_____

45. Number of close male relatives who have been seriously emotionally disturbed: _____ Number that have been hospitalized for psychiatric treatment, or have attempted suicide: _____ Number of close relatives who have been seriously emotionally disturbed: _____

_____ Number that have been hospitalized for psychiatric treatment, or have attempted suicide: _____

46. Additional information that you think might be helpful

_____

_____

_____

Some REBT therapists like to have their clients fill in a form that provides basic biographical information as well as information concerning the client's presenting problems. In Figure 4.1 the biographical information form routinely employed by therapists at the Institute for REBT in New York is presented.

In addition, therapists at the institute routinely ask clients to fill out the personality data form presented in chapter 2 (see Figure 2.1). This form provides the therapist with information concerning the Irrational Beliefs that are likely to underpin the client's problems. However, the use of this form is designed to supplement rather than to replace a thorough assessment of the client's problems.

Most REBT therapists like to structure the therapeutic process at the outset in order to emphasize that therapy will be problem-focused. For example, such questions as, "What are you bothered most about?" and "What is your major problem at this time?" are employed to encourage clients to adopt a problem-solving focus. Indeed, I (AE) routinely read aloud the information provided by the client on item 23 of the biographical information form and ask him or her to start talking about what is most bothersome among this list of problems.

Before proceeding to the assessment stage of therapy the REBT therapist often seeks an agreement with the client concerning the first problem to tackle. When this has been achieved, the therapist proceeds to help the client to understand his or her problems according to the ABC framework outlined in chapter 1. At this point the therapist both seeks to understand the client's problems according to the ABC framework and to teach the client the ABC model of emotional disturbance. During this process the therapist is also concerned to correct any misconceptions that the client may have about the therapeutic enterprise. Thus, the therapist endeavors to show the client that REBT is a form of therapy that is problem-focused and educational in nature and that the therapist will often adopt an active and directive approach. The therapist also encourages the client to see that his or her initial task is to learn to focus on the cognitive determinants of his or her problems.

Other tasks that REBT therapists strive to accomplish in the initial phase of individual REBT include the following: (1) helping the client to understand that in REBT the therapist is basically concerned with helping clients to solve their emotional and behavioral problems *before* encouraging them to solve their career and environmental problems (Grieger & Boyd, 1980); (2) putting the client at ease and helping the client to bring some order to and to achieve some insight into his or her problems by use of questions and structuring statements; and (3) seeking an understanding about what effects the client's symptoms have on his or her own functioning and relationships. This last task is carried out to determine whether or not the involvement of significant others at later phases of therapy is warranted. If it is, transfer to a more appropriate therapeutic modality may be kept in mind for later discussion.

Assessment We have already covered the issue of assessment in chapter 2. However, further discussion on this topic is relevant to the practice of individual REBT. We have already commented that REBT therapists frequently begin to discuss the client's most pressing problems. An alternative approach would be to work on the client's problem that is easiest to solve. This may be done to enhance the credibility of the therapist and to inspire hope. Whether the therapist adopts the "most pressing problem" approach or the "easiest to solve" approach will depend on which tactic best involves the client in the process of therapy.

During the assessment process the therapist is careful to help the client to understand the connections between A, B, and C and is particularly concerned to help the client understand the role of B variables. Furthermore, the therapist pays particular attention to the possible existence of "problems about problems" (as discussed in chapter 1). If such second-order problems are identified, it is important for the therapist to help the client to understand why such problems often are assessed and targeted for change *before* the client's primary problems. Thus, a client is shown that if she is, for example, guilty about her anger, she will be less successful at working on and overcoming her anger problem while she is feeling guilty about it. However, there are occasions when clients will not accept this rationale despite the therapist's explanations. A guiding rule under these conditions is for the therapist to work at a level that the client will accept.

Therapeutic Intervention After the therapist has successfully put the client's problem into the ABC framework and the client understands and accepts this formulation, the therapist can then move to the Disputing stage of therapy and use some of the techniques that have already been discussed in chapter 2. The initial goal of Disputing is to help the client to understand the poor results of his or her irrational musturbatory evaluation and the better results of its rational alternative. When this is done, the client is in a position to consider a homework assignment that is chosen to strengthen the client's rational Beliefs and to weaken his or her irrational ones. As discussed in chapter 2, homework assignments may be predominantly cognitive, emotive, and/or behavioral in nature, and the selection of a relevant homework assignment will be dictated by the nature of the client's problems and his or her present learning capability. As a supplement to a homework assignment (or as a separate assignment) most REBT therapists often suggest that clients read some REBT literature that is designed to help them gain greater insight into the role of dysfunctional musturbatory evaluations in their problems and the importance of replacing these Irrational Beliefs with their more functional alternatives. In this regard many therapists at the Institute for REBT in New York give their clients a package of leaflets and suggest that they read the opening chapters in *A Guide to Rational Living* (Ellis & Harper, 1997). However, this book may be too complex for some clients, who might derive more benefit from reading *A Rational*

Counseling Primer (Young, 1974a), *A Guide to Personal Happiness* (Ellis & Becker, 1982), *How to Stubbornly Refuse to Make Yourself Miserable About Anything—Yes, Anything* (Ellis, 1988), or one of Paul Hauck's texts (e.g., *Hold Your Head Up High* [Hauck, 1991]).

Toward the end of the initial phase of REBT the therapist should prefer- ably have an understanding of the client's major emotional and behavioral problems and have begun to start to prioritize these, with the client's cooper- ation, so as to give some structure to the therapeutic practice of individual REBT. Ideally, at this stage both therapist and client will know and agree to the order in which the client's problems are to be tackled.

In chapter 2 we outlined some of the major sources that contribute to resis- tance to therapeutic progress. In addition to this list, a number of additional "roadblocks" to therapeutic progress can often occur. Grieger and Boyd (1980) have noted a common therapist error at the initial stage of individual REBT concerning failure to bring adequate conceptual clarity to the client's prob- lems. This may occur when the therapist fails to spend sufficient time on each of the client's problems and moves from problem to problem in quick succes- sion. A second roadblock can occur when the therapist either focuses too much on the historical determinants of the client's problems or strives to gain a total picture of the client's past, present, and future before beginning an interven- tion program. In addition, the therapist may make the error of giving too much focus to the therapeutic relationship in the initial stages of therapy. Although we recognize that developing a cooperative relationship between therapist and client is important in REBT, we argue that this can be best done through a businesslike focus on the client's problems, the execution of a correct assess- ment of these problems, and an early start on helping the client to overcome these problems. We argue that focusing on developing the relationship per se *without* these task activities is less efficient and effective.

We have already stated that REBT is an educational therapy, and as such it is important for the therapist to help the client to learn at the client's own pace. Failure to do this provides another reason why roadblocks may occur at the initial phase of REBT. Here the therapist may become overly impatient and demand the client's cooperation at a stage when the therapist would do better to check out the client's level of understanding of what he or she is being taught. Impatience leading to the adoption of any overly lecturing style can often occur at this stage. We recommend that REBT therapists adopt a toler- ant attitude toward their clients' learning rate and urge that they experiment with different ways of communicating.

As we have underscored, it is important that clients be successfully inducted into the REBT process, and the bulk of this work often occurs in the initial phase of therapy. Clients may come to therapy anticipating a different kind of thera- peutic process than that offered by REBT. Thus, they may believe, from prior experience or previous knowledge, that therapy has a focus on past events or necessitates the dramatic expression of pent-up emotions or that it involves a close existential relationship between client and therapist. Failure to identify, confront, and deal with these incorrect anticipations often leads to premature client termination from REBT or needless client resistance during the therapeutic process. When such anticipations are discovered, it is often helpful to ask clients how they think that such factors can help them solve their problems. This initial inquiry can often lead to a productive discussion of the client's role in therapy.

During this discussion the therapist can use this opportunity to show clients that they have more appropriate tasks to execute in the process of REBT. When clients' anticipations and preferences for therapy are very different from the experience that they are likely to encounter during individual REBT, the therapist can continue to persuade them to relinquish these (thereby running the risk of the client leaving therapy prematurely), try to tailor REBT as closely to the client's preferences as possible without offering the client a type of therapy deemed ineffective by the therapist, or refer the client to a therapist who will more easily meet the client's anticipations and preferences.

Another roadblock to client progress that is encountered at this stage occurs when clients only focus on either the Activating events or adversity (A) or their feelings, or their behavioral problems or symptoms at C. Here the therapist might fruitfully inquire how talking about either A or C will actually help them to solve their problems at C. This approach can be used again to initiate a productive discussion about the respective tasks of therapist and client in the process of REBT. A final roadblock that sometimes occurs at this stage concerns clients who believe that once they have understood and agree with the fact that their dysfunctional beliefs cause their emotional and behavioral problems, such understanding is sufficient for them to effect lasting change in their problems at C. As discussed in chapter 2, it is important that therapists help clients see that such insight is rarely sufficient and that a thorough working through of their Irrational Beliefs is very likely to be necessary if they are to achieve a long-term solution to their problems at C.

The Middle Phase of Individual REBT

The middle phase of REBT is characterized by the therapist and client working toward strengthening the client's Rational Beliefs and weakening the dysfunctional Beliefs. In addition, the therapist works to identify obstacles to the client's progress in this respect and helps the client to overcome such obstacles. Particular attention is paid to what the client has learned from homework assignments and can make use of in the future. Attention is also paid to what the client has not learned from these assignments, and blocks to the learning process are uncovered and overcome.

Although it is possible to practice REBT by focusing at the beginning of each session on what the client has been most bothered about in the preceding week, we consider that this is not always an efficient way of practicing therapy. Rather, we encourage therapists to bring some order to the therapeutic process. This is achieved by the therapist's helping the client to work through a particular problem before moving to a different problem. Thus, there should preferably be some continuity from session to session with respect to the problems that are being dealt with.

As therapist and client work together on a particular problem over time, the therapist endeavors to help the client to internalize the following process. First, the client identifies troublesome emotions and behaviors, links them to Activating events, and then identifies his or her major dysfunctional Beliefs. The client then Disputes those Beliefs and puts the alternative rational Beliefs into practice by executing relevant assignments. Thus, in the middle phase of REBT the therapist is not only concerned with helping clients to solve their emotional and behavioral problems but also with helping them to internalize the scientific methods of REBT problem identification and problem solution.

As clients make progress on a particular problem, it often happens that the degree of therapist directiveness fades as the therapist encourages them to practice self-therapy. In addition, the therapist strives to help clients see that they can tackle similar problems that may occur in different contexts. Thus, therapists often plan and work to help clients achieve therapeutic generalization across situations. This process should preferably not be seen as occurring naturally. Thus, the client who believes, "I must be perfect at passing examinations" and is successful in challenging this Belief and acting on alternative rational Beliefs may not in fact be successful at challenging a similar belief with relevance to love relationships.

Thus, in the middle phase of REBT the therapist encourages the client to see the links between problems, particularly those that are characterized by common dysfunctional Beliefs. When a client has made significant progress on a particular problem, the REBT therapist then deals with a new problem and may in fact become more directive in the process of helping the client to identify, challenge, and change the Irrational Beliefs that underpin this new problem. However, the therapist continually looks for opportunities to encourage the client to use the skills that he or she has successfully demonstrated in helping to solve problem No. 1, which can then be used to solve problem No. 2.

Whereas in the initial phase of REBT the therapist is usually responsible for making suggestions concerning homework assignments, in the middle phase of REBT the therapist encourages clients to set their own homework assignments and also helps them to learn the effective ingredients that are involved in the selection of effective homework assignments.

Another major concern of the REBT therapist in the middle phase of therapy is to assess adequately the reasons for therapeutic change and to help the client to understand and learn from these. As noted in chapter 2, clients can make progress on their emotional and behavioral problems for a variety of reasons. Thus, a client may show therapeutic progress because he or she has successfully changed A or has effected an inferentially based change, a behaviorally based change, or, as is the ideal in REBT, a change in underlying philosophy (i.e., clients have successfully challenged their dysfunctional musturbatory evaluations and replaced these with rational preferential evaluations). Assuming that a client has shown therapeutic progress by effecting a philosophic change, the therapist may profitably move to another problem. However, when changes can be attributed to one or more of the other sources mentioned above, the therapist uses this information to help the client see that the core of emotional or behavioral problems has not been successfully tackled.

Grieger and Boyd (1980) consider that the middle phase of REBT is characterized by the therapist's helping the client to *work through* his or her emotional and behavioral problems and to achieve an REBT *reeducation*. Forms (such as the one printed in Appendix 1 of this book) are now given to clients to help them maintain their gains and guard against relapse. We have already mentioned some sources of resistance that occur on these two dimensions; the following additional sources of resistance are often encountered in this phase. We will focus initially on roadblocks that can be attributed to the therapist. Apart from failing to identify and deal with the client's unsuccessful attempts to carry out homework assignments (a common failing, particularly among novice REBT therapists), the therapist should preferably refrain from adopting an overly lecturing and philosophizing approach in this phase. Such a stance does not, in general, help the client to begin to internalize the REBT methods of problem identification and problem solution as outlined above.

Therapists can also impede client progress by failing to help clients to attain closure on a particular problem. If the therapist continually asks a client, "What has bothered you most this week?" at the beginning of a session, he or she may end up by working on a myriad of different client problems from week to week without successfully helping the client to work any of them through to a satisfactory conclusion. The therapist can also fail by uncritically accepting the client's report that progress has been made without determining that the client's progress can in fact be attributed to philosophic change. In addition, some REBT therapists fail to be sufficiently repetitive and persistent at this stage of therapy. Here the therapist assumes that reports of client progress in a previous session necessarily mean that lasting change has taken place. In response to their supervisors' inquiries about a given issue, novice therapists often say, "I dealt with that in the last session." These therapists make the error of thinking that once a topic has been dealt with the client has thoroughly learned what needs to be learned.

As noted above, one of the client's major tasks in the middle phase of REBT is to strengthen his or her rational Beliefs and weaken his or her irrational Beliefs. This often involves hard work and repetitious challenging of dysfunctional beliefs and instigating cognitive, emotive, and behavioral assignments to effect such change. Change itself can be an uncomfortable experience for clients, as Maultsby (1984) has shown. He refers to a process called cognitive-emotional dissonance, whereby clients feel "strange" as they work toward strengthening their rational Beliefs. Grieger and Boyd (1980) note that this issue can take a number of forms, for example, the "I won't be me" syndrome, and "I'll become a robot." Clients who are not helped to accept uncomfortable feelings as a natural part of relearning will often not persist in changing their dysfunctional ideas.

The major reason, however, that clients do not persist in sustaining the change process can be a philosophy of low frustration tolerance in which clients believe that "it's *too* hard to persist in bringing about change" and that "change *must* be easy." It is very important that therapists be alert for the existence of such a philosophy in their clients and appropriately help them to identify, challenge, and change it. Clients who internalize the theory of REBT as a body of knowledge but not as a working method often demonstrate resistance to change. Such clients are often quite knowledgeable about REBT theory and can quote passages from the various books, in some cases almost verbatim, but do not necessarily act upon this knowledge. Such clients often have a philosophy of low frustration tolerance and/or believe that knowing the theory is sufficient to effect a lasting emotional and behavioral change.

The End Phase of Individual REBT

The major purpose of the end phase of individual REBT is to prepare clients to execute the task of becoming their own future therapists. In the end phase of individual REBT the therapist strives to make himself or herself redundant. Individual REBT is terminated not when clients have necessarily solved all their problems but when they feel prepared to solve their remaining problems on their own and are confident in their ability to deal with any future difficulties. The therapist may work toward termination either by decreasing the frequency of sessions over time or by setting a definite termination date. In both cases most REBT therapists do schedule follow-up sessions to monitor client progress. In advance of termination the therapist can productively use session time to help the client to anticipate future problems and to imagine how he or she would productively handle those problems by using the skills of REBT that have hopefully now been internalized to a considerable degree.

Additionally, the therapist elicits and deals with any dependency needs that the client may have about terminating therapy. Some clients who have made considerable progress still believe that they *need* the continued help of a therapist in order to maintain their progress. Such problems may become manifest when clients who have made very good progress are reluctant to either set a termination date or to decrease the frequency of sessions. However, there is a minority of quite disturbed clients who do seem to find it hard to cope on their own, and in these cases therapists can productively schedule infrequent booster sessions of REBT for such people.

Some therapists may be reluctant to terminate therapy with clients who have shown considerable progress. These therapists may believe that they *need* the continued evidence of client progress to prove that they are competent therapists and therefore worthwhile people. Needless to say, it would be highly desirable for such therapists to identify and challenge such competency needs, using the methods of REBT outlined in this book.

INDIVIDUALIZING REBT

It is in the nature of individual REBT that because the therapist is dealing with only one client, he or she can strive to tailor the practice of REBT with this client free from the concern that such a style of interaction (and the use of an individually tailored treatment program) may have an adverse affect on the presence of other clients (e.g., in couples therapy, family therapy, or group therapy). Thus, as we have shown in chapter 2, the therapist can modify his or her style of participation in individual therapy according to the personality structure of a given client in order to maximize that client's learning and to minimize the possibility that the client's problems are being unwittingly reinforced. This refers in particular to individualizing REBT in the bond domain (i.e., the interpersonal relationship between therapist and client) of the therapeutic alliance (Bordin, 1979). Therapeutic bonds in REBT change over time according to the amount of progress that the client makes and according to which bonds the client best responds to.

In this latter regard, the therapist can at the outset attempt to assess what might be a productive bond to form with a particular client. Thus, the therapist might ask the client, either on a biographical form or in person, what constitutes helpful and unhelpful therapist behavior in the client's mind. The therapist might also ask the client about the latter's previous experiences of being helped, whether formally or informally, and in such exploration focus on what aspects of the other person's behavior the client found most helpful and what aspects were least helpful. It is important, however, to view such information critically because what a client has found helpful in the short term may not have been helpful in the long term. Thus, for example, therapists can help clients feel better in the short term without helping them to get better in the long term (Ellis, 1972a, 1994c, 1996a). Although the information that can be obtained from the client about possible helpful ways of intervening with that particular client may be useful, REBT therapists would be wise to answer by experimentation the question concerning *which* bond is most productive with *this* client at *this* particular time. Thus, the therapist might try particular ways of interacting with different clients and observe how they respond to different forms of therapist interaction.

Another way that REBT therapists can individualize therapy for their clients is to ensure that there is congruence between clients' goals and the goals of therapy. Ineffective REBT can often occur when the client wishes to achieve one goal and the therapist is working to help him or her achieve a different goal. However, we advocate that therapists do not uncritically accept their clients' goal statements as sacred. Indeed, a good REBT therapist sometimes spends some therapeutic time trying to talk a client out of goals that the client considers to be helpful but that the therapist considers to be harmful to the long-term welfare of the client. Good REBT therefore involves a fair measure of negotiation between therapist and client concerning the client's goals. It is helpful if the therapist does not dogmatically insist that a client give up his or her unrealistic or harmful goals because such insistence may add to the client's problems!

Clients' goals can and often do change over time, and therapists had better be sensitive to the changing nature of their clients' aims and attempt to track changes in their goal statements. It is particularly helpful for REBT therapists to understand (and to help their clients understand) what underlies such changes in therapeutic goals. Remember that clients' initial goals are often colored by the nature of their disturbances and that is advantageous for therapists to encourage them to postpone fixing on certain goals until they have achieved a fair measure of success in overcoming their emotional and/or behavioral disturbances. When this is done, REBT therapists are noted for helping their clients to pursue the latters' own individualized goals because they believe that a particular client does not *have to* achieve satisfaction in any given way. Thus, clients are encouraged to actualize their potential in their own individualistic way (preferably after having achieved a large measure of freedom from emotional and behavioral disturbance). Thus, in general, REBT therapists encourage clients to first work on the goals of overcoming their emotional and/or behavioral disturbances before working to pursue individualistic goals that will bring *them* happiness.

In addition to bonds and goals, another aspect of the therapeutic alliance where REBT can be practiced in an individualized way is in the task domain. Bordin (1979) has stressed that every therapeutic system favors particular therapists' tasks *and* clients' tasks, which then become embodied in the practice of that approach to therapy. In chapter 2 we outlined what these tasks are in the sections on therapeutic strategies and major treatment techniques. REBT can be practiced in an individualized way if the therapist encourages the client to carry out tasks that are best suited to that particular client and that are likely to encourage that client to achieve his or her therapeutic goals. In this way the practice of REBT can be seen as efficient as well as effective (Ellis, 1980d).

Some clients seem to progress better by carrying out techniques that are more cognitive in nature, whereas other clients seem to benefit more from executing tasks that are more emotive in nature (yet a further group of clients do best by carrying out behavioral tasks). We have already pointed out that a particular therapeutic technique draws upon all three modalities, yet it is also true that a particular technique may emphasize one modality over others. There are no firm guidelines for REBT therapists to use in determining, before the event, which therapeutic techniques are most appropriate for given clients. However, it may be helpful to explore with clients their past history of effecting productive changes while paying attention to their answers concerning which modalities they spontaneously used or were encouraged to use. In other words, it may be helpful for REBT therapists to pay attention to a client's prior learning style and modify the practice of REBT accordingly. Once again, perhaps the best indication concerning which techniques clients will benefit from most is experimentation. Whatever tasks clients execute, it is important that REBT therapists help them to (1) understand how the execution of such tasks is relevant to the achievement of stated goals, (2) overcome any obstacles to the successful execution of such tasks, and (3) specify when they might execute such tasks and in which setting. Cognitive and behavioral *rehearsal* methods that can be carried out within the course of a session can be of particular help in this regard.

When client resistance occurs it can often be attributed to problems in the task dimension. Thus, I (WD) have argued that

> client resistance can occur when (1) clients do not understand what their tasks are and thus cannot be expected to carry them out; (2) clients understand what their tasks are but do not understand how executing them will help them achieve their goals; (3) clients understand what their tasks are but do not believe that they are capable of executing them; (4) clients both understand their tasks and believe that they are capable of carrying them out but believe that they should not have to work to change . . .; (5) clients do not understand their therapists' tasks and/or cannot see the link between their therapists' tasks and their own tasks and goals; (6) clients may in fact be incapable of executing their tasks (e.g., some clients are not intelligent enough to do socratic disputing); (7) therapists do not adequately prepare their clients to understand and execute the latter's tasks; (8) therapists poorly execute their own tasks (i.e., they are poorly skilled in the techniques of REBT); (9) therapists compulsively carry out a limited number of tasks (e.g., they often use cognitive techniques but rarely employ behavioral methods); and (10) some tasks are not potent enough to achieve the clients' goals (e.g., disputing irrational beliefs without exposure is unlikely to help clients with agoraphobic problems (Emmelkamp, Kuipers, & Eggeraat, 1978). (Dryden, 1985a, p. xi)

A Typical Individual REBT Session

As we have shown, the practice of individual REBT varies to some degree, depending upon whether the client is in the initial, middle, or end phase of therapy. We wish, however, to give the reader an idea of how a "typical" session is conducted. In doing so we have chosen to provide an example from the initial phase of therapy. It is important to note that the following is meant to be a flexible guide rather than a rigid framework.

First, if the clients agreed to carry out a homework assignment from the previous session, it is important to spend some time discussing their experiences in doing the task. If the assignment has been carried out successfully, it is important to investigate whether the clients have achieved the success by making changes in their irrational musturbatory evaluations or their distorted inferences or whether they have changed their behavior or the activating event. If clients have not changed by modifying their musturbatory evaluations, then it is important for the therapist to help them to realize this and to understand the importance of carrying out another assignment in order to bring about such philosophically based change. If any problems with the homework emerge, the therapist had better spend some time on troubleshooting these problems. In particular, the therapist can help clients become aware of the existence of any irrational Beliefs that prevented them from executing the task. If this is the case, then the therapist spends some time Disputing these Beliefs and reassigning the task (if appropriate).

If sufficient closure has been achieved on the problem that the clients discussed the previous week, then the therapist can move on to discussing another of their problems. If insufficient closure has been achieved, then the therapist would do well to spend more time on the previous problem. Assuming that sufficient closure has been achieved, then the therapist asks for the clients' most pressing primary problem that has not already been discussed. The therapist encourages the clients to briefly disclose the nature of this problem and uses opportunities to help them assess the problem using the ABC framework outline in chapter 1.

Using inference chaining, the therapist helps clients to identify the most relevant inference that provided the context for their emotional and/or behavioral problem. The therapist temporarily encourages clients to assume that the inference is correct. Before progressing to the Disputing stage the therapist checks out whether clients have a secondary problem about the primary problem (e.g., a depression about feeling depressed or anxiety about feeling anxious). If a secondary problem does exist, the therapist gives a persuasive rationale concerning why it is important to devote therapeutic time to this problem before moving to the primary problem. If no secondary problem exists, the therapist can reiterate the problem in ABC form and proceed to help clients to see the connections between A factors, B factors, and C factors, paying particular attention to helping them to see the connection between B and C. This framework can also be used if the therapist is spending time on the clients' secondary problem. If so, the therapist can help clients understand that in order to reduce their emotional or behavioral problems they had better first devote their time to Disputing their irrational

Beliefs. The therapist then Disputes the clients' major dysfunctional Belief by asking for any evidence that supports it, for example, "Where is the evidence that . . .?" The therapist helps clients to see that any "evidence" that they provide is virtually always in support of their Rational Belief and not of their Irrational Belief. For example, there is evidence that it is preferable for clients to do well and be approved but not that therefore they "must" do well or be approved.

The therapist then goes over this process until clients acknowledge that evidence can be provided only for the existence of the Rational Belief but not for that of the Irrational Belief. The therapist then helps them to see the relationship between the Rational Belief and the constructive and desired emotional and behavioral changes. The therapist then underscores the importance of clients continuing to dispute their dysfunctional Beliefs in the setting outlined in A and other relevant situations.

After this has been done, the therapist negotiates a homework assignment with clients that will give them the opportunity to Dispute the Irrational Belief and act on the new Rational Belief. As noted above, the therapist works carefully to ensure that clients can see the sense of doing their assignments and helps them to overcome any doubts they may have concerning the practice of the assignment. The therapist encourages clients to be specific in determining when and where their assignments will be executed and generally troubleshoots possible obstacles to the successful completion of each task before it is done. If relevant, the therapist conducts in-session practice in which clients can rehearse the assignment using imagery or simulated exercises (e.g., role play).

If time allows and it is relevant, the therapist can help clients to identify and correct any distorted inferences that were assumed to be true when the ABC analysis was first conducted. In addition, and again if time allows, the therapist can engage clients in constructive skills training if they are deficient in any skills that are relevant to the problem outlined. The above framework indicates clearly that the typical REBT session is sequentially structured. It is important to reiterate that it is highly desirable that clients can make sense of and agree to their active participation in this structure.

Whenever possible, the therapist attempts to individualize the therapy session for clients, using the therapeutic strategies and techniques that are assumed to be of particular benefit to this particular client at this particular time. If any written homework assignment or tape material is to be suggested, it is important that it meets the therapeutic requirements of the client. Thus, for example, for clients who do not often read books or do not profit from reading, the therapist may suggest that they listen to a tape. If a client often reads but is not used to complex material, the therapist may suggest a book such as Young's *A Rational Counseling Primer* (1974) instead of Ellis and Harper's *A Guide to Rational Living* (1997).

CASE EXAMPLE

Mrs. Haynes (pseudonym), at the time that I (WD) saw her, was a 35-year-old professional married woman who had recently discovered that her husband had been having an affair and had decided to leave her for the other woman. There were no children in this marriage. Mrs. Haynes's general practitioner referred her to me for psychotherapy for depression and anxiety. In the initial session she made it clear to me that she did not want to involve her husband in therapy but rather wanted an opportunity to focus on her own problems. She further did not think that joining a group would give her sufficient time or privacy to discuss her problems in as much depth as she considered to be most productive for her. We thus decided on a course of individual REBT.

In the initial session, Mrs. Haynes reported having had a previous spell of individual counseling with a marriage counselor who, from her description, appeared to practice a kind of nondirective, psychoanalytically oriented therapy. She felt that she did not benefit from this kind of therapy, mainly because she was confused and put off by the therapist's passivity and seeming lack of active involvement. I gave her a thumbnail sketch of what she might realistically expect from REBT, and her initial reaction was favorable. We agreed to meet initially for five sessions. I like to make an initial time-limited contract to enable clients to later make a more informed decision about whether or not they wish to continue with me as an REBT therapist.

Mrs. Haynes saw depression as more of a pressing problem for her than anxiety, and it was the one that she wanted to make a start on. She was particularly depressed about her own failure to make her marriage work and blamed herself for her husband's preference for another woman. I helped her to see that it was not his preference for another woman that made her depressed but her beliefs about the situation, which were, "I must make my marriage work and I am a failure if I don't!" Before proceeding to help her to dispute this belief in the initial session, I worked patiently with her to enable her to see the connections between A, B, and C.

I started to Dispute her demanding belief only when she said that she saw clearly that it was this Belief that caused her depression rather than her husband leaving her and that in order to overcome her depression she needed to change her Belief. While disputing her Belief, I helped her to develop a list of self-Disputes that she could ask herself in the coming week whenever she felt depressed about her presumed failure in marriage. I gave her a copy of *A Guide to Rational Living* and suggested that in particular she read chapter 2 ("You Feel the Way You Think") and chapter 11 ("Eradicating Dire Fears of Failure"). I also offered her an opportunity to take away a tape of our session, which she gratefully accepted.

At the beginning of the following session I asked her for her reactions to both the tape and reading material. It transpired from this that she had a positive response to both the tape and the reading material, and she commented that she particularly liked the method of bibliotherapy. Her depression had lifted considerably since our first session, and she was able to use her own self-disputes to come up with plausible answers. In order to reinforce her progress I asked her if she would find it helpful to use one of the written self-help forms that exist for this purpose and showed her three. She decided to start off with the one that I invented (see Figure 2.3). We first worked on an episode of depression—even though she had progressed on that since our initial session—after we decided that it was better to get closure on her depression before we tackled her anxiety. We spent the rest of session 2 filling out this form, and at the end I gave her a number of these forms and suggested that she read chapter 15 of *A Guide for Rational Living* ("Conquering Anxiety") and to use such insights to fill in a form whenever she became anxious.

At the beginning of session 3 she reported that she benefited from reading the chapter on anxiety but had experienced some difficulty in zeroing in on the irrational Beliefs that underpinned her anxiety. Using the inference chaining procedure, I helped her to see that she was anxious about ever finding another man again and ending up an old spinster. As is typical in REBT, I encouraged her to assume the worst and to imagine that she was an old spinster and asked her for her feelings about that. Her reply was instructive: "Oh God, I couldn't stand the thought of living like that." I Disputed her Belief that she needed a man in her life in order to be happy and helped her to see that she could in fact gain a fair measure of happiness in her life if single even though she would prefer to be married and have a family. This led to a discussion of her immediate anxiety, that is, of her feeling that she could not go out on her own because this would be shameful.

Often feelings of shame are related to feelings of anxiety, and assuming this to be the case with Mrs. Haynes, I helped her to see that she was saying: "If I go out on my own then other people will see that I am alone and that would prove that I am worthless." The rest of the session was spent putting this into A, B, C, D form using the self-help form. I then suggested that we try rational emotive imagery as a bridge between changing her attitude in her mind's eye and putting into practice her new Belief, "I have every right to go out on my own, and if other people look down on me, then I refuse to look down on myself." Mrs. Haynes had a great deal of difficulty in using rational emotive imagery in the session and between sessions 3 and 4.

At the beginning of session 4, I went over the rational emotive imagery and suggested instead that she say her new rational Belief quite vigorously to herself. She was able to do this, first of all out loud and then internally, and felt a mood shift that was much more profound than what she was able to achieve by using rational emotive imagery. Let me add that her feelings of depression were no longer considered by her to be a problem since session 1.

At the end of session 4 we negotiated an assignment in which she would go out socially on her own on two occasions (on one occasion to a local evening class and second to a dance hall) while vigorously repeating the rational self-coping statements we developed. This apparently was very helpful to Mrs. Haynes, for she reported that she was able to go out on both occasions without undue anxiety. This was our fifth session, the last of our therapeutic contract, and I discussed her progress with her and how she wished to proceed in the future. She said that she felt very pleased with her progress and wanted to continue to have sessions every 2 weeks rather than weekly.

From sessions 5 to session 10, Mrs. Haynes made great progress. She had a number of dates with men and was able to resist the sexual advances of two of them, which to her was a great stride because in the past she had had great difficulty saying no to men and had for a period prior to her marriage been quite promiscuous, out of desperation rather than out of choice. Between sessions 5 and 10, I gave her *Why Do I Think I Am Nothing Without a Man* by Penelope Russianoff (1981) and *Living Alone and Liking It* by Lynn Shahan (1981) to read. She also continued to listen to the tapes of her sessions, although I suggested that she review them only once, rather than her accustomed three times, because I wished to encourage her to rely on her own resources rather than to rely on my direction, albeit secondhand, through the tapes. She also continued going out on her own and used vigorous self-Disputing to increasingly good effect.

As I attempted to move the therapy from the middle phase to the end phase, Mrs. Haynes became quite anxious. She said that she felt she had become quite dependent upon my help and was anxious about whether or not she could cope on her own. First of all I Disputed her Belief that she needed my help, and second, I encouraged her to view a break from therapy as an experiment and suggested a 6-week gap between our 10th and 11th sessions, stressing that she rely more on self-Disputing than on bibliotherapy. I also suggested that she not listen to any of the past tapes so that we could conduct a fair experiment of her inference that she could not cope on her own.

The experiment proved to be a success. When she came in, she wondered why she even thought that she could not cope on her own, because she had managed the 6-week gap very well. I commented that I was pleased with her progress, to which she replied, "That's nice to know, but even if you weren't, I am. I don't need your approval." Having been firmly put in my place in this regard, we discussed whether she needed any future sessions and finally agreed that we would have a 6-month follow-up. I did suggest that she could contact me if she wanted to in the interim, on the condition that she use her own skills for a 2-week period and if she could not cope with any emotional problems that came up in that period, then she could contact me.

At the 6-month follow-up session, Mrs. Haynes had attained and enhanced her therapeutic gains. She was productively involved in many social and voluntary activities and had ongoing casual relationships with three men, one of which included sex out of choice, not out of desperation. Her relationship with her husband was reasonably cordial, and they were proceeding toward an amicable divorce. In my keenness to encourage her to cope on her own, I made the error of moving toward termination without helping her to anticipate future problems and encourage her to see that she could use her new coping methods to deal with these problems. Although this was an error at the time, Mrs. Haynes was able to cope in the intervening period. In addition, I had to do very little work in helping her set goals for increased satisfaction because she was able to do this on her own.

5

Couples Therapy

I (AE) began my career in the helping professions as a sex, marital, and family counselor in the early 1940s. As a result of my experiences as a marital counselor, I concluded that in most instances disturbed marriages (or premarital relationships) are a product of disturbed spouses and that if people are truly to be helped to live happily with each other they first had better be shown how they can live peacefully with themselves. This conclusion led me to embark on intensive psychoanalytic training, believing then that psychoanalysis was the preferred mode of treatment for such disturbances. As has been already mentioned, in the early 1950s I became increasingly disillusioned with both the theoretical validity and the clinical effectiveness of psychoanalytic treatment and began to see more clearly that human disturbance had profound ideological roots. Drawing upon the work of early Asian and Stoic philosophers (e.g., Marcus Aurelius and Epictetus) who stressed that people are disturbed not by events but by their views of these events, I began to develop a therapeutic approach based upon a perspective of human disturbance that stressed philosophic determinants and deemphasized psychoanalytic psychodynamics. I applied this approach to a number of therapeutic modalities, including couples therapy.

Rational emotive behavior couples therapy (REBCT) has developed considerably since those early days. A number of REBT therapists have maintained an active interest in couples therapy, and there are a number of events that can be regarded as important in the history of its growth.

An early important development was the publication of my first book on REBT, *How to Live with a "Neurotic": At Home and at Work* (Ellis, 1957). In this book I advanced the thesis that partners could alleviate couple discord, first by working to remain undisturbed about their partners' neurotic problems, and then by experimenting with various solutions to help their partners get over their neurotic difficulties. In a later text, written with Robert Harper, entitled

Parts of this chapter were adapted from W. Dryden, "Marital Therapy: The Rational-Emotive Approach," in Dryden (1985b). Used by permission.

A Guide to Successful Marriage (Ellis & Harper, 1961b), I developed this thesis and also made an important distinction between couple disturbance and couple dissatisfaction, which has remained a cornerstone of REBCT ever since. In the same book, Harper and I also wrote on the important role that unrealistic expectations about intimate relationships play in the development and maintenance of both couple dissatisfaction and disturbance. Although the term "expectation" in psychotherapy is problematic in that it does not clearly differentiate between "hopes," "assumptions," "predictions" of varying certitude, and "absolutistic demands," we made the valid point that there is often a large discrepancy between what actually happens in intimate relationships and what one or both partners assume or predict will happen. Thus, unrealistic expectations are often the breeding ground for the later development of relationship problems.

In 1962 my seminal book, *Reason and Emotion in Psychotherapy*, was published. This contained a chapter entitled "A Rational Approach to Marital Problems," which was adapted and expanded from two earlier articles. Here I clearly outlined that one of the major tasks of the marriage counselor was to "tackle not the problem of the marriage, nor the neurotic interaction that exists between the marital partners, but the irrational ideas or beliefs that cause the neurosis à deux" (Ellis, 1962, p. 210).

As will be discussed later in this chapter, another cornerstone of REBCT is its position on the role and treatment of angry and hostile reactions in intimate relationships. I published an important paper on this topic (Ellis, 1976g) in which I clearly outlined both the rational emotive behavioral position on anger—namely, that it is a dysfunctional emotion that severely interferes with relationship harmony—and its management in therapy.

Apart from myself, a number of other REBT therapists have made important contributions to the field of REBCT. Among others, the writings of McClellan and Stieper (1973) on a structured rational-emotive approach to group marital counseling, and Hauck on (1) the reciprocity theory of love and marriage (1981, 1983a) and (2) parenting styles (1983b) are particularly noteworthy. Special mention should be made of Walen, DiGiuseppe, and Wessler's (1980) chapter entitled "A Rational Approach to Marriage and Divorce Counseling" in their book *A Practitioner's Guide to Rational-Emotive Therapy*. Finally, in 1989, the first text was published that provided a comprehensive exposition of the theory and practice of REBCT (Ellis, Sichel, Yeager, DiMattia, & DiGiuseppe, 1989).

THE NATURE OF DISTURBED
INTIMATE RELATIONSHIPS

REBT therapists clearly distinguish between couple dissatisfaction and couple disturbance. Couple dissatisfaction occurs when one or both partners are not getting enough of what they *want* from their partner and/or from being in an intimate relationship. Couple disturbance arises when one or both partners become emotionally disturbed about these dissatisfactions. Thus, they may make themselves anxious, angry, hostile, hurt, depressed, ashamed, guilty, and jealous—emotions that usually interfere with constructive communication, problem-solving, and negotiation processes that aid the solution of couple dissatisfaction problems. In addition, when one or both partners are emotionally disturbed, they generally act in a self- and relationship-defeating manner, thus perpetuating couple disturbance. REBCT theory states that, assuming they have the necessary constructive communication, problem-solving, and negotiation skills, couples are likely to solve their dissatisfaction problems on their own. When they are deficient in such skills, the focus of couples is on training them to develop and use these skills. However, once couples are in the disturbance stage of a relationship, unless their emotional problems are dealt with, relationship problems usually remain, no matter how skillful one or both partners are in communicating, solving problems, and negotiating workable compromises. Couples, interestingly enough, often misdiagnose their own problems. They often conclude, for example, that their problems are due to deficits in communication skills, whereas in reality they find it difficult to talk to one another when one or both are hurt, angry, depressed, or anxious.

Couple Disturbance

As we have shown in chapter 1, emotional disturbance, C according to REBT's ABC theory, stems not merely from events at A but mainly from a certain type of evaluative thinking or Belief at B. This type of thinking, which is absolutistic, devout, and grossly exaggerated in nature, is called "irrational" in REBT theory, mainly to denote that it hinders people from actualizing their basic goals and purposes. Thus, Irrational Beliefs that lead to such disturbed emotions as anxiety, anger/hostility, hurt, depression, shame and embarrassment, guilt, and jealousy largely stem, according to REBT theory, from a thinking process known as "musturbation." In the couple context, this process is characterized by one partner making *absolute* demands and commands on self, the other partner, and/or the relationship situation.

In the main, three further self-defeating and grossly exaggerated thinking processes tend to stem from musturbation (Ellis, 1994c). Once humans absolutistically demand that something, for example, "must" not occur, they tend, if that event occurs, to conclude that the event is "awful," "horrible," or "terrible," that they "can't stand it" or "can't bear it," and that the perpetrator of the event that must not have occurred is "no good," "worthless" (or "less worthy"), or "bad"—whether the perpetrator is self, another person, or life conditions in general. I (AE) noted that these four thinking processes, known colloquially in REBT literature as (1) "musturbation," (2) "awfulizing," (3) "I-can't-stand-it-itis," and (4) "damning," represent a philosophy of devout belief, in which the person adopts a godlike position and *insists* (not just desires or prefers) that the world (and the people in it) be as he or she wants it (or them) to be (Ellis, 1991b).

The rational (or self-enhancing) alternatives to these absolutistic beliefs are framed within a nondemanding, nonabsolutistic philosophy of desire. Here, in the relationship context, it is acknowledged that couples do have desires, are probably happier when these are met, and become dissatisfied when these remain unfulfilled. However, as has been stressed above, dissatisfaction is not synonymous with disturbance; the latter mainly develops if one or both partners escalate their nonabsolute desires into absolute demands. Couple dissatisfaction occurs when one or both partners' important desires are not being fulfilled (and neither is insisting that they get what they want). Couple disturbance occurs when one or both partners demand their desires must be met. Parenthetically, couples therapy is normally more difficult when both partners are emotionally disturbed about the relationship than when only one partner is thus disturbed.

The rational versions of the four dysfunctional thinking processes are as follows:

1. *Desiring* (vs. musturbation). Here the partner acknowledges his or her desires, does not insist that they be met, but is dissatisfied when they are not. Such dissatisfaction often serves to stimulate constructive attempts at problem solving that have a better chance of succeeding with a spouse who is also not musturbating. Rational thinking processes tend to follow from nondemanding desiring, just as dysfunctional thinking processes follow from musturbation.

2. *Rating as bad* or *anti-awfulizing* (vs. awfulizing). REBT theory holds that "awful" really means totally or 100% bad because such a definition stems from the belief that this *must* not be as bad as it is." Thus "awful" is seen to be on a different continuum from "bad." If a partner is not getting what he or she really wants but is not insisting upon it, this person will tend to define the deprivation as "bad" but not "awful." The general principle is that the more important the unfulfilled desire, the more "bad" the definition of the deprivation is likely to be. It is, thus, only under very unusual conditions that an event can be legitimately rated as 100% bad. Nonabsolutistically defining something as "bad" but not "awful" tends to help the partner to try to ameliorate the "bad" situation.

3. *Tolerating* (vs. I-can't-stand-it-itis). "I can't stand it" literally means disintegrating or dying on the spot. It more often seems to mean not being able to have any happiness whatsoever under any conditions, rather than actually dying. However, tolerating something means (1) acknowledging that some unwanted event has occurred and believing that there is no law that says it must not occur, (2) rating it as "bad" but not "awful," and (3) determining whether change is possible. If it is possible, constructive attempts are made to

produce the desired change; if change is not possible, the person accepts but definitely dislikes this "grim" reality. When partners are thinking rationally, they are likely to see that, although they *can* tolerate a bad relationship, there is no reason why they *have to* do so. Tolerating adverse conditions is an attitude that may lead to constructive change attempts, whereas I-can't-stand-it-itis often leads to destructive manipulative strategies.

4. *Accepting* (vs. damning). This attitude can be applied to self, others, and the world. When a woman, for example, unconditionally accepts herself in this way, she recognizes that she is a fallible human being who has an "incurable error-making tendency" (Maultsby, 1984), meaning that she can and will make mistakes. If she is able to accept herself as such, she will more likely be able to acknowledge these errors, regard them as bad if they impede her goals, and take responsibility for committing them. Moreover, if she does not *insist* that her partner act well, she will more likely be able to accept him or her as fallible, dislike the fact that he or she is acting badly, and initiate constructive negotiations for future improvement. Finally, if she does not dogmatically *insist* that her relationship be the way she wants it to be, she will tend to see it as a fallible institution with good and bad components that can only be improved but not perfected.

As Young (1975) has shown, rational thinking can and does (especially in the arena of intimate relationships) lead to strong, healthy negative emotions, such as concern, annoyance, sadness, disappointment, regret, and dislike. However, these emotions tend to motivate marital partners to take constructive steps to improve matters if their shared goal is to remain partnered.

Couple Dissatisfaction

REBCT theory notes that there are two major contributing factors to couple dissatisfaction: relationship myths and important incompatibilities.

Couple dissatisfaction may occur if partners adhere to one or more myths (Ellis & Harper, 1961b; Lazarus, 1985; Lederer & Jackson, 1968). Such myths tend to be unrealistic in that they idealize the state of the relationship and encourage partners to overestimate what they can realistically expect to derive from being partnered. Some examples of commonly held relationship myths* that are often implicated in marital dissatisfaction include the following: love equals good sex; romantic love will endure throughout the partnership; my partner will be able to know what I want without my having to communicate my desires; good sex will always be spontaneous; I will not suffer any deprivations or penalties as a result of being partnered; my partner will help me get over my feelings of unworthiness; my partner will make up for my past frus-

---

*Partners often express such myths in idiosyncratic form.

trations; my partner will make allowances for my bad behavior; my partner will always be on my side, always be loyal, and always love me (no matter how badly I behave). If partners do not modify these myths in line with their experiences, they will tend to become dissatisfied, as reality proves to be discrepant from their assumptions of what is "expected" to happen in the relationship. Furthermore, it can be easily seen how such myths can further lead to couple disturbance when linked to a philosophy of musturbation.

Couple dissatisfaction may also occur when partners are revealed to be incompatible in one or more areas of the relationship. Generally, the more important the area, the greater the dissatisfaction, especially if negotiations for compromise fail to resolve the issues.

Couple incompatibility may stem from naive and superficial partner selection in which partners do not really get to know one another, or it may occur as a result of changes in outlook on the part of one or both of them. A commonly encountered example of emergent incompatibility occurs when a woman seeks to develop a more independent life-style. If this exceeds the role expectations of her partner, then neither is likely to get what he or she wants in a significant area of their relationship. If she does not act on her newly discovered desire, she is likely to become dissatisfied and act less responsively toward him so that he becomes dissatisfied. However, if she spends less time in the house, he becomes dissatisfied because his desires for a well-kept house are not being met; and if he begins to nag her, she becomes dissatisfied because her desires for support are not met. Dissatisfaction based on emergent incompatibility can often be a stimulus for constructive renegotiation of roles and responsibilities, but equally often, especially if the incompatibility occurs in a centrally important area for one or both partners, it may lead to relationship breakdown even if couple disturbance is not involved. In such a case one or both partners conclude that the relationship no longer meets a very important desire and is not likely to in the future. If the incompatibility is in a less important area, it may lead to less intrusive dissatisfaction and may hardly affect the relationship, especially if the partners can find expression for the desire elsewhere and this is accepted by the other.

The Development and Perpetuation of Couple Disturbance

REBCT theory holds that couple disturbance can develop and be perpetuated in a number of different ways. Conflict may occur soon after the relationship has been established if one or both partners are quite disturbed as individuals. Similarly, conflict might develop at various stages of an ongoing relationship when change occurs in the couple system. This change becomes a stimulus for one or both partners to bring their philosophy of musturbation to the new situation. Thus, a dissatisfaction can quickly become a disturbance if, for example, a man demands that his mate *must* not ask to see his pay packet or if the woman insists that her mate *must* telephone to tell her that he will be staying late at the office. Here partners give themselves an emotional problem about the problem of dissatisfaction. In addition, partners may give themselves secondary emotional problems about their newly developed primary emotional problems (Ellis, 1994c, 1995a, 1996c). Thus, a man may get angry with his mate because he is demanding that she *must* not act in a certain manner; he may then notice his angry reaction and condemn himself for reacting in such a *terrible* manner. He thus becomes guilty for reacting angrily. It is unlikely that constructive communication or problem solving could ensue while he is experiencing anger alone and doubly unlikely if he adds guilt to his emotional menu.

Unhealthy anger, stemming from the absolutistic demand that you, my partner, must not act this way either because it is "wrong" or because it is a threat to my "self-esteem," is probably the most prominent reason why couple dis-

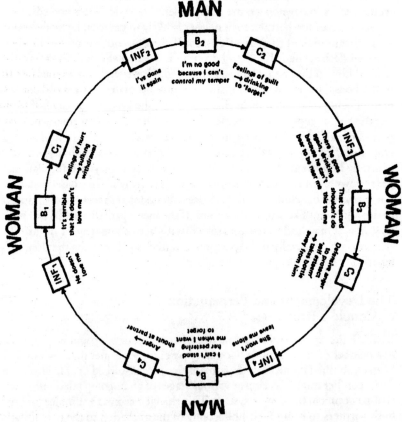

FIGURE 5.1 The ABCs of dysfunctional couple interaction.

turbance is perpetuated (Ellis, 1976g, 1977a). Indeed, when both partners are damning each other, couple disturbance can be perpetuated indefinitely with little chance of a constructive solution being found. Another core reason that couple disturbance is perpetuated is anxiety over confronting basic issues. One or both partners may be scared that if they shared their feelings of dissatisfaction with one another something "awful" would ensue. They thus withdraw from one another and feel lonely, guilty, and depressed about the growing distance between them.

Partners with emotional disturbances tend to act in dysfunctional ways (behavioral C's). These then serve as the stimulus for the second partner's inference (INF). Vicious circles of disturbed couple interaction result when a dysfunctional behavior (C) on the part of one partner serves as the trigger (INF2) for an irrational Belief (B2) of the other partner that in turn leads to disturbed feelings and behavior (C2). This serves as a new trigger (INF3) for the first partner . . . and so on. An example of such a vicious circle is shown in Figure 5.1. As this interaction pattern demonstrates, partners often make inferences of each other's behavior (which have been included under INF). These inferences may be correct but, especially in the phase of couple disturbance, are likely to be faulty, colored as they often are by dysfunctional evaluative thinking. Nevertheless, REBT therapists do draw on Beck's (1976) work on "cognitive distortions" and note that partners often make errors in processing interpersonal information and that these errors often serve to perpetuate couple disturbance (see chapter 1). These also become the focus for therapeutic work, but normally after partners' musturbatory evaluative thinking has been tackled.

PRACTICE

Contextual Considerations

REBT therapists are guided by the principle of flexibility throughout the therapeutic process in working with couples. Thus, there are no absolute rules to guide REBCT practitioners concerning whether to see partners conjointly, concurrently, or consecutively in individual sessions. Therapeutic decisions concerning the working context are suggested by therapeutic exigencies. Ellis (in Dryden, 1984d) and Bard (1980), for example, consider that the decision whether to see both partners together or separately at the outset of therapy should preferably be made by clients themselves. However, individual sessions may be indicated for three main reasons:

1. When the two partners persist in arguing nonproductively in the context of conjoint sessions and thus negate the potential benefit of the therapist's interventions.

2. When the joint presence of the partners in the therapy room unduly inhibits one or both of them. They may be so anxious about the possible negative effects of speaking their minds that they do not disclose significant material in therapy. In such cases a period of concurrent individual sessions is often helpful.
3. When the goals of the individual partners are sufficiently incongruent to preclude the establishment of a productive therapeutic alliance in conjoint therapy, for example, when one person wishes to leave the relationship while the other wishes to preserve it.

When both partners wish to be seen together, share basically congruent goals, are not inhibited by their joint presence in therapy, and can contain their strong angry feelings, then conjoint couples therapy is usually the most beneficial context for productive work.

Some REBCT practitioners prefer to work concurrently with the partners in individual sessions in the "overcoming couple disturbance" phase of treatment. They hypothesize that partners are more likely to disclose their genuinely held "deep" feelings (e.g., of hurt, jealousy, anger, and fear) if they see the therapist alone. Partners can thus give their full attention to the therapeutic process while the therapist helps them to see the connections between their dysfunctional emotions/behavioral patterns and their irrational Beliefs and helps them to Dispute and change these ideas. Because REBCT is by nature an educational process, its practitioners are mindful of choosing environments that best facilitate learning. We note, however, that partners *can* learn the ABCs of REBCT in the context of conjoint therapy in the "disturbance" phase. Here, our experience has taught us that while the therapist works with one partner, helping him or her to identify, challenge, and change core irrational Beliefs, the "listening" partner often learns the ABC framework of emotional/behavioral disturbance better than the "working" partner.*

Although REBCT practitioners differ concerning their views about the supremacy of conjoint versus concurrent therapy in the "overcoming couple disturbance" phase of treatment, they generally agree that the presence of both partners is highly desirable in the "enhancing couple satisfaction" phase. In this phase both partners have, ideally, made some progress overcoming their emotional disturbances about their differences and are ready to explore possible ways of improving their relationship if they have decided to stay together. REBT therapists use a variety of methods to facilitate such exploration. Communication, problem-solving, sex education, and negotiation training are used

---

*A similar phenomenon often occurs in individual REBT. When clients are given audiotape recordings of therapy sessions they often learn the ABCs of REBT better after they have listened to these recordings than when they are in the therapy room. It may be that this is due to the fact that later they are less emotionally involved with the material and can thus listen more attentively to what the therapist and they themselves are saying.

in this phase, and the presence of both partners is highly desirable to enable the therapist to instruct them *both* to communicate more effectively, solve problems, and negotiate more constructively so that they can improve the quality of their relationship.

Conjoint REBCT is usually conducted with a single therapist, although there are occasions when a cotherapy arrangement would be desirable, particularly if, say, a woman feels unduly adversely affected by the presence of a male therapist. Here a female cotherapist would be helpful to strengthen the therapeutic alliance, and such a four-person arrangement might be particularly desirable in sex therapy.

In conclusion, the conduct of REBCT is not bound by strict rules of procedure; flexibility is encouraged, and changes in context may occur throughout the therapeutic process. Such changes are made according to therapeutic purposes that are generally made clear and agreed to by clients. It is in keeping with REBT philosophy that REBCT practitioners are against dogmatically *insisting* that therapy must be practiced in any predetermined context.

Developing and Maintaining a Therapeutic Alliance

It is important to note at the outset that REBCT practitioners consider that their therapeutic contract is with the individuals in the relationship and not only with the couple system (Ellis, Sichel, Yeager, DiMattia & DiGiuseppe, 1989; Harper, 1981; Walen et al., 1980). As Harper (1981) argues, the couple system is an abstraction, and as such, REBCT therapists have great difficulty seeing how a therapeutic alliance can be made with it. They prefer, whenever possible, to develop alliances with each of the involved partners. It is preferable that this is made clear to both partners at the outset of couples therapy so that they can see that the therapist is not interested in trying to preserve, or indeed destroy, their relationship. As has already been stressed, a primary objective of REBCT therapists is to help both partners over their emotional disturbance about their situation and then help them work on forging a more mutually satisfying relationship if that is their goal. However, partners often come into couples therapy with overt *and* hidden agendas, and it is often helpful to have separate interviews with each of the partners early in the process to determine whether the goals of each partner are sufficiently concordant to make conjoint couples therapy (which is the best working forum for partners who have similar objectives) feasible. Since the therapeutic alliance is with the individuals and not with "the relationship," the most appropriate therapeutic arena is sought to help the individuals actualize their goals.

Because therapeutic goals can be based on irrational as well as rational thinking, it is our practice to explain to both partners that they are more likely to make productive decisions about whether to stay partnered (and if so, what improvements are desired) or to separate when they are not emotionally disturbed about what is presently happening in the relationship. Thus, we like to set goals appropriate to particular phases of couples therapy. If the partners are disturbed, we attempt to have them identify and set goals that involve minimizing such disturbance; and if they are dissatisfied but not disturbed, we attempt to work on relationship enhancement goals after a decision has been made by both that they wish to stay partnered. Too often we have seen non-REBCT therapy founder because the therapist is working on couple enhancement goals when one or both partners are emotionally disturbed, with the result that goal-sabotaging needlessly occurs.

Another common error made by non-REBCT practitioners occurs when the therapist is only prepared to see the partners in conjoint therapy. Thus, if one partner wishes to preserve the relationship and the other has a hidden agenda to leave it but will not declare this openly in the therapeutic triangle, such therapy is either terminated by the latter soon after its inception or is marked by little or no improvement, to the detriment of both partners, REBCT therapists would be more likely to identify such a situation earlier in individual assessment interviews.

In the "overcoming emotional disturbance" phase of REBCT it is important for the therapist to work with each partner individually, either in conjoint therapy or in separate interviews. In conjoint therapy the therapist gives each partner roughly equal amounts of time in order to maintain a productive alliance in the three-person situation—a social system that can easily be destabilized if the therapist, for example, excludes one partner for lengthy periods of time. The therapist explains at the outset of this phase that the goal is to help each of the partners overcome his or her own disturbance (intrapersonal focus) so that they can more productively work on their disagreements later (interpersonal focus). Productive REBCT occurs when both partners clearly understand and agree to this modus operandi. In our experience, highly skilled REBCT therapists who can present a convincing rationale concerning this important point are usually, but not always, successful at developing a good therapeutic alliance with both partners when such an alliance is based on this principle. Failure to form a productive alliance with both partners at the outset of therapy usually leads to problems later in the therapeutic process and does not bode well for successful outcome. Such failure is due to either poor therapist skills or various partner factors, which include severe emotional disturbance, rigid adherence to the Belief that the other person is totally responsible for relationship problems, and various hidden agendas. In such instances the therapist is advised to consider changing the therapeutic context or to consider various systems-inspired interventions that are designed to change A factors in the ABC schema. If the therapist can successfully manage the "overcoming emotional disturbance" alliance, then the alliance necessary to effect productive change in the "enhancing couple satisfaction" phase is much easier to manage because both partners are in a position to make sound decisions about goals and are sufficiently free from emotional disturbance to work toward goal achievement.

MAJOR TREATMENT TECHNIQUES

REBCT is a multimodal form of therapy in that it employs a variety of cognitive (verbal and imagery), emotive, and behavioral techniques to help partners overcome their emotional disturbances and couple dissatisfactions.

"Overcoming Couple Disturbance" Phase

The goal of the REBCT practitioner in this phase of couples therapy is to help each partner become relatively undisturbed about the couples' problems so that they can constructively work, if they wish, to improve their level of relationship satisfaction. The therapist helps both partners to think functionally about themselves, their partner, and their relationship, which means feeling healthily frustrated, sorry, annoyed, and sad about their predicament when their desires are not met—emotions that will motivate them to work to improve their relationship or separate without needless emotional pain.

In this phase the REBCT practitioner helps both partners to see how they are needlessly upsetting themselves about their problems and often adopts a "let's assume" approach with both of them. Both partners are encouraged to assume that their negative inferences—about, for example, their partner—are correct, for the time being, to offset unproductive arguments about what actually occurred at A in the ABC framework. In this way the therapist helps each partner to identify his or her underlying dysfunctional Beliefs and replace them with rational alternatives. The therapist had better persistently encourage both partners to focus on their own upset if the goals of this phase of treatment are to be achieved.

A variety of cognitive methods are used at this stage. Partners are shown how to use realistic, logical, and heuristic questioning to dispute their irrational Beliefs. They are taught to ask themselves such questions as "Where is the law of the universe that states that my partner *must* do the housework perfectly well?"; "How does it follow that she is *bad* for acting badly?"; "Is it true that I *cannot stand* her behavior?"; "If I insist that my partner must be a perfect father, what will happen to our relationship?" They are helped to see that there is no evidence for such absolute statements, only evidence for their "preferential" form and that their dogmatic insistences will get and keep almost any relationship in trouble.

A number of clients appear less able to perform this kind of Socratic questioning, and here the therapist would help them develop and employ rational coping statements, such as "I don't like my partner's behavior but she has a right to act badly"; "She is a fallible human being who is doing the wrong thing"; "I can stand her behavior although I may never like it." These statements can be further written down on index cards and rehearsed between sessions.

Some couples can be shown, similarly, how to Dispute each other's irrational Beliefs and thus serve as therapists for each other between formal therapy sessions. Other cognitive techniques employed in this phase of REBCT include the use of (1) general semantics methods (Korzybski, 1988); (2) self-help forms (see chapter 2); (3) audiotape recordings (of the couple's therapy sessions or recorded lectures on various rational themes); (4) bibliotherapy, especially the use of books that present the REBT perspective on how to overcome emotional and behavioral disturbance; and (5) a variety of imagery techniques (Lazarus, 1984)

Emotively, the therapist can employ several evocative and vivid methods of REBT to help change the couple's irrational philosophies (Dryden, 1984b). Such methods include the use of (1) rational-emotive imagery (Ellis, 1993d; Maultsby, 1971)—where the partners deliberately imagine "upsetting events" at A and practice making themselves feel healthily sad, annoyed, or frustrated about these at C, which is achieved by spontaneously thinking more rationally at B; (2) vigorous and forceful repetition of rational statements (Ellis, 1979c); (3) role playing—to uncover hidden feelings that can then be traced back to the relevant irrational Beliefs and Disputed; (4) shame-attacking exercises—where couples deliberately seek out various "shameful" experiences and practice accepting themselves for acting "shamefully"; and (5) therapist self-disclosure and humor to help couples not take themselves and their partners *too* seriously.

Behaviorally, in this phase partners are encouraged to face and not avoid potential problems so that they may have real-life opportunities to stay in these situations until they have made themselves undisturbed about them (Grieger & Boyd, 1980; Ellis, Sichel, Yeager, et al., 1989).

"Enhancing Couple Satisfaction" Phase

Once both partners have made some progress at helping themselves and their partner overcome their emotional disturbances about their dissatisfactory relationship, they are in a position to constructively look at ways of enhancing their degree of relationship satisfaction or to be helped to amicably separate. Assuming that they wish to stay partnered, there are a number of well-established methods that can be used to help them to live more happily together. These include communication training (Crawford, 1982; Ellis, 1993b, 1993c; Guerney, 1977), negotiation training (Stuart, 1980), and a variety of behavioral techniques designed to help them to develop appropriate relating and sexual skills and to get more of what they want from each other (Mackay, 1985). Bibliotherapy is often used in conjunction with these methods.

A hallmark of REBCT is that homework assignments are negotiated to encourage couples to put into practice what they have learned in therapy. Assuming that such assignments are carefully designed by the therapist and agreed to by both partners, failure to execute them often reveals further emotional disturbance, particularly that which stems from a philosophy of low frustration tolerance (LFT). REBCT practitioners are alert to such possibilities and strive to help both partners, if appropriate, overcome their LFT so that they can follow through on the difficult task of changing the nature of their relationship.

A final task of REBCT practitioners in this stage is to address the topic of relationship myths (see the "Couple Dissatisfaction" section above) and help partners develop more realistic perspectives concerning what they can legitimately expect from intimate relationships.

Problems Encountered in REBCT and Their Solutions

The conduct of couples therapy is fraught with potential problems, no matter which approach the practitioner adopts. The more flexible the practitioner can be, the better, and in general it is highly desirable for REBCT therapists to dispute their own irrational beliefs concerning how therapy *must* proceed, how clients *must* behave, and what harmonious relationships *must* be like. Practitioners are advised not to be invested in either preserving or destroying relationships if they are to truly help couples negotiate what is in *their* best interests. Apart from therapist-derived problems, the following problems are often encountered in REBCT.

Secrets Because REBCT therapists conceive their basic task to be one of helping both individual partners rather than the relationship, they will frequently see the partners alone in individual sessions, particularly at the beginning of therapy. Consequently, they will sometimes be called upon to keep "secrets." They are prepared to do this, and in order to help both partners disclose what is really on their mind they will tell clients in individual sessions of their willingness to do so. This tactic also helps therapists to quickly uncover hidden agendas. Consequently, they had better be mindful of what information is confidential to a particular partner and keep a mental note not to disclose this in front of the other. It should again be noted that this is done in order to develop productive contracts with both partners. Some REBCT therapists stress to both partners that whatever is discussed in individual sessions is confidential to each partner concerned, so that if directly asked about what occurred in an individual session with the other partner, they can refer to this principle. Moreover, partners are advised to talk about their individual sessions with each other in general terms rather than in detail.

Persistent Other-Blaming It sometimes happens that one or both partners refuse to acknowledge that they make themselves disturbed about their mate's behavior and cling rigidly to the assertion that their mate is the cause of their upset. In certain of these cases it transpires that they are anxious that if they admit that they make themselves upset, their mate will not be motivated to change. In other cases such "defensiveness" is often motivated by fear of self-criticism: "If I admit that I make myself disturbed, as I *must* not do, then I will condemn myself." In these two instances good REBCT practitioners will test such hypotheses rather than assume that their hunches are correct. Such defensiveness can also be, in certain instances, a sign that the partner is profoundly disturbed. One technique that sometimes helps clients who persistently blame their partner is to stress that if they want their partner to change one of the most effective ways of achieving this is to change their own behavior first.

When Disputing Fails In certain cases REBCT therapists will fail to encourage one or both partners to identify, challenge, and change their Irrational Beliefs that mediate their disturbance. When this occurs, the practitioner can use some of the methods that are ideally intended for use in the "enhancing couple satisfaction" phase. In the case where one partner is overcoming his or her emotional disturbance and the other is not, the therapist may focus his or her efforts on encouraging the former to be unusually nice to the disturbed partner to encourage that partner to change. I (AE) originally advocated this tactic in my book *How to Live with a "Neurotic"* (Ellis, 1957), and it is one that sometimes proves successful. When both partners remain disturbed after disputing fails, REBCT practitioners may use a number of systems-theory-inspired interventions that are designed to change A. Thus, for example, reframing and various paradoxical procedures can be employed to help the couple extricate themselves from a vicious circle of negative interactions. If this is successful, it occasionally provides the stimulus for one or both partners to *then* focus on their disturbance-creating Beliefs. However, although such interventions may be successful in the short term, if both partners remain emotionally disturbed, they might, as a result, experience more problems later, because unresolved emotional disturbance is the driving force behind the development and maintenance of much disturbed interactions.

Extremely Hostile Interchanges These are difficult to manage when they occur in couples therapy sessions, and when they become a regular occurrence it is advisable to see the partners individually. However, in dealing with such a situation at a given time, I (WD) have found it helpful to do something unusual to gain the couple's attention. Thus, I have, in the midst of a heated interchange, got up and commenced speaking to a picture on the wall or tried to catch an imaginary mouse. These attention-getting techniques are, in my experience, generally more effective in defusing the situation than trying to shout the couple down, which tends to increase the heat in an overly hot kitchen.

The Change Process In the same way that a good navigator plots his favored course but plans several different alternative routes should they be needed, so do effective REBCT therapists have their preferred and alternative game plans. Because couples differ markedly, the REBCT therapist who adheres rigidly to a single game plan is likely to fail with a number of couple clients.

When therapy goes smoothly, REBCT practitioners are able to keep to their preferred game plan. In cases where this applies, they help both partners see that they have two different kinds of problems: those related to couple disturbance and those related to couple dissatisfaction. They succeed at (1) showing the couple that they had better work on disturbance issues first; (2) explaining that their disturbance results in the main from their Irrational Beliefs about their unsatisfactory relationship; (3) inducing them to work at Disputing and changing those Irrational Beliefs and replacing them with rational alternatives; (4) inducing them to work at identifying whether their differences can be reconciled; (5) if so, helping them to negotiate more satisfying relationship arrangements; and (6) encouraging them to work to actualize these desired alternatives. When both partners are only dissatisfied and not disturbed, only stages 4, 5, and 6 apply.

Problems still tend to occur even in this smooth change process and can be generally attributed to one or both partners believing that change *must* be easier than it is (LFT) or to one or both partners testing the solidity of change (Stuart, 1980). Here the therapist (1) helps the couple to tolerate the discomfort that change almost inevitably brings and to see that change is rarely easily achieved, and (2) explains to the couple (preferably in advance) that testing behavior is a common occurrence in the change process, that is, that one or both partners sometimes tests the solidity of change by returning to dysfunctional patterns. When partners are prepared for this eventuality, they are less likely to disturb themselves about it. The therapist also explains that change is rarely a linear process because humans easily return to well-ingrained but dysfunctional patterns of behavior, thought, and emotion.

When both partners are disturbed at the inception of therapy and only one changes for the better in this respect, the therapist will often, as noted above, encourage that partner to make an extra effort for his or her own sake and for the sake of determining the future prospects of the relationship. This involves the less disturbed partner being unusually understanding and tolerant of the still disturbed partner, a tactic that often serves as the fulcrum and lever that encourages the more disturbed partner to begin to change. For it sometimes happens that he or she needs to see that the other partner has shown an extra amount of good faith before beginning to work on his or her own disturbance. If such a tactic fails to yield beneficial results for the disturbed partner, then the other partner has useful information when coming to determine the viability of the relationship.

As has also been noted above, when both partners remain disturbed even after the therapist's interventions in the "overcoming couple disturbance" phase of treatment, the therapist is prepared to use a variety of behavioral and systems-theory-inspired interventions to change A in the ABC framework, even though he or she acknowledges that this is an inelegant approach to producing philosophic change at B (Ellis, 1979d; Ellis, Sichel, Yeager et al., 1989). If these interventions are successful, then the couple has been helped to see that they can extricate themselves from a negative pattern and thus may be encouraged to do so for themselves. There is always the danger, however, that if they reencounter the original problem situation they will again become disturbed and thus may need further help to change A.

It needs to be reiterated that REBCT practitioners tend to be flexible in their use of different therapeutic contexts and thus may suggest changing the therapeutic modality at various points in the process of couples therapy (e.g., from conjoint couples therapy to concurrent individual sessions with each person). Such changes are usually instigated for positive therapeutic reasons but can also be made if the therapy has become unproductively stuck in a given modality.

The Personal Qualities of Effective REBCT Therapists

In the practice of couples therapy effective REBCT practitioners will preferably be (1) comfortable using the structure of REBCT but flexible enough to work in less structured ways when the occasions arise; (2) drawn to adopting an active-directive teaching style and credible enough to teach their client couples the principles of REBT in ways appropriate to the learning abilities of the people involved; (3) "authoritative without being authoritarian; . . . bring up discussions of basic values without foisting their personal values on to clients; . . . push, coach, persuade, and encourage clients to think and act against their own self-sabotaging tendencies" (Ellis, 1982d, p. 316); and (4) prepared to reveal their own feelings and Beliefs and show their clients that they are not scared to take risks in helping them over their relationship difficulties. Moreover, they will tend to be philosophically inclined, scientific, empirical, multimodal, and antiabsolutistic in their approach to the problems of their couples and will be drawn to REBCT because it allows them to fully express these tendencies. They will be comfortable working with more than one person in therapy and raising difficult issues with both partners, particularly in the area of sexual relations.

It is not essential for effective REBCT therapists to have had firsthand experience of cohabiting relationships, but in our opinion this is desirable for a number of reasons. First, they will be able to talk with clients about their difficulties from a more authoritative and credible position, particularly if they have been successful in dealing with some of their own problems. Second, they will tend to have a deeper understanding of the stresses of intimate relationships and see the potential for growth and for harm that such relationships hold. Finally, they will be able to share specific examples from their own experiences to help show their clients the advantages of an REBT approach to coupled life. However, it is noted that some REBCT practitioners are quite successful without such firsthand couple experience.

CASE EXAMPLE

Mr. and Mrs. Rogers (pseudonym), married with no children, were seen when I (WD) worked as a part-time counseling psychologist for an East Birmingham (England) general practice. Mrs. Rogers, a 35-year-old housewife, was initially referred to me for "depression." In an initial intake interview it transpired that she was depressed about what she described as her husband's cold attitude toward her. I decided, with her permission, to invite Mr. Rogers to come and see me to determine his opinions about his wife's depression and the marital situation. In cases where one partner is referred to me whose disturbance is rooted in an interpersonal context, I prefer to interview the significant other because this contact facilitates his or her later involvement in therapy if this is indicated. Mr. Rogers, a 38-year-old businessman, angrily complained about his wife's "low mood." He also expressed concern that he could not "get through to her." They both stated in these initial individual interviews that they would be interested in having counseling for their problems. They wanted to stay married, but both stated that they would like to be seen separately at first. I saw no reason to refuse their requests.

"Overcoming Couple Disturbance" Phase

I began by helping Mrs. Rogers to see that she was absolutistically *insisting* that she must have her husband's love and that she was unlovable because he did not seem to love her at present. I showed her that it was her insisting attitude rather than the assumed lack of love on his part that determined her feelings of depression and proceeded to help her to accept herself even if her husband did not love her. I helped her to Dispute her dysfunctional *need* for love but encouraged her to keep to her *desire* for his love. I showed her that she could be healthily sad but did not have to be unhealthily depressed if her assumption that her husband did not love her proved to be correct now and/or in the future.

When working with Mr. Rogers, I zeroed in on his demand that his wife absolutely *should* not be depressed and helped him to see that this was related to another demand that his wife *must* be supportive, which in turn was related to his fear of failure at work. His wife used to help him by doing important typing and bookkeeping, and this helped him maintain a high standard of work performance. The fact that she was no longer assisting him in this way confronted him directly with his own anxiety, which, as often occurs, was masked by anger. I encouraged Mr. Rogers to face this fear and helped him to Dispute his underlying Irrational Beliefs, namely, "I *must* do well and continue to do well at work or I'd be an inadequate person."; and "I *must* keep getting promoted or I may not be able to improve our living standards, which would be terrible." For good measure, I showed him that, although he wanted his wife to support him, there was no law in the universe that decreed that she had to do so. When he changed these Beliefs, he consequently became more tolerant and sympathetic toward his wife when she was depressed.

At this point, it would have been tempting to bring Mr. and Mrs. Rogers together for conjoint sessions; she was becoming less depressed and he was less anxious and angry. However, I decided to continue to see them separately for two more individual sessions each to help them deal more thoroughly with the worst examples of A in the ABC framework that they could imagine. This strategy, in fact, elicited Mrs. Roger's acute fear of divorce. I helped her to identify and challenge her Belief that divorce would be "awful" and helped her to see that she could lead an independent, happy life and therefore was not impelled to stay in the marriage.* I also helped Mr. Rogers deal with his morbid fear of unemployment and showed him that his value as a human being was not dependent on his work status and that he could become vitally absorbed in other pursuits if he ever faced unemployment.

When I felt satisfied that they had made progress in dealing with their worst fears, I then arranged to see them in conjoint marital therapy, having seen them individually for six sessions each.

"Enhancing Couple Satisfaction" Phase

This phase of treatment began with a shared review of what Mr. and Mrs. Rogers had both learned in individual couples therapy. They reiterated their desire to stay together and work toward increased marital satisfaction. At the outset of this phase, Mrs. Rogers experienced a greater degree of dissatisfaction than her husband. Although she had made great strides in accepting herself, she stated that, in her opinion, he was still taking her for granted and

---

*This procedure, known as "de-awfulizing" divorce, is very helpful in reducing anxiety in partners who feel impelled to stay married out of obligation rather than out of desire.

expected that she would devote much of her life to helping him gain a managerial position, to which he had always aspired. She said that she was no longer prepared to devote as much time to helping him in this respect and wanted more time to pursue her own emerging interests. Although Mr. Rogers initially appeared to understand her desire for self-actualization, his actual behavior in subsequent weeks belied his words.

Despite the fact that I had helped them to negotiate a more equitable allocation of time to different tasks, Mr. Rogers failed to keep his part of the bargain. At this point Mrs. Rogers decided to get tough with him. She was able to do this because she was less anxious about the prospect of being alone. When Mr. Rogers saw that his wife was really serious about pursuing her own goals, he was jolted into realizing the implications of continuing to act in an unsupportive way toward her.[†] At this point he was able to articulate his fears about what living with an independent woman might mean for him. He feared that she might find another man, whereas in reality Mrs. Rogers wanted not only to spend some time pursuing her own interests but also to spend more time socially with him: "I no longer want to be a doormat," she said.

At this point I did some individual work with Mr. Rogers in the context of conjoint couples therapy. I helped him to see that he could still accept himself even if his wife did in fact leave him for somebody else and that he could be relatively happy if this happened. Mrs. Rogers tried, on several occasions, to reassure him that she was not interested in other men, but I showed her and her husband that this was not the central issue and that the real point was that Mr. Rogers was anxious about the *prospect* of this happening. As he successfully Disputed his dysfunctional Beliefs that he would be less of a man if his wife left him, he calmed down and listened to her desires with greater empathy. At this point I taught them how to listen and respond accurately to each other's statements and how to check out their hunches about the meaning of such statements rather than assume that their hunches were indeed facts. I further helped them to consider the implicit contracts that they had made with each other, at the time of their marriage, about their roles as husband and wife and showed them that these role expectations could be renegotiated (Sager, 1976). This led to a full discussion of their aspirations for themselves as individuals and as a couple, and they were able to determine for themselves how they could achieve "I-goals" and "We-goals." At the end of 10 conjoint sessions they decided that they had achieved enough to keep working on "enhancing couple satisfaction" on their own.

---

†I (WD) have often found that it is only when wives are prepared to take drastic action in pursuing their own goals that their husbands are "shocked" into realizing the implications of not listening to them. This shock is often the motivating factor for initiating constructive change.

Observations

This example clearly demonstrates the major features of REBCT. Issues of couple disturbance were dealt with first, in this instance in individual couples therapy sessions for both partners. Conjoint couples therapy sessions were employed to deal with issues of relationship dissatisfaction. Communication, problem-solving, and negotiation training procedures were all employed in this second phase. The case also shows that REBCT practitioners are often called upon to deal with further disturbance issues that emerge in the "enhancing couple satisfaction" phase. As is commonly found, emotional disturbance is often uncovered as a result of the failure of one or both partners to execute carefully negotiated homework assignments. In this case, Mr. Rogers's anxiety about his wife having "affairs" was elicited as a consequence of his failure to follow through on an assignment that was negotiated on two separate occasions. He was helped to see that his "excuses" were in fact defensive in nature and served to protect him from his own self-condemnation. Mr. Rogers confirmed my own hypothesis that it was my early focus on Disputing his Irrational Beliefs in the first phase of treatment that encouraged him to disclose this core fear. In his words, "I feel that I was helped to acquire the skills to actually deal with this particular fear. I doubt whether I would have revealed it if I felt unable to deal with it."

Follow-up

I conducted a follow-up session 6 months after treatment was terminated. Mr. and Mrs. Rogers maintained the gains that they had achieved in therapy and, according to them, were experiencing the most productive period of their marriage. They reported that they were more able to express their desires to one another and be supportive of each other's goals as well as spend more time together. Mrs. Rogers had taken up volunteer work, pottery classes, and yoga. She spent about an hour a day typing her husband's business correspondence, compared to the 4 hours daily work she used to do for him. She had not experienced any depressive episodes since treatment had ended. Mr. Rogers had still not acquired his coveted managerial position. He occasionally experienced bouts of panic about this fact but said that on these occasions he was able to identify and Dispute the underlying irrational Beliefs. He had come to realize that work was not the "be-all and end-all" of his life and had started to manage a local junior soccer team. He seemed genuinely pleased with his wife's improvement and rarely got angry with her, and she felt that he showed sincere interest in her activities. Together they had taken up ballroom dancing lessons and enjoyed regular Saturday evenings at the local dance hall. They reported that they were more able to challenge one another in a constructive way when problems began to emerge and that they were able to resolve matters without undue upset.

Interestingly enough, both Mr. and Mrs. Rogers pointed to the gains that they had made in the first phase of treatment as the most significant feature of their therapy experiences. Mrs. Rogers summed this up well when she said "Although it was painful, you helped me most by showing me that divorce wasn't the end of the world. I thought it was, you see. Yes, that really helped. Before, we stayed together more out of fear and obligation than anything else, but now we are together because we want to be together." That statement beautifully encapsulates the goals and spirit of REBCT!

6
Family Therapy

Rational emotive behavior family therapy follows the principles and practice of rational emotive behavior therapy (REBT). REBT holds what when family members become emotionally disturbed or upset (e.g., anxious, depressed, hostile, self-pitying, or behaviorally dysfunctional) at point C (emotional and behavioral Consequence) following a significant Activating experience or Activating event (point A), A may significantly contribute to but actually does not "cause" C. Instead, disturbed Consequences (in individuals and in families) are largely (though not exclusively) created by B—the family members' *belief system.* When undesirable or disruptive Consequences (C) occur, these can largely be traced to people's Irrational Beliefs (Bs)—absolutistic, musturbatory, or unrealistic demands, commands, or expectations on (1) themselves, (2) others, and/or (3) world conditions. When these dysfunctional Beliefs are effectively disputed (at point D) by challenging them logically, empirically, and pragmatically, the disturbed consequences are minimized or disappear and ultimately seldom recur.

When still using psychoanalysis, I (AE) began to do conjoint marital counseling and family therapy but found these techniques to be much more efficient and less time-consuming as I replaced analytical with REBT. REBT for families, as will be shown below, not only gets to the fundamental philosophic premises that underlie people's disillusionment with themselves and their family arrangements but also uses cognitive, emotive, and behavioral methods of teaching them communication, sexual, relating, and other skills that will help them enhance their family relationships.

Scores of studies have shown that RET and CBT are effective (DiGiuseppe, Miller, & Trexler, 1979; Ellis & Whiteley, 1979; Engels, Garnefski, & Diekstra,

Parts of this chapter are adapted from Albert Ellis, "Rational-Emotive Family Therapy," in A. M. Horne and J. L. Passmore (Eds.), *Family Counseling and Therapy* (pp. 403–434), Itasca, IL: Peacock, 1991; from Albert Ellis, "Family Therapy: A Phenomenological and Active Directive Approach," *Journal of Marriage and Family Counseling*, April 1978, pp. 43–50; and from Albert Ellis, "The Rational-Emotive Therapy (RET) Approach to Marriage and Family Therapy," *The Family Journal*, 1993, 1: 292–307. Used by permission.

1983; Haaga & Davidson, 1989; Hajzler & Bernard, 1991; Hollon & Beck, 1994; Lyons & Woods, 1991; McGovern & Silverman, 1984; Miller & Berman, 1983; Silverman, McCarthy, & McGovern, 1992). The use of controlled studies of the rational emotive behavioral and cognitive behavioral approach to family therapy is still meager. However, it has already produced some findings that tend to show that REBT can be used effectively in helping couples and families with emotional problems. Outcome studies that support REBT hypotheses include papers and books by Baucom and Epstein (1990), Eisenberg and Zingle (1975), Epstein, Schlesinger, and Dryden (1988), Jacobson (1992), Margolin and Weiss (1978), McClellan and Stieper (1973), Saxon (1980), and Tsoi-Hoshmand, 1976.

The first major books applying the principles of REBT to marriage and family problems were *How to Live with a "Neurotic"* (Ellis, 1957) and *A Guide to Successful Marriage* (Ellis & Harper, 1961b). Subsequently, a large number of articles have been published that demonstrate how REBT can be efficiently applied to marriage and family therapy and to parenting problems, and a number of books on REBT and CBT marital family issues have appeared, including those by Barrish and Barrish (1985), Baucom and Epstein (1990), Grieger (1986), Hauck (1977, 1981, 1984), Huber and Baruth (1989), and Ellis, Wolfe, and Moseley (1966).

REBT APPROACH TO FAMILY THERAPY

The ABC theory of REBT states that the basic or main "cause" of disturbed emotional Consequences (C) in family life (or in any other kind of human activity) does not rest in the Activating experiences that happen in the family at A but in the spouses' and children's Irrational Beliefs (IBs) with regard to these A's. Although people can theoretically have a large number of IBs, 12 of these are exceptionally common (Ellis, 1962). These, in turn, can be reduced to three major absolutistic *musts*, each of which includes several important subcategories (Ellis, 1994c, 1996a; Ellis & Abrahms, 1978; Ellis & Grieger, 1977; Ellis & Harper, 1977; Ellis & Whiteley, 1979). These are (1) "I *must* (or *should* or *ought to*) perform well and/or be approved by significant others. It is *awful* (or *horrible* or *terrible*) if I don't! I *can't stand* it! I am a pretty rotten *person* when I fail in these respects!" (2) "You *must* treat me considerately and fairly. It is *horrible* if you don't! When you fail me, you are a *bad individual*, and I *can't bear* you and your crummy behavior!" (3) "Conditions *must* be the way I want them to be, and it is *terrible* when they are not! I *can't stand* living in such an awful world! It is an *utterly abominable place!*"

If family members subscribe to one or more of these three basic *musts* and their many derivatives, various forms of emotional disturbance and dysfunctional behavior will almost inevitably follow. If they clearly see these absolutistic and unrealistic commands on themselves, on others, and on the universe and work hard at surrendering them and replacing them with strong preferences, they will rarely disturb themselves about almost anything—although they will still often have strong appropriate feelings of displeasure, frustration, disappointment, and sorrow.

Although REBT places great emphasis on cognition, it does not hold that psychoanalytic or psychodynamic insight leads to significant personality change but that, instead, this kind of insight is usually wasteful and sidetracking. Therefore, it stressed three different kinds of insight and awareness that clients had better achieve. *Insight No. 1* is that the "causes" of the practical problems of family members may lie in environmental situations but that the "causes" of their emotional problems (or their problems about the practical problems) mainly lie in their Irrational Beliefs (IBs) about the Activating experiences that the family undergoes. *Insight No. 2* is that regardless of how family members originally became (or made themselves) disturbed, they feel upset today because they are still indoctrinating themselves with the same kinds of IBs that they originated in the past. Even if they learned some of these IBs from their parents and other early socializing agents, they keep repeating and retaining them today. Therefore, their *self*-conditioning is more important than their early external conditioning. *Insight No. 3* is that if family members achieve Insights No. 1 and 2 and thereby fully realize that they have created and keep carrying on their own disturbed feelings, these two insights will not automatically make them change their irrational Beliefs. Only if they constantly *work and practice*, in the present as well as in the future, to think, feel, and act *against* these IBs are they likely to change them and make themselves significantly less disturbed.

REBT takes the humanistic and existentialist position that family members largely create their own world by the phenomenological view they take of what happens to them. It also accepts the philosophy that people had better define their own freedom and cultivate a good measure of individuality but at the same time, especially if they are to live successfully in family ways, adopt an attitude of caring, sharing, and social interest. In accordance with its humanistic outlook, REBT especially emphasizes what Carl Rogers calls unconditional positive regard and what REBT practitioners call unconditional self-acceptance (USA) and unconditional acceptance of others (UAO) (Ellis, 1962, 1972b, 1973, 1994c, 1996a). As a consequence, REBT takes the unusual stand that we had better not rate ourselves, our essence, or our being but only our deeds, acts, and performances. We can choose to do this limited kind of rating not in order to prove ourselves—that is, to strengthen our ego and self-esteem—but in order to be ourselves and enjoy ourselves.

REBT introduced the concept of acceptance into the field of marriage and family therapy in the late 1950s (Ellis, 1957, 1958b, 1960). This is because, as Neil Jacobson (1992) and other behaviorist family therapists realized many years later, showing family members how to condition their partners and children to be more cooperative and loving often just doesn't work. They may have their own agenda and sometimes are too disturbed to respond to even the best marital training methods. Therefore, they present a somewhat grim reality to other family members who cannot easily change them or leave them.

Acceptance is stressed in REBT family therapy in several important ways:

1. *Acceptance of human fallibility.* REBT teaches family members to accept the reality that all humans—including their partners, siblings, and other relatives—are exceptionally fallible. No matter what they agree to do, they frequently do not do it; and whatever they agree to refrain from doing, they still frequently do. To be happy with themselves and others, family members preferably should fully accept their own fallibility and that of others to whom they are attached. *Then* try to change what they can change.

2. *Acceptance of human demandingness.* All normal humans strongly prefer, wish, and desire. Fine. But they also have an innate and learned tendency to easily escalate their wants into absolutistic demands and commands: "Because I very much *want* you to treat me lovingly, you always *must* do so!" "Because it would be *highly preferable* if you saw things my way, you *absolutely have to* agree with me!"

REBT shows family members that unless they understand and *accept*—though not necessarily *like*—this almost universal condition of their intimates, they will tend to demand that family demanders not be the way they indubitably are. And their own demandingness will usually get them nowhere.

3. *Acceptance of uncaringness and unlovingness.* Children and adults are born and reared with strong tendencies to care for others, particularly their family members (Bowlby, 1988). Great! But most people are also born and raised with sturdy proclivities to be often uncaring, uninterested in others, and unloving—not to mention, at times to be antagonistic and hostile. Even family members who really love each other can be affectionate with notable inconsistency. So REBT points out to family clients: "If you find one person in your entire lifetime who is not this way, you are extremely lucky. If you find several, it is a miracle! So accept, accept, and accept this reality."

4. *Acceptance of proneness to human disturbance.* In some ways, nobody is fully responsible for his or her own emotional and behavioral disturbance. First, we are born with a strong tendency to upset ourselves over frustrations and difficulties; otherwise we might not be motivated to minimize them and to survive (Ruth, 1992). Second, we are often beset with tribulations and traumas, including childhood abuse, assault, rape, incest, accidents, diseases, and handicaps. Once seriously assaulted, we tend to remember these traumatic incidents and strongly keep reacting—and often overreacting—to them. Third, our family, school, and cultural teachings often show us that we *should* upset ourselves when unfortunate Activating events occur.

Because important environmental and biological factors predispose family members to various kinds of disturbability, REBT teaches family clients to *expect* some of their intimates to behave irrationally and to *accept* that eventuality without unduly upsetting themselves about it.

Even though, as we pointed out in the beginning of this section, people are in some ways *not* responsible for being easily upset, they still *are* responsible for creating and indulging in *some* of their feelings of depression and rage. As REBT shows, they have some *choice* about not upsetting themselves about family affairs. REBT family therapy therefore tries to help each member accept himself or herself *with* his or her disturbances while also accepting responsibility for these disturbances and for trying to reduce them.

5. *Unconditional self-acceptance and other acceptance.* As we keep emphasizing in this book, REBT particularly shows family members (as well as single individuals) how to have unconditional self-acceptance (USA) even when they act poorly and sabotage family living. It shows them how to fully accept *all* people *whether or not* they perform well and to rate their own and others' *behavior* but not to rate their *self* or *personhood* for this behavior. Throughout the many years we have practiced couples and family therapy we find that one of the best techniques we can use to help family members reduce their anger at each other is to have some of them—or preferably all of them—first give themselves USA and then to achieve the same kind of unconditional acceptance of others (UAO) to their close relatives (Ellis, 1957, 1962, 1988, 1991d, 1993e, 1994c, 1996a).

6. *Accept unchangeable frustrations.* Hassles and frustrations of living are the inevitable human condition. Although family life, especially for young children, greatly relieves life's difficulties, it also considerably adds to them. As a mate, parent, or child one has to go along with many domestic restrictions, including room arrangements, money expenditures, meal scheduling, and a hundred other limitations. Too bad—but that's it!

REBT therefore shows people how to accept family conditions that they distinctly dislike but cannot—or will not—very well change. As Hauck (1984) has shown, when a family setup is seen as "bad," one can (a) do nothing about it, (b) work to change it, or (c) leave the situation. Most people, however, often take one of these three paths and unduly disturb themselves—that is, whine!—about taking it. REBT shows them how, instead, to uncomplainingly take one of these choices without defining it as *awful* or *horrible* (Dryden & Ellis, 1990, 1991; Ellis, 1988, 1994c, 1996a).

REBT FAMILY THERAPY AND OTHER SYSTEMS OF FAMILY THERAPY

There are almost innumerable systems of family therapy today, but the main (or at least most popular ones) seem to be the psychoanalytic systems, and behavioral schools. The following is a brief attempt to show how REBT family therapy overlaps with and differs from these systems.

REBT and Psychoanalytic Family Therapy

REBT differs considerably and radically from what might be called "pure" or "genuine" psychoanalytic therapy as originally presented by Freud (1965) and his close followers. Fortunately or unfortunately, psychoanalysts and psychoanalytically oriented therapists rarely stick to Freudian theories or techniques these days; and what has been called neo-Freudian therapy—such as that of Karen Horney, Erich Fromm, Franz Alexander and Thomas French, and Harry Stack Sullivan—is actually much more neo-Adlerian than neo-Freudian. Thus, what Paul Wachtel (1994) calls psychoanalysis really emphasizes clients' understanding and changing their current interpersonal relationships (rather than mulling around endlessly in their past lives) plus what might be called low-level or mild REBT—that is, showing them how to acknowledge and dispute their unrealistic and Irrational Beliefs about themselves, others, and the world.

Classical Freudian psychoanalysis includes several basic assumptions that psychoanalytic family therapists such as Nathan Ackerman (1958) partially adopt. These include the theories that (1) current family problems largely stem from people's past experiences in their own original families, which they then transfer to their present mates and family members; (2) deep-seated family difficulties stem largely from the fairly severe emotional disturbances of the individual family members; (3) only by understanding the early origins of their own disturbances and working through these in prolonged psychoanalytic therapy will people really overcome their current family upsets; (4) the main therapeutic tool is the transference relationship between the therapist and his or her client(s), and only by the therapist arranging for the client(s) to experience a transference neurosis during treatment and by using his or her personal relationship with the client(s) is this neurosis, as well as the original neurosis, of each family member to be truly resolved; (5) at bottom, virtually all disturbed individuals, including family members, have unresolved Oedipal complexes, castration fears, and repressed hostilities toward their parents and siblings; and the understanding of and working through these complexes and hostilities largely comprises cure; (6) all serious family disturbances result from people's deeply unconscious or repressed thoughts and feelings, and when they are made fully aware of these they no longer act or feel disturbed; (7) severe emotional disturbances, such as schizophrenia, are largely caused by the treatment of children during their early childhood and also by generations of poor family conditions; (8) intellectual and emotional insight leads to behavioral change, and behavioral solutions in themselves are almost useless and do not lead to intellectual and emotional changes; (9) resistance to therapeutic change largely results from early family-inculcated disturbances and from unconscious resistances to childhood-imbibed feelings and to transferring these feelings to the therapist.

All of these basic psychoanalytic theories of personality formation of psychotherapy, except the second one listed above, are strongly opposed by the theory and practice of REBT. The REBT view is that these theories are based on fictional "evidence," are not backed by research, and often lead to more therapeutic harm than good (Ellis, 1968, 1994c). Though it agrees with the analytic view that family members are usually disturbed in their own right and that elegant therapeutic resolution involves their overcoming their intrapersonal (as well as their interpersonal) disturbances, REBT has few other agreements with classical psychoanalysis. We would hold, in fact, that the closer therapists stick to "pure" or "real" psychoanalysis, the more ineffective and the more iatrogenic they almost invariably are. When they significantly deviate from psychoanalytic theory and practice mildly analytically oriented psychotherapy, they then are much more helpful to individual and family clients.

REBT AND SYSTEMS FAMILY THERAPY

REBT largely goes along with a great deal of the systems theory perspective, including its endorsement of the following propositions that tend to be held by different kinds of systems therapists, such as Gregory Bateson, Don Jackson, Paul Watzlawick, Jay Haley, Salvador Minuchin, Virginia Satir, and Murray Bowen: (1) In studying families and family therapy, we had better pay attention not only to interpretation of individual thoughts, feelings, and behaviors but also to wholeness, organization, and relationship among family members; (2) we had better also seriously consider general (as well as reductionist) principles that might be used to explain biological processes that lead to increasing complexity of organization (for the organism); (3) we had better concentrate on patterned rather than merely on linear relationships and on a consideration of events in the context in which they are occurring rather than an isolation of them from their environmental context; (4) the study of communication among family members shows how they often become disturbed and what they can do to ameliorate their disturbances (Ellis, Sichel, Yeager, et al., 1989; Huber & Baruth, 1989).

While agreeing with these basic views of systems-theory-oriented family therapy, REBT would offer a few caveats as follows:

1. Focusing on wholeness, organization, and relationship among family members is important but can be overdone. Families become disturbed not

merely because of their organization and disorganization but because of the serious personal problems of the family members. Unless, therefore, these are considered and dealt with, too, any changes that are likely to occur through changing the family system are likely to be superficial and unlasting, and family therapy will tend to be wasteful.

2. Family systems therapy tends to require an active-directive therapist who makes clear-cut interventions and who engages in a great deal of problem solving. REBT is highly similar in these respects. But most family systems therapists tend to ignore the phenomenological and self-disturbing aspects of family members' problems and mainly or only deal with the system-creating aspects (Ellis, 1978a). In REBT terms, they focus on solving A-type (Activating events–type) family problems and not on the more important B-type (Belief system–type) problems. REBT first tends to show family members how they philosophically disturb themselves about what is happening to them at point A and how, at B, they basically create their own disturbances. It then also shows them how to change their family and personal situations at A. Its approach is double-barreled rather than single-barreled in this respect.

3. Because they focus largely on family situations and interpersonal communications and problems, family therapists, for all of their cleverness and use of many cognitive methods, usually miss the main reasons behind most people's emotional and behavioral problems, namely, their absolutistic "must's" and "should's" and their other irrational beliefs. In this respect, systems family therapy is partially effective but still superficial.

REBT AND BEHAVIORAL FAMILY THERAPY

REBT subscribes to virtually all the main principles of behaviorally oriented family therapy because it is a form of cognitive-behavior therapy itself and invariably uses (as noted above) many behavioral theories and methods. However, it uses behavioral techniques mainly to help family members change their basic philosophic assumptions and to make an "elegant" change in their thinking, feeling, and acting (Ellis, 1972b, 1980c) rather than the symptomatic change that some of the "pure" behavior therapists, such as Joseph Wolpe, aim for (Wolpe, 1990). And it recognizes that some behavioral methods of individual and family change, such as social reinforcement and gradual desensitization of fears, not only have distinct limitations but also have profound philosophic implications that may lead to antitherapeutic results. Thus, if therapists reinforce family members' changes by giving them social approval, these clients may become overdependent on the therapist and may increase rather than decrease their dire needs for approval, which are often one of the main sources of their disturbances (Ellis, 1983b).

REBT AND EXISTENTIAL FAMILY THERAPY

Robert Levant's (1978) phenomenological-humanistic critique of conventional family therapy, including the approaches of the psychodynamic and the family systems therapists, includes some excellent points that have been rather neglected in the literature, and it may well serve as something of a corrective influence in the future. As longtime skeptics of both the approaches that he criticizes, we are inclined to endorse many of his views and to enthusiastically join him in calling for a radically different, "third force" method of family therapy that makes up for the grave deficiencies and distinct inefficiencies of the two highly popular systems and that utilizes some of Levant's valuable suggestions. However, in espousing a phenomenological-humanistic outlook toward marriage and family counseling, Levant unfortunately sees this outlook as being incompatible with an active-directive, information-giving approach, whereas we see the two as being highly compatible. Let us try to show how they are compatible.

We start off with several propositions that Levant, along with existentialist, humanistic, experiential, and client-centered therapists, is likely to agree with:

1. Disturbed martial and family relationships stem not so much from what happens among family members as from the perceptions these members have and the views they take of these happenings.

2. Consequently, no matter what family members do, with or without therapeutic aid, to bring about more favorable events and relationships within the family context, these events and relationships are not likely to remain favorable if one or more of the members perceive themselves and/or the other participants in a highly distorted, negative way.

3. Almost all individuals who live in family settings have strong innate self-correcting and self-actualizing tendencies so that even though they have distorted, self-defeating, and family-sabotaging perceptions and behaviors, they have a considerable ability, by dint of their own resources or with the help of a therapist, to change their ways and to bring about more favorable events and relationships within the family system.

4. A therapist can be of considerable help to family members who see themselves as being in trouble by conveying to them his or her empathic understanding of their misperceptions of themselves and others; by accepting them fully, even with their foolish and self-sabotaging behavior; by encouraging them to unconditionally accept themselves, no matter how badly they behave; and by serving as a good model of an open, genuine, congruent individual who is able to accept himself/herself in spite of personal deficiencies and in spite of the hassles and uncertainties that life presents to all of us (Ellis, 1991c, 1993e, 1994c, 1996a).

This kind of phenomenological approach to human disturbance (inside and outside family systems) and to the therapist's helping clients with such disturbance appears, as Levant points out, indigenous to client-centered therapy but not to most psychodynamic and system-oriented therapy. What he fails to note is that it is also part and parcel of several kinds of active-directive therapy—for example, Perls' Gestalt therapy, Frankl's existential therapy, and REBT—that radically differ from client-centered procedures. And we contend that approaches that combine a phenomenological view of human disturbance with a highly active-directive methodology not only include all the advantages that Levant claims for client-centered family therapy but also are more efficient than client-centered or other passive-nondirective forms of treatment.

Our main reasons for believing in the efficacy of a phenomenological and active-directive approach to family therapy arise from several propositions about human disturbance and personality change that Levant (and other client-centered proponents) significantly omits. Here are some of these propositions: (1) Just as humans are born and reared with strong self-actualizing and self-correcting tendencies, they are also born and reared with exceptionally strong tendencies toward misperception, overgeneralization, self-damning, deifying and damning others, omnipotence, magical thinking, low frustration tolerance, and other forms of irrationality (Beck, 1976; Ellis, 1962, 1976a, 1976b, 1979e, 1980b); (2) once people begin to think and act in self-defeating ways they easily become habituated to doing so and resist changing, not because of the unconscious motivations to which psychodynamic therapists attribute their resistance but because it is intrinsically hard for virtually any person to change his or her habitual dysfunctional thinking, feeling, and behaving (Ainslie, 1974; Ellis, 1962, 1979a, 1979e); (3) although the most serious kinds of individual and group disturbance probably stem from misperception and faulty personal constructs (Kelly, 1955), a considerable amount of sex, love, and marital difficulty, as well as individual dysfunction, partially arises from people's misinformation and lack of training for marital and family living (Ellis, 1957; Ellis & Harper, 1961b; Raimy, 1975); (4) people who have emotional difficulties, within or outside a family framework, almost always require some kind of concrete, monitored homework assignments that they can do by themselves or in between therapy sessions (Ellis, 1994c, 1996a; Ellis & Grieger, 1977; Masters & Johnson, 1970; (5) some individuals and some families have special handicaps such as low educational and/or socioeconomic status, and there is evidence that such handicapped persons would have enormous difficulties changing themselves or improving their family structures solely with the help of relatively passive, client-centered methods of counseling (Ellis, 1994c, 1995b). It seems likely that even if many educated, middle-class clients can appreciably benefit from phenomenological and nondirective family therapy, many other types of clients require a more active-directive approach.

For reasons such as these, which are hardly exhaustive, we would suggest that even though the active-directive approach taken by many psychodynamic and family systems therapists leaves much to be desired in helping people resolve their individual and family problems, other kinds of active-directive approaches are suitable and will tend to bring about better results than passively oriented client-centered therapy. What specific kind of directive family therapy would we recommend? Naturally, REBT, a comprehensive method of treatment that consciously employs a large variety of cognitive, affective, and behavioral methods, and that does so within a distinctly phenomenological and humanistic framework (Ellis, 1973, 1976g, 1988, 1991c, 1993c, 1993d; Ellis & Harper, 1997).

REBT FAMILY THERAPY

The most popular forms of family therapy today, psychodynamic and systems-oriented therapy, leave much to be desired because they tend to ignore and to lose family members as individuals, as people in their own right. They often fail to help clients to see themselves as the creators and perpetrators of their own intrapersonal and interpersonal problems, not merely as the victims of early childhood upbringing or of contemporary environmental difficulties. A phenomenological-humanistic view of families who come for therapy, such as the client-centered view espoused by Levant (1978), would serve as something of a corrective for the one-sided methods of family therapy espoused by most of today's leading practitioners and writers. This view itself, however, omits some of the realities of human individual and group disturbance and consequently ends up being somewhat pollyannaish and ineffectual.

A "third force" in family therapy is therefore suggested here that combines a phenomenological-humanistic approach with a highly active-directive attempt to help family members surrender their misperceptions of themselves and others and to make profound philosophic changes in their intrapersonal and interpersonal attitudes and behavior. As an example of this kind of a phenomenological-humanistic and active-directive approach to family therapy, some of the principles and practices of REBT help individuals change themselves and help each other within the family unit. In REBT family therapy clients are shown how to acknowledge, understand, and minimize their own emotional problems, as well as how to help other family members become more rational, experience more enjoyable and appropriate emotional responses, and act in a less self-defeating and family-defeating manner.

WHERE REBT FAMILY THERAPY IS MOST EFFECTIVE

All forms of therapy seem to be especially effective with clients who are young, intelligent, verbal, and not too seriously disturbed; and REBT, too, works best with family clients who are in this range. However, it is one of the few forms of treatment that also is effective with DCs (difficult customers), that is, individuals who are in the psychotic, borderline, organic, or mentally deficient category. Naturally, it does not work as well with these DCs as it does with the less disturbed clients. But it particularly helps such clients to accept themselves with their disturbances, to stop downing themselves for being emotionally inadequate. Then, because it is realistic and can easily accept the concept of limited gains for some individuals, REBT helps family members with severe personality disorders to train themselves to be less seriously aberrated, although it does not pretend to "cure" them (Ellis, 1994b, 1994c, 1994d, 1996a, 1996b).

Moreover, rational emotive behavioral family therapy is particularly effective at helping less seriously disturbed family members fully accept and nicely put up with more aberrated members. If children are, as they often are, dyslexic, overimpulsive, antisocial, or psychotic, REBT shows their parents that although they may have significantly contributed to these children's disturbances, they usually did not directly cause them. It teaches such parents that there are almost inevitably strong biological factors in their children's over- or underresponsiveness and that they, the parents, are hardly to blame for such factors. It also shows parents how to fully accept their emotionally or physically handicapped offspring and how to try to help them be less (though not necessarily non-) disturbed (Ellis, 1957, 1995b; Ellis et al., 1966).

At the same time, REBT frequently shows children, such as older children and adolescents, how to accept their alcoholic, psychopathic, borderline, and psychotic parents with their handicaps and how to stop roundly criticizing and excoriating them for being the way they currently are. Thus, in the case of 14- and 12-year-old sons who were extremely incensed about their alcoholic father's irresponsibility and their mother's neglecting them for a lover only a few years older than themselves, they were able to see, after only a few sessions of REBT family therapy, that both their parents were acting in a highly irresponsible manner—since they had some choice about drinking and about neglecting their children and were choosing to exert this choice in nonparental ways—but that they, like all humans, had a *right to be wrong*, were fallible, disturbed individuals who decided to act the way they did but who could be accepted and forgiven in spite of their antifamily behaviors. Once these two youngsters learned, in family therapy, to accept their parents with their irresponsible behaviors, they were able to maintain reasonably good and loving relationships with these parents and to focus on what they, the children, were going to do to get along better in this poor family environment. Their school-work and their relations with their own friends then considerably improved; they were even, to some degree, able to help their parents face their problems and to act somewhat more responsibly. This is what frequently happens in rational emotive behavior therapy: by accepting the "poor" or "bad" behavior of other family members, parents, or children are then able to help these oth-ers improve their behavior and act somewhat more responsibly.

GOALS OF THE FAMILY THERAPEUTIC PROCESS

The main goals of rational emotive behavioral family therapy are usually the following:

1. To help all the family members, or at least as many as possible, to see that they largely disturb themselves by taking the actions of the other members too seriously and that they usually have the choice, no matter how these others behave, of not seriously upsetting themselves about their behavior.

2. To help the members continue to keep, and even augment, their desires, wishes, and preferences (including their desires for family love, amity, and responsibility) but to be keenly aware of and to largely surrender their "must's" demands, and commands that others in the family act the way they would pre-fer them to act.

3. To encourage parents and children to feel strongly sad, regretful, frus-trated, annoyed, and determined to change things when they are not getting what they want or are getting what they do not want in and out of the family setting, but to clearly demonstrate how to differentiate these healthy negative feelings from feelings of severe anxiety, depression, hostility, self-pity, and low frustration tolerance and to minimize the latter while acknowledging, feeling, and at times even augmenting the former.

4. To pinpoint and be closely in touch with their Irrational Beliefs—their absolutistic "should's," "ought's" and "must's"—that usually seem to underlie their unhealthy feelings and dysfunctional behaviors and to keep disputing and challenging these ideas and replacing them with preferential, more sensible philosophies of living.

5. To learn a variety of cognitive, emotive, and behavioral techniques that will be available to them for combatting their dysfunctional ideas and encour-aging them to think, feel, and behave more healthily and self-enhancingly.

6. As they change their basic disturbance-creating attitudes and philosophies, to investigate more effective problem-solving ways of changing the practical issues—the real frustrations and annoyances—that are preventing them and other family members from being as happy and effective as they would like to

be. In REBT terms, as they particularly work on their Irrational Beliefs (IBs), the goal is to simultaneously work on changing their A's (Activating events or Activating experiences) that accompany and contribute to these IBs and that also contribute to their C's (disturbed and dysfunctional Consequences).

7. Not only to learn to deal effectively with the present crises in their families and to stubbornly refuse to upset themselves about these crises but also (and even more important) to realize that, no matter what occurs to them and their close relatives in the future, they can develop a sensible way of accepting these exigencies, again refusing to upset themselves about what occurs, and striving to achieve both practical and emotional solutions to their family (and other) problems.

CLIENTS' RESPONSIBILITIES

REBT teaches clients that, in the course of therapy as in the course of the rest of their lives, their primary responsibilities are to themselves—not to the therapist, the therapeutic situation, nor even to other family members. They are shown that therapy can be a most helpful procedure but that there is no reason why they *must* undergo it or *have to* follow its rules or teachings. As in everything else, it is highly *preferable* that they do so but not *necessary*.

At the same time, all family members (or those old enough to understand) are shown that if they really want to be responsible to themselves first and to other family members second, they had better fully accept the decision to do this; and that such acceptance only truly exists when they decide, and act upon their decision, to *work and practice* at helping to change themselves and others. They are continually shown that there is no free lunch and that the most desirable behaviors, on their own and others' part, do not automatically come into existence but almost always had better be the result of strong determination to change and hard work at changing themselves.

In REBT for families, therefore, each family member is pretty much made responsible for his or her inner changing and for trying to modify the practical aspects of family problems. As in the family counseling methods of Dreikurs (1974), it is recommended that children be given a chance to set family policies, along with their parents and other adults; but that they also take responsibility for their actions and try not to cop out by blaming others for what they do. Adult family members, too, are shown how to acknowledge their own activities and take responsibility for them, even when other individuals in the family are acting badly and are contributing to difficulties. It is continually emphasized that one family member has little ability to change others (though he or she can encourage such changes) and that changing oneself had better largely depend on one's own attitudes and efforts, not on the manner in which others treat one.

Clients are held to be responsible for their attendance at family therapy sessions and for doing their homework assignments. If they do not like what is happening during the therapy, they are encouraged to speak up about their feelings and to object to what is going on. They are also encouraged to express their feelings about other family members and to voice clearly what they would like to see and would not like to see accomplished within the family system.

Clients are held responsible for their own change because no therapist can really change them. They can only modify their own behavior (or refuse to do so), and they are never blamed for choosing not to change. They are consistently shown that they are in control of their own emotional destiny and that they distinctly have the power to alter their own thinking, emotion, and behavior. But if they stubbornly persist at self-defeating actions, they are merely shown that this is their way and that they are fully entitled to keep it but that they still have strong options to change.

THERAPIST'S ROLE AND FUNCTION

REBT is one of the most active-directive forms of therapy, and this applies to REBT family therapy. The therapist is presumably a highly trained individual who understands how people needlessly upset themselves and what they can usually do to stop doing so and to actualize themselves in (and outside) the family setting. REBT therapists, therefore, are expected to be authoritative without being authoritarian; to bring up discussions of basic values without foisting their own personal values on clients; to be sensitive to and considerate of multicultural influences on family members from different ethnic, religious, and cultural backgrounds; and to push, coach, persuade, and encourage clients to think and act against their own self-sabotaging tendencies (Ellis, 1978b, 1994c).

Some of the specific skills that REBT practitioners had better display in family therapy are the following:

1. They can empathize with clients' thinking and feeling and also with their basic disturbance-creating philosophies.
2. They can monitor clients' reactions to other family members and to the therapist and show them how to become highly involved but not overinvolved and dependent on others (including the therapist).
3. They can show clients how they are relating well and poorly and teach them communication inside and outside the therapeutic sessions.
4. They can teach the general principles of self-upsetness and self-help and instruct clients how to specifically apply these to themselves and to other family members.
5. They can confront clients with their avoidant, defensive, and resistant

behavior, show them the irrational beliefs behind this kind of behavior, and persuade them to change these beliefs and to become much less defensive.

6. They can at times be intrusive, questioning, forceful, and action-assigning, just as a successful teacher of children or adults would be.

7. They can be self-revealing of their own feelings and ideas and show clients that they are not afraid to express themselves during therapy sessions nor to take risks in the therapeutic process.

8. They can unhesitatingly teach a variety of sex, love, marital relating, and other skills as these seem appropriate for different clients but at the same time, as noted above, not overdo practical skill training as opposed to teaching the specific REBT disputing skills.

9. They can specifically focus on teaching themselves and clients the unique REBT-oriented skills, such as (a) actively listening, probing, and evoking clients' statements of what they are telling themselves, of their irrational and rational beliefs; (b) showing clients the connections between thinking and emoting—between B (their Belief system) and C (the emotional and behavioral Consequences) of this thinking; and (c) Disputing (D) or challenging Irrational Beliefs (IBs) and giving follow-through homework assignments to aid the achievement and maintenance of the corrected misperceptions (Ellis, 1978b, 1991d, 1993e; Wessler & Ellis, 1980; Woods & Ellis, 1996).

PRIMARY TECHNIQUES USED IN REBT FAMILY THERAPY

The main techniques used in REBT family therapy include the following.

Cognitive Family Techniques

In REBT family therapy clients are shown what they do to largely create their own disturbances: how they have dysfunctional (as well as functional) Beliefs; and how they demand that they must do well and be approved, that others (especially family members) must treat them fairly and lovingly, and that conditions must be nice and easy. They are especially shown how to use realistic, logical, and pragmatic methods to dispute their irrational Beliefs and to surrender them. On a lower or less elegant level of disputing, they are shown how to give themselves coping statements to replace their irrational beliefs, including such statements as, "I am a *fallible* human who doesn't *have to* behave competently!" "Others will do what *they* want and not necessarily what is right or what *I* want!" "I do not *need* what I want and can be a reasonably happy human being even when frustrated or deprived!" They are taught to use some of the principles of general semantics, promulgated by Alfred Korzybski (1933), and to interrupt their all-or-none thinking when they make such statements as, "I *always* fail," "I *can't* change," and "I'll never get what I want."

Family members are given several different forms of cognitive homework to do, such as to look for their absolutistic *should's* and *must's* and to steadily fill out the Self-Help Report Form (Sichel & Ellis, 1984) published by the Institute for Rational Emotive Behavior Therapy. They are shown special cognitive methods, such as "Disputing Irrational Beliefs" (DIBS) (Ellis, 1974a), which they can use on their own (see chapter 2). They are helped to figure out several choices and actions that are better alternatives to the ones they are now utilizing. They are taught sensible philosophies, such as "Nothing is awful— only inconvenient!" "There's no gain without pain!" and the philosophies of tolerance, flexibility, humanism, and unconditional acceptance of themselves and others (Ellis, 1972b, 1994c). They are vigorously and consistently shown some of the present and evil consequences of their self-defeating behaviors and how they will inevitably suffer more from their low frustration tolerance, short-range hedonism, and insistence on trying to get away with things. They are taught imaging techniques that will help them in their marital and sex lives. They are shown how to use methods of cognitive distraction, such as Edmund Jacobson's (1938) relaxation technique or the sensate focus, to divert them from their anxiety and depression.

Emotive Family Techniques

REBT family therapy employs a good many emotive, evocative, and dramatic techniques of therapy that are also designed to show people how they feel and think and to encourage them to make profound philosophic changes. Thus, REBT therapists use rational-emotive imagery (Ellis, 1993a; Maultsby, 1971) to help clients get in touch with their worst feelings, such as horrors, despair, and rage, and to change them to healthy feelings, such as disappointment, sorrow, and annoyance. They use role-playing methods to help clients to express and work through some of their feelings and self-sabotaging behavior. They employ shame-attacking exercises (Ellis, 1971a, 1973; Ellis & Abrahms, 1978) to induce clients to deliberately bring on and then surrender their feelings of intense shame and self-downing. They resort to dramatic and evocative confrontation, especially with clients who refuse to acknowledge or work through some of their feelings (Ellis, 1962). They often use forceful language to help loosen people up and get them to face some of their "unfaceable" problems and emotions. They encourage clients to vigorously and powerfully repeat to themselves in a highly emotive manner, sensible statements such as "I do *not* need what I want!" "I never *have* to succeed, no matter how *desirable* it may be to do so!" "People *should* sometimes treat me badly—for that's the way they naturally behave!" (Ellis, 1993g). They often use humor and paradoxical intention to strongly attack some of their clients' irrational beliefs and to show how silly they are (Ellis, 1977b; 1977c, 1987b). They give clients, as noted above, unconditional acceptance and thereby show them that they can accept themselves, even when their behaviors are abominable (Ellis, 1994c, 1996a).

Behavioral Family Techniques

REBT has always been exceptionally behavioral as well as cognitive, more so in some ways than the behavioral therapies of some of the main behavior therapists, such as Joseph Wolpe. Some of the behavioral techniques it frequently utilizes are these: It gives clients activity homework assignments, most of them to be done in vivo rather than merely in these clients' imaginations. Frequently, these assignments consist of clients staying in an unpleasant marital or family situation until they make themselves unupset about it—and then perhaps leaving it. REBT also makes use of a good deal of operant conditioning and contracting methods: helping family members to contract with other members to do one thing (such as communicate more often) if the other will also do something else (such as be more tidy around the house). Parents are also frequently shown how to use operant techniques to help their children change their undisciplined or other self-defeating behaviors. Skill training, such as assertion training, is often taught, cognitive and behaviorally. Other deconditioning and reconditioning methods are also used in REBT family therapy, including overt desensitization, emotional training, sexual resensitization, and flooding. In regard to the latter technique, in vivo implosion or flooding is recommended for some family clients because it has been found to be one of the most effective means to help them overcome long-standing phobias, compulsions, and obsessions that seriously interfere with their marital and family lives (Ellis, 1988, 1990, 1991c, 1993b, 1993e, 1994c, 1995a, 1996a).

GUIDELINES FOR FAMILY
MEMBERS TO BE SEEN

REBT has no special guidelines for family members that presumably have to be followed to do effective family therapy. The preference is for all the family members to be seen at some time during the therapy process, but there are no compulsive rules about this, and different conditions and circumstances are taken into account.

Different ways of seeing family members, all of which may be used in REBT, are (1) seeing all the family members together for all of the sessions; (2) seeing the family members usually together but sometimes seeing one or more of them separately (e.g., seeing a more disturbed member more frequently than the others); (3) seeing mainly the husband and wife and only sometimes the other family members; (4) usually excluding very young family members, seeing them a few times with the others but, especially if they are children below the age of 4 or 5, not seeing them as regularly as the other members; (5) seeing the parents together but the children, for the most part, separately, either singly or together; (6) seeing mainly one parent and preferably trying to see the other parent and the children but working with the one parent who will come for therapy if the others will not come too.

It is desirable for all family members to be seen, preferably often all together. But, again, this is not an REBT rule, and when only other kinds of sessions can be arranged, REBT family therapy can still be effective.

CASE EXAMPLE

The following is a typescript of part of the initial family treatment session with a mother, father, and their 15-year-old daughter. The mother is 45 years of age and is a housewife who had done a little professional dancing during the first few years of her marriage. The father is also 45 and runs his own business in the garment center. They have 21-year-old and 17-year-old sons, both of whom are doing well in school and not having any serious difficulties. But both parents are very upset about their daughter because she has always shown herself to be quite bright, with an IQ of 140 on regular intelligence tests and the ability to think very clearly in certain respects, but she does not do her schoolwork, refuses to cooperate in regard to family chores, does not get herself a job when she promises to do so for the summer or after school, fights with her brothers, steals from her family and from the neighbors, and is quite disruptive in several ways. She acknowledges some of these behaviors but makes innumerable excuses for or denies the other things that her family members accuse her of doing.

At the beginning of the first family therapy session with me (AE), the daughter, Debbie, admits that she is a "kleptomaniac" and that she uncontrollably steals, but she only partially admits that she steals to provide herself with money for alcohol and pot and that she uses them steadily. She and her parents agree that she had two good years, in the seventh and eighth grades, when she was in a strict Catholic school, but since that time she has lost her purpose in life, which was to be a lawyer and politician, and that she now feels purposeless and hopeless and has no incentive to work at school or anything else. Early in the session she noted that she had a goal during those two good years: "I knew I wanted to be a lawyer."

THERAPIST: Yes?
    DEBBIE: And I worked on that process.
THERAPIST: But you've now given that up?
    DEBBIE: Yeah.
THERAPIST: Why did you give that up?

DEBBIE: Because I really wanted to become a politician.

THERAPIST: And you don't want to become a politician anymore?

DEBBIE: No. They have bad practices and stuff.

THERAPIST: So that's out of the window?

DEBBIE: Yes, I have no goal.

THERAPIST: You're right. If you had a goal in life, that would probably help you be happier and keep out of the trouble you're getting in. But if you no longer want to be a politician, what stops you from picking some other profession and working toward achieving that?

DEBBIE: Well, I usually only pick on one goal and don't think of other things.

THERAPIST: Well you could still choose to be a lawyer, even if not a politician. And there are lots of other things that you could pick that you are capable of doing. Do you think you're capable of doing what you really want to do?

DEBBIE: For the most part, yes.

THERAPIST: You had really better give some more thought to that. When bright people like you screw up and give up on goals, they frequently feel that they're incapable of succeeding at those goals. So perhaps you are in that category, too.

DEBBIE: Maybe.

The therapist's main hypotheses, which he would hold on theoretical grounds in most cases like Debbie's, are that she has low frustration tolerance and refuses to do things, such as disciplining herself, that are hard and uncomfortable and that she has severe feelings of inadequacy that prevent her from trying too hard to achieve anything and encourage her to cop out at school and at other tasks at which she perfectionistically thinks that she might not do well enough. He tries to get her to bring out information to back these hypotheses and only partly succeeds in doing so. But the manner in which she answers his questions and responds to the statements of her parents, who are present during the entire session, lead him to believe that there is considerable evidence to back his hypotheses.

THERAPIST: Do you want to keep getting into the kind of trouble that you're in, with your parents, with the school, and with your brothers?

DEBBIE: No.

THERAPIST: Why do you think you steal?

DEBBIE: 'Cause I can't control myself.

THERAPIST: That's a nutty hypothesis! Horseshit! You have *difficulty* in controlling yourself. But that doesn't mean that you *can't*. Suppose that every time you stole, the authorities cut off one of your toes. How long do you think you'd continue to steal?

DEBBIE: [Mumbles something like "Many times."]

THERAPIST: Many times? Well, that's a strong belief you have—but it's not true. You most probably wouldn't. You would then have a powerful *impulse* to steal, but you don't have to give in to your impulses. For two years you weren't doing many self-defeating things and did well at school and at home and didn't steal. Doesn't that show that you're able to control your impulses?

DEBBIE: Yes, to some extent.

THERAPIST: Yes, for two whole years you were apparently okay. You were obviously able to control yourself to some degree.

DEBBIE: Because I was allowing myself to have a purpose. And I was working on that purpose.

THERAPIST: Yeah. And that was fine. If you have a purpose, you'll use your energies in that direction, and then you won't be using them in the other, self-defeating directions.

Although it is quite early in the first session, the therapist wants to try to show Debbie and her parents that, in REBT terms, Activating events (A) do not mainly cause or create emotional Consequences (C), but instead, Beliefs (B) do. So he tries to help Debbie to see that just before she gives in to her urge to steal she is telling herself something and that this set of Beliefs is the main cause or contributing factor to her dysfunctional Consequences.

DEBBIE: I want it.

THERAPIST: You mean, " I want the money I take?"

MOTHER: I think the main thing she wants is to buy liquor or dope with the money.

THERAPIST: That may be. But let's go along with Debbie's views. You're saying that you want the money. Right?

DEBBIE: Yes.

THERAPIST: But if you only stuck to that belief—"I want the money"—you probably wouldn't steal. Do you know why?

DEBBIE: Because I'd see that I often get caught and wouldn't want to get caught stealing it.

THERAPIST: Right! Whenever we have a want or a wish, we tend to see the consequences of having it, and we often reject it. So you're probably saying something much stronger than "I want the money" when you steal. Do you know what that stronger belief probably is?

DEBBIE: No. Uh, maybe, "I need it."

THERAPIST: Correct! "I *need* the money that I want! I *must* have it because I want it!" And that *need* and that *must* will often drive you to steal, even when you know you may get caught and suffer the consequences. But is that *need* or *must* true? *Must* you have the money? Or *must* you have what you get with the money—alcohol, pot, or anything else?

DEBBIE: No.

THERAPIST: That's right! No! But if you keep insisting that you *must* have the money (or anything else), you're going to feel not only uncomfortable but horrible, off the wall, when you don't have what you *think* you *must*. Then, when you feel exceptionally uncomfortable, you may well go on to another *must*: "I *must* not feel uncomfortable. I *can't stand* this discomfort of not having what I *must* have!" Is that what you're saying, too?

DEBBIE: Yes, I *can't* stand it. I *can't*!

THERAPIST: Stop a minute, now! *Can't* you really stand it? *Can* you stand the discomfort of being frustrated and not getting exactly what you want at the very moment that you want it?

DEBBIE: I don't like it.

THERAPIST: Right. But you're not merely sticking to "I don't like it." That would be fine, if you did. I hear you saying, "*because* I don't like it, I *can't stand* it! It's *awful* if I don't have it!"

DEBBIE: But I really want it!

THERAPIST: Yes, of course. But your want is not what drives you to stealing. Your basic attitude, "I *must have* what I want!" is what does so. And we call that attitude low frustration tolerance. You're apparently telling yourself, "I want, and *must have*, what I want right now! I *can't bear* frustration and deprivation." Isn't that what's really going on in your head?

DEBBIE: Yes, I *can't* stand it.

THERAPIST: Well, as long as you have that basic philosophy—"I absolutely *need* what I want and I *can't stand* not having it!"—you'll be driven, driven by those ideas, to steal, fight with your family, break things, goof at school, and do the other things that tend to get and keep you in trouble. But you could have, instead, the philosophy: "I want what I want and am determined to try to get it. But if I don't get it right now, tough! So I don't! I do not *need* everything I immediately want!" But you are saying to yourself, as far as I can see, "I *do* need it!"

DEBBIE: Well, perhaps I'm doing it because I'm escaping.

THERAPIST: Escaping from what? What are you escaping from? Feelings of inadequacy, you mean? The feeling that you haven't the ability to get some of the things that you want or think you need?

DEBBIE: That could be one.

THERAPIST: Let's talk about those inadequacy feelings for a moment. What are they? Are you willing to talk about them in front of your parents?

DEBBIE: It doesn't matter.

THERAPIST: Well, what do you feel inferior about?

DEBBIE: I'm confused. I haven't figured out what's the purpose of it all. I don't see how to react to certain problems.

THERAPIST: Such as?

DEBBIE: Well, some domestic problems. And I just don't get along with people. I like them but I don't understand them.

THERAPIST: And you think that you *should*, you *must* understand them?

DEBBIE: Yes. And that's why I often try to get high.

THERAPIST: And do you blame yourself, then, for getting high?

DEBBIE: Yes, sometimes.

THERAPIST: Well, let's assume that getting high won't solve things and make you understand people better, and it's therefore something of a mistake. And let's suppose you're not yet very good at understanding and getting along with people. Why do you put yourself down for these errors or deficiencies?

DEBBIE: Because I know that it's not right.

THERAPIST: Yes, well, let's assume that. Suppose what you're doing is wrong. How does that make you a worm, that wrong behavior?

DEBBIE: [silence]

THERAPIST: Suppose your mother and father do something wrong. Are they shits for doing that wrong thing?

DEBBIE: No.

THERAPIST: Then why are you?

DEBBIE: Because then I'm a wrong person.

THERAPIST: But you're *not* a wrong person! That's your nutty thinking! That's what we call an overgeneralization. If we can get you to give up that kind of irrational thinking and get you to completely accept *yourself*, even when you are doing the wrong *thing*, then you can usually go back and correct your error. But if you put *yourself* down and define yourself as a shit for acting shittily, there's no good solution to the problem! For how can a shit be deshittified? [Debbie and her parents all laugh fairly heartily at this statement.] And feelings of inadequacy don't come from doing the wrong thing. They come from *condemning yourself* for doing it—putting yourself into hell. Then that makes things much worse.

DEBBIE: Yes, it does.

THERAPIST: But do you really see all of what's going on here? You first do badly—or think that you will do badly at something. Then you put yourself down, *make yourself* feel inadequate as a person. Then you tend to do something like drink or take pot to make yourself relax temporarily and feel a little better. But then you get into more trouble because of the alcohol or pot or the stealing that you did to get the money for it, and then you blame yourself more and go around and around in a vicious self-damning circle.

DEBBIE: I guess I do. I keep thinking that I'm really no good. And then things get worse.

THERAPIST: Right!

DEBBIE: But how can I stop that?

THERAPIST: The best solution is to see very clearly what I said before: that some of your acts are poor or self-defeating but that *you* are not a worm for doing them. If we could get you to fully accept *yourself*, your *being*, your *totality*, even when you are screwing up and acting stupidly or badly, then we could get you to go back and work on improving your screwups. And you could change most of them, which you are quite capable of doing if you weren't wasting your time and energy and making things worse by your self-blaming. That isn't going to work.

DEBBIE: It doesn't. I just feel worse. And then I think that I have to keep repeating this, uh, inadequate behavior.

THERAPIST: Right! The more you condemn *yourself* for your poor *behavior*, the more you lose confidence in your ability to correct that behavior.

DEBBIE: [smiling] A shit can't be deshittified!

THERAPIST: Exactly! If you are, to your core, a thorough turd, how can you change your turdiness? No way!

DEBBIE: But how do I stop blaming myself?

THERAPIST: By getting rid of your fundamental *musts*. For, at bottom, you seem to be saying: "I *must*, I *have to* do well." Not "I'd *like* or *prefer* to do well." And you're also saying to yourself, and very strongly, "I *must* not suffer inconveniences. It's *awful* if I do." Not "I'd *like* to avoid inconveniences. But if I don't, I don't! I can still abide them—and still be a happy human!"

DEBBIE: I see what you mean. But how am I going to keep seeing that and believing it?

THERAPIST: By damned hard work! By continuing *to think about* what you say to yourself and do. And by changing your perfectionistic, demanding thinking into preferences and desires.

The therapist, without knowing too much about Debbie and her parents, takes the main information he does have—that she demands that she do well and that the universe treat her kindly—and quickly and forthrightly attacks these unrealistic, dysfunctional Beliefs and tries to show her that she can do this herself and can give them up. As he talks to her, he interrupts from time to time to show the parents that they, too, have *musts* about Debbie and that they are unrealistically demanding that she act well and are condemning her and upsetting themselves when she doesn't. So he lets them listen to his disputing of her dysfunctional beliefs but also indicates that they are often doing the same thing she is, that they are acting irrationally, too—and do not have to continue to do so. Toward the end of the session the therapist speaks to Debbie and then to her parents:

THERAPIST: If I can help you to keep your desires and to give up your *must's*, you'll get somewhere in feeling better and acting better. By so doing, you'll most probably get more of what you desire and less of what you don't want. But you won't get *everything* you desire. [To Debbie's parents]: She has normal desires, but then she tells herself, "I *must*, I *must* fulfill them!" And: "I *must* get what I want *immediately*!" Now, if I can get all of you, including her, to look for the *should*, look for the *must*, which you are all bright enough to do, and I can persuade you to tackle these absolutes and give them up, you will be able to stop upsetting yourselves and usually solve the original problem of getting along together and living happily in this world. [To Debbie, again]: If I can help you do that, then you'll get along with your parents and siblings and live more successfully. But what you tend to do is to give up your desires because of your *must's*. "I *must* do this and *must* do that! But maybe I won't. And that would be *terrible*!" Then you feel depressed and anxious and start goofing. Then you blame yourself for the goofing and feel more anxious and depressed. A very vicious circle! Have you read any of my writings on this?

The therapist closes the session by assigning all three of them, Debbie and her parents, to read a group of pamphlets on REBT that the Institute for Rational Emotive Behavior Therapy gives to all clients at its clinic in New York and also to read *A Guide to Rational Living* (Ellis & Harper, 1997) and *A Guide to Personal Happiness* (Ellis & Becker, 1982), which many clients are encouraged to read. They are to make another appointment, for next week; in between, they are to make a note of all the times they feel upset during the week, especially about each other and what is happening in the family; to look for the "should's" and "must's" that lead to these feelings; and to find them or fail to find them and to bring up their feelings during the next session, so that they and the therapist can look for the *must's* that largely create them.

Following this first session, Debbie and her parents were seen once a week for a total of 16 weeks. Debbie was largely seen for individual sessions by herself, but usually one or both parents were also seen with her for a half hour, and she was seen by herself for a half hour. On a few occasions her parents were also seen by themselves to deal with their anger and other feelings of upsetness about her "rotten" behavior and about their own problems with each other and with outsiders (especially her father's problems with his business associates and her mother's problems with her women friends).

It would have been preferable as a part of the REBT for families that was done with Debbie and her parents to see her two brothers too during some of the sessions. But the parents insisted that the brothers had no problems and might be harmed by participating in the therapy. The brothers themselves also resisted coming because they thought that their sister had a serious emotional problem and they did not. Under more usual conditions the brothers would have been seen along with the other members of the family in REBT for families.

The main REBT techniques for family therapy that were used with Debbie and her parents during these sessions were as follows.

Cognitive Methods

Whenever Debbie or her parents showed any feelings of anxiety, depression, anger, or self-pity (which they frequently did) or when Debbie continued her antisocial and antifamily behavior and failed to go for job interviews or to work at the jobs she temporarily obtained, they were shown the ABCs of REBT: that their C's (emotional Consequences) did not stem only from their A's (Activating experiences) but largely from their own IBs (Irrational Beliefs) about these A's. They were shown their absolutistic "should's" and "must's" and how to Dispute these (using the logical, empirical, and pragmatic method of questioning and challenging these "must's"). They were given the cognitive homework of working on the REBT Self-help Form published by the Institute for Rational Emotive Behavior Therapy (Sichel & Ellis, 1984), and these were gone over with them and corrected by the therapist. They were given, as noted above, bibliotherapeutic materials on REBT to read and discuss with the therapist, particularly *A Guide to Rational Living* (Ellis & Harper, 1997); *How to Live with a "Neurotic"* (Ellis, 1957); and *Overcoming Procrastination* (Ellis & Knaus, 1977). They were also encouraged to listen to some of the cassette recordings distributed by the Institute, such as *How to Stubbornly Refuse to Be Ashamed of Anything* (Ellis, 1971b), and *Conquering Low Frustration Tolerance* (Ellis, 1976b). They also participated in some of the 4-hour workshops on parent-child relationships and overcoming depression that the institute regularly holds.

Cognitively, too, the members of this family, especially Debbie, were given useful advice and suggestions on how to solve certain practical problems that arose (such as how Debbie could get and keep a job, in spite of her poor reputation in the community and her poor record of holding a job up to that time). They were shown how to write down and focus on the real disadvantages of their avoidant behaviors. They were taught some of the principles of general semantics dealing with overgeneralization and allness (Korzybski, 1933). They were made aware of their wrongly attributing motives and intentions to others (e.g., Debbie continually thought that her parents were against her when they were merely trying to get her to become more self-disciplined) and how to challenge these misattributions. They were shown how to use cognitive distraction methods, such as Edmund Jacobson's (1938) progressive relaxation methods, when they wanted to temporarily calm themselves down or overcome insomnia. The therapist sometimes used humor and paradoxical intention with them—for example, tried to get Debbie to deliberately fail at certain tasks, to prove to herself that the world did not come to an end when she did, and tried to help her to see the humorous side of her taking things too seriously and blaming herself for her poor behavior. And they were continually taught how to accept themselves fully and to stop condemning themselves for anything, even when they indubitably screwed up and made stupid mistakes.

Emotive Methods

Emotively, even though I (AE) pulled no punches in showing Debbie how she was being irresponsible to herself and others and did not let her get off the hook with her clever rationalizations in this respect, she could always see that I fully accepted her as a human being, with her failings, and that I had confidence that she definitely could—if she would—change. I also encouraged her, as a homework assignment, to do rational-emotive imagery—to imagine that she really did very badly, at work or socially, and that others despised her for her poor behavior—and to make herself feel only sorry and disappointed rather than depressed and self-downing. I did role playing with her and her parents and let her confess to them some of the things she hadn't yet told them, let her feel very ashamed, and then had her persist at the confessions and work through the shame and be able to handle their responses. I gave her out-of-session homework assignments to deliberately do "foolish" or "shameful" things—such as wear very "loud" clothing—and to work at not making herself feel embarrassed or humiliated when she did this. I got her to write out some rational self-statements—such as "I do not *need* immediate gratification, no matter *how* much I really want it"—and to repeat these to herself very vigorously 10 or 20 times a day. I deliberately used "obscene" language with her parents, who were very prim and rigid in this respect, to help loosen them up and to show them that they could even use this kind of language themselves (Ellis, 1985c). I used George Kelly's (1955) dramatic enactment method of fixed role playing with both Debbie and her parents and had them write scripts about the kind of people they would like to be and then enact these scripts for a week, until they became used to acting in that unfamiliar way.

Behavioral Methods

With Debbie in particular I used several behavioral methods and taught her parents how to use them with her. Whenever she spent at least 2 hours a week looking for a part-time job, she was permitted to socialize with her friends or do other things she enjoyed. And whenever she lied or stole, she was confined to her room for several hours at a time. When her parents failed to do their homework and criticized her in an angry, damning manner, they were also to refrain from socializing with their friends, in person or over the phone, for that day. These reinforcements and penalties worked fairly well, as long as they were enforced. But her parents had to enforce them with Debbie, and she, to some extent, had to enforce them with her parents.

Debbie agreed to take several different kinds of activity homework assignments, including looking for a job, doing various family chores, and behaving in a cooperative instead of disruptive manner with her parents and her siblings. Some of these she quickly carried out and got a great deal of benefit from the fact that she saw was able to do them and was not totally out of control, as she often said she was. Other assignments, such as the chores, she did sporadically, but she still seemed to derive some benefit from doing them.

Outcome

At the end of 16 weeks of family REBT, Debbie was doing her schoolwork regularly, had ceased stealing, and was getting along much better with her family members. Better than that, she was accepting herself much more than before, even when she goofed and failed to do something up to her own standards. Her mother and father were considerably less angry at her, even when she fell back into her old disruptive behavior; and though the emphasis of the family therapy was not very much on their relations with each other, they voluntarily used some of the rational ideas we were all discussing and began to feel less angry at one another and to behave more cooperatively. The parents' sex life also improved considerably, though there was little discussion of this during the therapy sessions. They especially understood Debbie much better and were able to take her with her failings. The father returned for several therapy sessions a year and a half later because he was avoiding some of his office work and was putting himself down for this. At that time it was ascertained that Debbie was still acting remarkably well and that a considerable degree of family harmony had been achieved.

CONCLUSION

As noted at the beginning of this chapter, REBT and CBT have a good record as far as their basic personality hypotheses and claims for clinical effectiveness are concerned. In the field of marriage and family therapy in particular, several favorable outcome studies have been published (as also noted above), but research in this area is still in the formative stage. Clinically, REBT appears to work very well, whether clients are seen separately or conjointly, and it works in premarital, marital, and divorce cases (Ellis, 1962, 1978a, 1991c, 1993e). However, studies and anecdotal reports of the effectiveness of any form of therapy, especially family therapy, are highly suspect. In the final analysis, family REBT will show proven effectiveness only when a considerable number of controlled experiments have been performed to show that it brings better results than other schools of family therapy, no therapy, or placebo therapy.

7

Group Therapy

Several methods of psychotherapy, such as psychoanalysis, employ group therapy for expediency reasons—because it is more practical and less expensive for clients, not because it notably fits in with the theory underlying these methods. Rational emotive behavior therapy (REBT), however, distinctly uses an educational rather than a medical or psychodynamic model (Ellis, 1962, 1971a, 1973; Ellis & Grieger, 1977; Ellis & Whiteley, 1979). Consequently, like most teaching, it distinctly favors group as well as individual sessions.

Although it is usually employed in small group processes—with from 8 to 10 clients on a once-a-week basis—REBT is also done with much larger groups, such as a class of 20 or 30 students or a public workshop or a Rational Emotive Behavior Training Intensive at which more than 200 people may be present (see chapter 8). Its group aspects are also adaptable to audiovisual presentations because it can be taught and practiced by tape recordings, films and videotapes, live radio and television presentations, bibliotherapy, programmed instruction, and other forms of mass media presentations (Ellis, 1976b, 1976c, 1982b, 1993a; Shostrom, Ellis, & Greenwald, 1976). More than most other methods of psychotherapy, therefore, REBT is truly group-oriented, and its practitioners frequently use groups as the method of choice rather than because of special circumstances.

DEFINITION OF GROUP THERAPY

As indicated in the previous section, REBT includes three main forms of psychotherapy: (1) small-scale groups such as the seven regular groups of 8 to 10 individuals that I (AE) and Janet L. Wolfe lead every week at the Institute for

Parts of this chapter were adapted from Albert Ellis, "Rational-Emotive Family Therapy," in G. M. Gazda (Ed.), *Basic Approaches to Group Psychotherapy and Group Counseling* (pp. 381–412). Springfield, IL: Charles C Thomas, 1982; and from Albert Ellis, "Group Rational-Emotive and Cognitive-Behavioral Therapy," *International Journal of Group Therapy*, 1992, 42:63–80.

Rational Emotive Behavior Therapy in New York; (2) large-scale groups of 50, 100, or even more people, such as the regular workshop, Problems of Everyday Living, that I and my associates give every Friday evening at 8:30 pm at the institute; (3) special Rational Emotive Behavior Training Intensives, which were started at the institute and in other cities in 1983 and which preliminary research findings on several hundred participants indicate can produce favorable results in a single 8-hour large-scale intensive. Because small-scale group therapy is more prevalent today than is large-scale, most of the present chapter will discuss this type of group work using REBT principles and practices.

SPECIAL ASPECTS OF REBT GROUP THERAPY

In small-scale group REBT the main goals are for the members (1) to understand the roots of their emotional and behavioral problems and to use this understanding to overcome their current symptoms and function better in their intrapersonal and interpersonal affairs; (2) to understand the difficulties of other group members and be of some therapeutic help to these others; (3) to minimize their (and the others') basic disturbability so that for the rest of their lives they will tend to feel healthily rather than unhealthily emotional and to upset themselves needlessly less often than when they first joined the group; and (4) to achieve not only a behavioral but also a pronounced philosophic change, including accepting (though not necessarily liking) unpleasant reality; surrendering magical, self-sabotaging thinking; desisting from considering life's misfortunes and frustrations awful; taking full responsibility for their own emotional difficulties; and stopping all forms of self-rating and instead learning to fully accept themselves and others as highly fallible and exceptionally error-prone humans.

In group REBT the therapist not only actively and directively shows members who are bringing up their emotional problems that they are largely creating these problems themselves by devoutly and rigidly inventing and holding on to Irrational Beliefs (IBs), vigorously questions and challenges these beliefs and helps rip them up, encourages and pushes all the group members to look for and dispute the *should's*, *ought's*, and *must's* of the other members, and helps them give up their perfectionism and dictatorialness. All group participants are steadily taught to think realistically and logically and to vigorously undermine, and to logico-empirically contradict, the disturbance-creating philosophies of the other members. They are also shown how to Dispute their irrational Beliefs by showing themselves the self-sabotaging consequences to which they usually lead.

Both the therapist and the group consistently suggest activity-oriented homework assignments to participants. Some of these assignments (such as speaking up in the group itself) may be carried out and monitored during the regular sessions. Other assignments (such as making social contacts) are carried on outside the group but are regularly reported and discussed during the sessions. It has often been found that such assignments are more effectively given and followed up when given by a group than by an individual therapist.

REBT includes a number of role-playing and behavior modification methods—such as assertion training, in vivo risk taking, and behavioral rehearsal—that can be done during individual therapy sessions but that are more effective in group. Thus, if a woman is afraid to tell people what she thinks of their behavior, she may be induced to do so with other group members.

The group is deliberately arranged as a kind of laboratory where emotional, gestural, and motor behavior can be directly observed rather than obtained through clients' secondhand reports. Angry or anxious individuals who might feel at home with an individual therapist and be able to hide their feelings from him or her can often be more easily unmasked in group, where they are asked to interact with several of their peers.

In REBT clients frequently fill out written homework report forms and give them to the therapist to correct (Sichel & Ellis, 1984). During group sessions a few homework forms are often read and corrected so that all members, not merely the individual handing in the completed form, may be helped to see specifically what are that person's Irrational Beliefs (IBs), and how he or she can effectively dispute them. By hearing about other group members' main problems and how they dealt with them on the homework report, clients are helped to use these reports more efficiently themselves.

Members of REBT groups give each other valuable feedback as to how they malfunction and what they are foolishly telling themselves to create this malfunctioning. They also learn to view others and to give them feedback; even more important, they get practice in talking other group participants out of their Irrational Beliefs (IBs) and thereby consciously and unconsciously begin to talk themselves out of their own self-defeating ideas.

One main purpose of REBT group sessions is to offer members a wider range of possible solutions to their practical problems and their neurotic problems (that is, their problems about having the practical problems) than they might normally receive in individual therapy sessions. Out of 10 people present at a given session, 1 may finally zero in on a presenter's central problems (after several others have failed), and another may offer an elegant solution to it (after various lower-level solutions have been offered). Where a single would-be helper may give up on a difficult issue (or person), some group members may persist and may finally prove to be quite helpful.

Revealing intimate problems to a group of people may itself be quite therapeutic for clients. In regular REBT group therapy they disclose many ordinarily hidden events and feelings to a dozen or so of their peers; in large-scale REBT group procedures (such as at a large workshop on stress or on anger) they may reveal themselves to a hundred or more people. Especially if clients are shy and inhibited, this kind of disclosure may serve as a useful shame-attacking or risk-taking experience. In its behavioral aspects, REBT specializes in this kind of shame-attacking or self-disclosing exercise and helps train its group members to be able to do "shameful" acts without actually feeling ashamed or putting themselves down in any way (Ellis, 1969, 1971b, 1996a).

SELECTION OF GROUP MEMBERS

REBT therapy groups often include many different kinds of individuals, including those who are moderately disturbed, severely neurotic, sociopathic, borderline, and psychotic. At the Institute for Rational Emotive Behavior Therapy in New York, where a number of groups meet regularly every week, group clients are required to have at least one session of individual therapy for screening purposes, to determine whether they are suitable for and are likely to benefit from the group process. The vast majority of people interviewed for this purpose are allowed, at least tentatively, to join a group. The relatively few who are screened out are those who are (1) too undisciplined, talkative, or manic to listen to what is taking place in group and to respond to others, (2) too autistic or schizoid to participate, and (3) too hostile or too disruptive to be easily controlled by the group leader and taught by the group to cooperate with the others.

If people are mistakenly permitted to join a group and it is later discovered that they are too disruptive, require too much personal attention, and/or seriously interrupt the fairly organized group process that normally is part of REBT, they are first shown how to be more effective group members (for their own sake and for that of the other participants). If this does not work, they are told that they will, for the present, have to leave the group and go into individual therapy until their therapist agrees that it is suitable for them to return to group. In the course of the almost 40 years that I (AE) have been working with REBT group therapy, fewer than 15 people have been specifically asked to leave group and return to individual therapy.

GROUP COMPOSITION AND SETTING

The preferred composition of REBT groups is from 8 to 10 members, covering a wide range of diagnostic categories. An attempt is made to have about an equal number of males and females in each group. Group members are of all ages in the adult groups, ranging from about 18 to 60; most of them are between 25 and 45. Adolescent groups include individuals from 13 to 17, again with a fairly even distribution of males and females. Most of the group members would be diagnosed as severely neurotic, a large minority as having personality disorders, and a few as psychotic. I (AE) have a large number of clients for individual REBT sessions at the clinic of the Institute for Rational Emotive Behavior Therapy in New York; and a great many of these clients, after they have had from 5 to 15 sessions of individual treatment, are encouraged to join a group and to finish their therapy by staying in the group from 6 months to a year. This gives them time to work on their own emotional problems and to relate to group process.

Once a member joins a group, he or she may have concomitant individual therapy sessions regularly or irregularly. Most group members choose to have them irregularly and therefore mainly learn the principles and practice of REBT in the course of their group work. Clients who are shy or who have interpersonal problems are particularly encouraged to join a group because it is often more therapeutic for them to work out their problems with their peers than to work on them only with an individual therapist (who may be a special kind of person to them and therefore not representative of the people they associate with in real life).

Originally, REBT groups were limited to 8 individuals. It was accidentally discovered that when some members who had temporarily quit the group and who wished to return were allowed to do so, the number could be raised to 10 or more. With groups of this size, usually about 8 or 9 attend each session (because of absences); with this number in attendance, the group tends to become more interesting and less repetitive.

The group is run in an organized manner, with the leader making sure that only one member speaks at a time, that spontaneity is encouraged but a good deal of order maintained, that silent members are pushed to speak up about their own and others' problems, and that most members who bring up a problem are given specific homework assignments, which are later checked up on. The leader also paces things so that no one is allowed to monopolize too much of the group's time and no one is allowed to cop out and avoid participation. Observation has shown that although REBT groups can be run regularly with a small number of people, the presence of about eight persons at each session is probably optimal for efficient and involved functioning.

My (AE's) groups meet once a week in my regular office in New York City, which is furnished with three large sofas and extra-comfortable chairs. The room is large (13 by 19 feet), is paneled, and has bookcases on most of its walls. It is comfortable and attractive, has a special coat hanger for members' extra clothing, and is equipped with adequate air conditioning in summer and heat in winter. It has a high ceiling and two large windows. Every effort is made to have the group members feel comfortable. The room is quite suited to group marathons, which may continue for 10 or 14 hours a day.

When my groups go to another room for the second part of their session with one of the group leaders who is in training, they go to another large and fairly comfortable room. However, REBT group therapy is not dependent on any particular kind of setting and may be done in much less comfortable surroundings.

FREQUENCY, LENGTH, AND DURATION OF GROUP SESSIONS

REBT groups usually meet once a week for 2 1/4 hours. My (AE's) groups are also used to train leaders; therefore, they include a leader and an assistant leader who is in training. The group stays with both these leaders for the first 1 1/2 hours and then goes to another room with the assistant leader for another three-quarters of an hour. REBT groups, however, do not require two leaders and can easily be run by one trained person without any assistance. Groups are given a free 8-hour marathon every year, in addition to the regular once-a-week group process.

All groups are open-ended; once members join, they can attend group for a minimum of 5 weeks and then (after giving 2 weeks' notice) can drop out at any time. Those who drop out are usually soon replaced by new members. New people therefore enter a group filled mostly with members who have been in attendance for a period of several months and who help teach them "some of the ropes" of REBT.

It is preferred that members stay in the group a minimum of 6 months because it takes some time for them to learn the principles of REBT and to have some group supervision of their homework assignments. Some less disturbed individuals, however, are able to stay in group only 2 or 3 months and get considerable help with their emotional problems.

PROCESS OF GROUP REBT THERAPY

Group REBT differs from other common forms of group procedures, such as psychoanalytic and experiential group therapy, in several important respects. To show what its process is like, let me (AE) describe its aspects in my regular groups.

Transference Aspects

REBT views transference, first, as overgeneralization. Thus, because group members were once treated badly by their father and treated well by their mother, they may tend to put other males in the same category as their father and may feel hostile or indifferent to men and warm toward women. They may—or may not—also react to the therapist as a father/mother figure and to other group members as siblings. These are overgeneralizations but, unless they are extreme, may not lead to major emotional and behavioral problems. Because REBT is not preoccupied with this kind of transference (as psychoanalysis is), it does not obsessively look for it and consequently invariably "find" it.

When normal, nondisturbed transference reactions are observed in my groups, I largely ignore them; but when they escalate into disturbed reactions in the group itself or in the members' personal lives, the other group members and I pounce on these reactions and show members how destructive they are and how to minimize or eliminate them. Thus, if Miriam avoids sex-love relationships because her father kept rejecting her, we show her that all males are *not* her father, that she can sensibly choose a different type of man, and that if she makes a mistake and picks a partner who is as unloving as her father, that doesn't prove that she needs his love, that she is worthless without it, nor that she'll never be able to have a long-term loving relationship. The group and I dispute her disturbed overgeneralizing but not her normal generalizing.

Similarly, if a male member deifies or devil-ifies me, the group leader, whom he sees as a loved or hated father figure, we point out his disturbed transference reactions, show him the distorted thinking that lies behind it, and encourage him to adopt less dysfunctional thoughts, feelings, and behaviors. Or if a woman fights with female group members just as she fights with her sisters, we point out her transference and the irrational cognitions behind it and show how to break her rigid women-are-all-like-my-sisters reaction.

The term *transference* is also used in psychotherapy to denote the close relationship that usually develops between clients and their therapist. I find that such relationship factors do develop in my group but not nearly as intensely as they do with my individual therapy clients. However, REBT actively espouses the therapist's giving all clients close attention, showing real interest in helping them solve their problems, and—especially—giving what Rogers (1961) calls unconditional positive regard and what I have called unconditional acceptance. So, although I am quite often confrontational with group members, I try to show them that I really care about helping them; that I will work hard during every session to hear, understand, empathize with them; that I have great faith that they can, despite their handicaps, change; that I can poke fun *at their unhealthy ways of thinking* without laughing *at them*; and that I totally accept them as fallible humans, no matter how badly they often think and behave. I also use my *person* in my group sessions and consequently am informal, take risks, reveal some of my own feelings, tell jokes and stories, and generally am myself as well as a group leader. In this way, I hope to model flexible, involved, nondisturbed behaviors.

Countertransference Aspects

I frankly like and dislike some of my group members more than I do others, and I especially tend to dislike members who often come late, act unhelpfully to others, fail to do their homework, and behave disruptively in group. When I see that I am feeling this way, I look for my possibly telling myself, "They *absolutely shouldn't* be the way they are and are rotten shits for being that way!"

I immediately dispute that damning Belief and convince myself that they *should* act the poor way that they do because it is their nature to act that way right now. I dislike what they *do* but I can accept *them* with their unfortunate doings.

By ridding myself of my *demands* of my clients, I largely (not completely) overcome my negative countertransference, and I am able to deal with "bad" group members more therapeutically. Sometimes, depending on their vulnerability, I confront them and honestly tell them, "I try not to hate *you*, but I really do dislike some of your *behavior*, and I hope for my sake, the group's sake, and especially your own sake, that you change it." When I find myself prejudicedly favoring some members of my groups, I convince myself that they are not gods or goddesses, and I make an effort to keep liking them personally without unduly favoring them in group.

Levels of Intervention

Most of my interventions take place with each individual member as he is telling about his homework, talking about his progress and lack of progress, presenting new problems or returning to old ones. I speak directly to him, ask questions, make suggestions, ferret out and dispute his dysfunctional thoughts, feelings, and behaviors, and suggest homework. My interventions are mainly about his personal problems, especially as they relate to his outside life but also as they relate to what he says and doesn't say in group.

I often show the member that her actions (and inactions) in group may well replicate her out-of-group behaviors. Thus, I may say, "Johanna, you speak so low here that we can hardly hear what you say. Do you act the same way in social groups? If so, what are you telling yourself to *make* yourself speak so low?"

My interpersonal interventions include commenting on how group members react to each other; noting that they often fail to speak up to or interact with other members; noting their warm or hostile reactions to others, encouraging the former and questioning the latter; giving them relationship exercises to do during group sessions; having a personal interaction with some of the members; and, especially, pointing out that their group interactions may indicate how they sabotage themselves in their outside relationships and giving them some in-group skill training that may help them relate better outside the group.

My intervention with the group as a whole largely consists of giving all of them cognitive, emotive, and behavioral exercises to be done in the group; giving them all the same homework exercise (such as a shame-attacking exercise) to do before the next group session; giving them a brief lecture on one of the main theories or practices of REBT; explaining to them some of the group procedures and discussing with them the advantages and disadvantages of these procedures.

Most of the time, as noted above, I intervene on the individual level, but when interpersonal problems (such as two or more members failing to relate to each other) arise, I often intervene with duos or trios. I also plan in advance group-as-a-whole interventions, or else I spontaneously promote them as I deem advisable (or as the spirit moves me!).

Process Versus Content Orientation

By far most of the time in my group sessions I use an individualized content focus. I assume that the group members come to therapy to work on their own individual problems and mainly to help themselves in their outside lives. Therefore, I induce them largely to talk about the things they are disturbing themselves about in their self-oriented and interpersonal relationships and, with the help of the group, try to show them exactly how they are needlessly upsetting themselves in their daily lives and what they can do to think, feel, and act more healthily.

The purpose of REBT group (and individual) therapy is to show clients how they are not only assessing and blaming what they do but also damning *themselves* for doing it; how they are also evaluating others' behavior *and* damning these others for "bad" behavior, and how they are noting environmental difficulties and (externally and internally) whining about them instead of constructively trying to change or avoid them. Therefore, whenever members bring up any undue or exaggerated upsetness and feel unhealthily panicked, depressed, self-hating, and enraged (instead of healthily sad, disappointed, and frustrated), the other members and I focus on showing them what they are doing to upset themselves needlessly, how to stop doing this, and how to plan and act on achieving a more fulfilling, happier existence. When they are, as it were, on stage in the group, almost everyone focuses on them and their difficulties and tries to help them overcome these in the group itself and in the outside world. So a majority of the time in each session is spent on dealing with individual members' problems.

When, however, any of the members display a problem that particularly relates to the group itself, this is dealt with specifically and group-wise. Thus, if a member keeps coming quite late to group or is absent a good deal of the time, I (or other members) raise this as an issue, and we speak to this member about it. We determine, for instance, why he comes late, what core philosophies encourage him to do so, how he defeats himself and the other members by his lateness, how he can change, and what kind of homework assignment in this respect he will agree to carry out. At the same time, the general problem of lateness—as it relates to group and also as it relates to the members' outside life—is also frequently discussed, and it is brought out how latecoming is disadvantageous to other members and how it interferes with a cohesive and beneficial group process.

Similarly, if a group member speaks only about her own problems and doesn't take the risk of speaking to the others, disputing their self-defeating thoughts and behaviors, and making some suitable suggestions for their change, she is questioned about this and shown how and why she is blocking herself in group and how and why she probably behaves similarly in her outside life. But the general problem of members being too reserved (or sometimes too talkative) in group is also raised, and various members are encouraged to speak up about this problem and to give their ideas about how the group process would be more effective if virtually all the members talked up appropriately, rather than said too much or too little.

Also, if the group as a whole seems to be functioning poorly—for example, being dull, uninterested, apathetic, or overly boisterous—I raise this issue, encourage a general discussion of it, get members to suggest alternative ways for the group to act, and check on these suggestions later to see if they are being implemented. Once in a while I go over some of the general principles of REBT—such as the theory that people largely upset themselves rather than *get* upset—to make sure that the members as a whole understand these principles and are better prepared to use them during the sessions and in their outside affairs.

Identifying Underlying Group Process Themes

I keep looking for cues for underlying issues that are not being handled well in group, such as members being interested only in their own problems and not those of other members; their not being alert during the group; their being too negative to other members who may not be working at helping themselves improve; their giving only practical advice to other members rather than disputing their dysfunctional philosophies; their being too sociable rather than being serious about their own and others' problems; their not staying for the after-group session, which immediately follows each regular session and is led by one of my assistant therapists after I leave the regular group session; and their subgrouping or rudely interrupting others when the group is going on. I usually intervene soon after these issues arise and raise the issue either with the individual who is interfering with the group process or with the group as a whole.

My strategy of intervention is usually direct and often confrontational. Thus, I may say, "Jim, you always bring up your own problems in group and seem to have no trouble speaking about them. But I rarely hear you say anything to the other group members about their problems. When you sit there silently while the rest of us are speaking to one of the group members, I suspect that you are saying quite a lot to yourself that you are not saying to the group. Am I right about this? And if I am, what are you telling yourself to *stop* yourself from speaking up to the others?"

A more general intervention will also usually be direct and will go something like this: "Several of you recently are not doing your agreed-upon homework or are doing it very sloppily. Let's discuss this right now and see if I am observing this correctly, and if so, what can we do about it to see that the homework assignments are more useful and to arrange that you tend to follow them more often and more thoroughly."

If the group process is going well and the members are fairly consistently bringing up and working on their problems, both in the group and outside the group, my interventions are relatively few in regard to the group process. But I frequently question, challenge, advise, and confront members about their individual problems. I am an active teacher, confronter, persuader, encourager, and homework suggester, and I usually talk more than any of the other members during a given session. I try to make sure, however, that I do not give long lectures or hold the floor too long. My questions and comments, therefore, are usually frequent but brief. Although I can easily run one of my groups by myself, without any assistance, because the Institute for Rational Emotive Behavior Therapy in New York is a training institute and because we want all of our trainees to be able to lead a group by themselves, I am usually assisted by one of our trainees, a Fellow of the institute, who is with me and the group for the first hour and a half of each session and who takes over the group by himself or herself for the after-group, for another 45 minutes. The assistant leader is also trained to make active-directive interventions but not to hog the floor at any one time and to encourage the other members to keep making interventions, too. A few of the members in each group usually become quite vocal and adept at making interventions, but I tactfully correct them if they seem to go too far off base. The assistant leader and I particularly go after the nonintervening members and keep encouraging them to speak up more and more about other people's problems. If they are recalcitrant or resistant in this respect, we fairly often give them the assignment of speaking up a minimum of three times in each session about *other's* issues.

Here-and-Now Activation

I keep showing the members how their behavior in group often—but by no means always—mirrors their behaviors and problems outside the group. Thus, if one member speaks sharply to another member, I may say, "Mary, you seem to be angry right now at Joan. Are you just objecting to her behavior, with which you may disagree? Or are you, as I seem to hear you doing, damning *her* for exhibiting that *behavior*?" If Mary acknowledges her anger at Joan, I (and the other group members) may then ask, "What are you telling yourself right now to make yourself angry? What is your Jehovian *demand* on Joan?" If Mary denies that she is angrily carping at Joan, I may then ask the rest of the group, "What do you think and feel about Mary's reactions to Joan? Am I just inventing her anger or do you sense it, too?"

We then get the group reactions to Mary; and if the group agrees that she probably is quite angry at Joan, we go back to the question: "What are you telling yourself right now to *make* yourself angry?" The others and I will also try to get Mary to see that in her outside life she is probably more often angry than she acknowledges and that she is telling herself the same kind of demanding things about those at whom she is angry as she is now telling herself about Joan in the group.

Again, if Ted only offers practical advice to the other members and never helps them to see and to dispute their self-defeating philosophies by which they are upsetting themselves, I, my assistant therapist, or one of the group members may say to him, "Look, Ted, you just ignored Harold's perfectionist demands that are making him refuse to work on the novel he is trying to write; instead, you only offered him some practical advice on how to take a writing course. You often seem to do this same kind of thing in group. Now isn't it likely that in your own life you don't look for and dispute your Irrational Beliefs and that you only look for practical ways of acting better *with* those irrationalities so that you do not have to tackle them and give them up?"

Working with Difficult Group Members

One kind of difficult group member is the one who interferes with the group process, such as Mel, who interrupted others, indicated that they were pretty worthless for not changing their ways, and often monopolized the group. Other members and I pointed this out to him several times, but he persisted in his disruptive behavior. So we insisted that he stop and consider what he was telling himself when, for example, he interrupted others.

His main *must*urbatory Beliefs appeared to be (1) "I *must* get in what I have to say immediately or else I might lose it and never get to say it and that would be *awful!*" and (2) "If I don't make a more brilliant statement to the group than any of the others make, I am an inadequate person and I might as well shut my mouth and say nothing at all!" We showed Mel how to dispute and change these ideas to preferences but not necessities that he speak and be heard and that he make fine contributions in group, and we have him the homework assignment of watching his interrupting tendencies and forcing himself for a while to speak up in group only after he had given some other member the choice of speaking up first. After several more sessions he had distinctly improved his interruptive tendencies and reported that he was doing the same thing in his group participations and individual conversations outside the group.

Another difficult type of member is the one who rarely completes the homework assignment he has agreed to do or else completes it occasionally and sloppily. I (and other group members) then ask him to look for the self-defeating ideas that he is overtly or tacitly holding to block his doing these assignments, such as: "It's hard to do this god-damned assignment; in fact, it's *too* hard and it *shouldn't* be that hard! I can get away with improving myself *without* doing it, even though other people have to do their homework to change. Screw it, I won't do it!" We keep after this member to look at the Beliefs he holds to block his doing the homework, to make a list of the disadvantages of not doing it and to go over this list at least five times every day, to dispute his Irrational Beliefs strongly and forcefully and to keep telling himself functional coping self-statements in their stead, to use rational emotive imagery to make himself feel sorry and displeased but not horrified and rebellious about having to do the homework, to reinforce himself whenever he does it and perhaps also to penalize himself when he doesn't do it, and to use other suitable methods of REBT to undercut his dysfunctional thinking, feeling, and behaving about doing the homework.

Another type of difficult group member is the one who is overly passive, polite, and nonparticipative. I usually do nothing about such a member until she has been in the group for several weeks and has had a chance to acclimate herself to its procedures and to some of the principles of REBT. But then I directly question her about her passivity and lack of participation; if she acknowledges these behaviors, I encourage her to look at her blocking thoughts and actively dispute them. Thus, one member, Josephine, kept telling herself, just before she thought of speaking up in group, "What if I say something stupid! They'll all laugh at me! I'll be an utter fool! They are all brighter than I and know much better how to use REBT. I'll *never* be able to say something intelligent or to be helpful to the other group members. I'd better quit group and only go for individual therapy, where it is much easier for me to speak up because I only have to talk about myself and don't have to help others with their problems."

In this case, the group and I did what we usually do: we disputed Josephine's empirically false or unrealistic attributions and inferences and showed her that she wouldn't necessarily say something stupid; that the group might well not laugh at her even if she did; that all the members were not necessarily brighter than she; and that if she kept trying, she most probably would be able to say something intelligent and to be helpful to the other members. As usual, however, we went beyond this—as we almost always do in REBT—by showing Josephine, more elegantly, that even if the worst happened, even if she did say something stupid, even if she was laughed at by the group, even if all the others were brighter than she, and even if she never was able to say something intelligent or to be helpful to the others, she still would never be an inadequate or rotten person but would only be a person who was now behaving poorly and who could always accept and respect herself while remaining unenthusiastic about some of her traits and behaviors.

This is what we usually try to achieve with difficult clients who continually down and damn themselves and who therefore steadily feel depressed, panicked, and worthless: the group members and I persist in showing her that we accept her as a fallible human and that she can learn to consistently do the same for herself. Group REBT (like individual REBT) is particularly oriented toward helping all clients give themselves unconditional self-acceptance, that is, to reject and to try to change many of their dysfunctional behaviors but always—yes, always!—to accept themselves as humans. Yes, *whether or not* they perform well and *whether or not*, they are approved or loved by significant others.

This is one of the cardinal views of REBT and one that often—though, of course, not always—works well with difficult clients. This aspect of REBT is probably more effective in group than in individual therapy, because all the members of the group are taught to accept both themselves and others unconditionally so that when an arrant self-denigrator comes to group, she is not only accepted unconditionally by the therapist (who is especially trained to do this kind of accepting) but is almost always accepted by the other group members, thus encouraging and abetting her unconditionally accepting herself.

Activity Level of Therapist and Group Members

In cognitive-behavioral therapy in general and in group REBT in particular, the activity level of the therapist tends to be high. I (AE) am a teacher who often shows my clients how they upset themselves and what they can do to change, but I also keep encouraging and pushing them to change. The romantic view in therapy is that if clients are provided with a trusting and accepting atmosphere they have considerable ability to change and will healthfully use this ability to get themselves to grow and develop. I take the more realistic view that they can but that they often won't choose to modify their thoughts, feelings, and behaviors unless I actively and directively push them to do so. Consequently, as noted previously in this chapter, I speak more than any other group member during each session; I purposely and purposively lead the group in "healthy" rather than "unhealthy" directions; and I keep each session going in an organized, no-nonsense, presumably efficient way. I try to make sure that no one is neglected during each session, that no one monopolizes the group, and that sidetracking into chit-chat, empty discussion, bombast, endless philosophizing, and other modes of problem avoidance is minimized.

As leader, I try to maximize honest revealing of feelings, cutting through defensiveness, getting to members' core dysfunctional philosophies, disputing these philosophies, accepting present discomfort, and carrying out difficult in-group and out-of-group experiential and behavioral assignments. For example, I (or the other members) may suggest that Sam, an unusually shy person, go around the room and start a conversation with every member who is present. I will then direct Sam to do so, will encourage him to keep going around the room, will ask him about his feelings as he does so, will get him to look at what he is thinking to create these feelings, will ask the other members for their reactions to his overtures, and will lead a general discussion on what has just transpired and how Sam and the other members can gain from this exercise. Once, when we did this exercise with an exceptionally shy man, he not only became much more active in group from that session onward but also, for the first time in his life, began to approach people in his neighborhood bar, where previously he had always waited for them to approach him. He noted that my actively persuading him and the group to participate in this encouraging exercise was a real turning point in his life.

METHODS EMPLOYED

The main technique employed in a regular group REBT is that of each member presenting a current problem, such as a feeling of anxiety, depression, worthlessness, hostility, or self-pity, or a dysfunctional behavior such as addiction, procrastination, or outbursts of violence. The therapist and several other members of the group then talk to this presenter and first try to discover his or her activating experience (A) and self-defeating emotional and behavioral consequences (C). Once this is determined, the therapist and the group try to help the presenter to zero in on the B's, the crucial Beliefs, and particularly the absolutistic Irrational Beliefs (IBs) that are mainly creating of "causing" the dysfunctional consequences (C). These dysfunctional Beliefs are then directly and vigorously disputed (D) by the therapist and the group members, and they try to help the presenter learn effective disputing and carry it on in his or her outside life. Group members also regularly suggest cognitive and behavioral homework assignments for the presenter to do to dispute Irrational Beliefs, and they check up, in subsequent sessions, to see if these homework assignments have actually been carried out and how they can be continued or modified in the future.

Many of the other cognitive, emotive, and behavioral techniques of REBT are also regularly or occasionally used with group members who bring up their problems (Ellis, 1992c, 1995a; Ellis & Abrahms, 1978; Ellis & Grieger, 1977; Ellis & Harper, 1997; Ellis & Whiteley, 1979). There are few of the regular REBT methods that are not equally effective when used in group; several of the methods are even more effective. Thus, group-given homework assignments are likely to be carried out more frequently and more thoroughly than are the same assignments given in individual therapy; and role playing in group is often more evocative, more anxiety-arousing, and more effectively critiqued than the same kind of role playing done in the course of an individual therapy session.

The following special methods are used in group REBT.

1. Structured exercises, such as risk taking, self-disclosing, and shame-attacking exercises, are regularly given to the groups in order to arouse, reveal, and deal with feelings that some of the members might not normally experience or might refrain from talking about when they do experience them.

2. All group members are encouraged to read some of the basic bibliotherapy writings of REBT, such as *How to Stubbornly Refuse to Make Yourself Miserable about Anything—Yes, Anything!* (Ellis, 1988), *How to Keep People from Pushing Your Buttons* (Ellis & Lange, 1994), *A Guide to Rational Living* (Ellis & Harper, 1997), *Overcoming Procrastination* (Ellis & Knaus, 1977), and *A Guide to Personal Happiness* (Ellis & Becker, 1982). All group members are given a series of REBT pamphlets when they start therapy and are urged to read these and other self-help materials that include the main REBT theories and practices. When group members see that other members do not understand some of the REBT philosophies, they frequently assign these readings in the form of homework.

3. At the Institute for Rational Emotive Behavior Therapy in New York City, group members have available to them a large variety of talks, workshops, seminars, and specialized skill training groups. Thus, a shy person may not only be a member of a regular REBT group but may, for a limited period of six or eight sessions, join a social skills group, where he or she will receive specific instructions in encountering and socializing with others. Group members may also use some of the other events at the institute—especially the famous Friday night workshop on Problems of Everyday Living—to meet and become friendly with other people who may be using the REBT philosophy.

THERAPIST ROLE

In REBT groups the therapist takes a very active-directive role in leading and running the group, keeping things in order, ensuring that silent people talk up and that others are not too talkative, and seeing that people consistently bring up their most serious problems and open up about them. In regard to disputing members' Irrational Beliefs and helping them with practical solutions to their problems, the therapist is one of the most active members of the group, frequently the most active. REBT group therapists ask questions, probe, teach, encourage, give homework assignments, present structured exercises, and perform all the other directive functions that are usually performed in individual REBT. The theory of REBT states that people not only severely disturb themselves but frequently hold on, powerfully and rigidly, to their absolutistic Beliefs, by which they make themselves disturbed; consequently, their basic irrationalities had better be quite strongly and persistently revealed and uprooted by REBT practitioners and by other group members. To this end, group leaders try to see that the active-directive process of REBT is steadily employed and that the group process practically never deteriorates into dullness, apathy, disorganization, unrestrained display of feelings, anarchy, or other forms of behavior that some other kinds of therapy encourage or allow. The REBT group leader, therefore, distinctly *leads* when he or she does not, therapeutic processes may ensue but, at best, might be called low-level or inelegant REBT (Ellis, 1978b).

GROUND RULES FOR THE GROUP

The REBT groups that are held at the Institute for Rational Emotive Behavior Therapy in New York are given printed ground rules that explain how the sessions are run, what the attendance rules are, to what extent they are encouraged to socialize with other group members, and so on. Some of the main rules follow.

1. All transactions during the group and the sessions outside the group that members have with each other are to be strictly confidential and are not to be revealed to others.
2. Group members are freely allowed to socialize with each other outside the group as long as they bring the information they thus learn about each other to the group sessions and as long as they do not make their whole lives an in-group process. They can even date each other and go seriously with each other, if doing so does not inhibit them from continuing to reveal themselves fully in group.
3. Group members are encouraged to help each other during sessions and outside the group, to be highly critical of others' behaviors but not to condemn other group members as *persons*, and to be especially cooperative with new people who join the group.
4. Group members are urged, in regular sessions and during rational encounter marathons, to push themselves as much as possible to reveal their most uncomfortable feelings and to bring out their serious problems. They are also encouraged to try to get others to reveal themselves and to refrain from politely letting inhibited and untalkative members get away with this kind of unrevealing behavior.

RESEARCH

An unusual number of outcome studies have been done on REBT that tend to show it is more effective as a form of psychological treatment than when emotionally disturbed individuals are left on a waiting list, given a placebo form of therapy, or subjected to non-REBT procedures. There now exist over 500 controlled experiments using REBT and related cognitive-behavioral forms of therapy; almost all of these experiments show positive results in favor of REBT (DiGiuseppe, Miller, & Trexler, 1979; Ellis & Whiteley, 1979; Haaga & Davison, 1989; Hajzler & Bernard, 1991; Hollon & Beck, 1994; Lyons & Woods, 1991; McGovern & Silverman, 1984; Miller & Berman, 1983; Silverman et al., 1992). A good many of the outcome studies that have shown that REBT and allied cognitive behavior therapy work effectively have been done with group rather than individual psychotherapy (Ellis, 1992c; McClellan & Stieper, 1973; Meichenbaum, Gilmore, & Fedoravicius, 1971).

In addition to these studies, a number of other controlled experiments have been published, indicating that REBT and allied cognitive-behavioral group therapy is effective when used in a classroom situation with children and adults who are taught rational emotive behavioral methods and through this psychoeducational group technique are enabled to change their self-defeating feelings and behaviors (Hajzler & Bernard, 1991; DiGiuseppe et al., 1979; Ellis & Whiteley, 1979; Lange, 1979; Lyons & Woods, 1991; Rose, 1980; Upper & Ross, 1979, 1980).

LIMITATIONS OF GROUP REBT

Rational emotive behavior therapy, like psychotherapy in general, has distinct limitations, as noted in the first major work in this area, *Reason and Emotion in Psychotherapy* (Ellis, 1962). This is largely because, at bottom, people seem to be biologically as well as sociologically disturbed and self-defeating, and so far no way of curing them that is even near-perfect has yet been discovered. REBT, moreover, has its own limitations and, like all therapeutic systems, works only some of the time for some individuals. We would still hypothesize, as in the first paper on REBT, given at the American Psychological Association Convention in Chicago in September 1956 (Ellis, 1958a), that, compared to other systems of therapy, REBT brings better results more quickly for more disturbed people more of the time. However, it still leaves much to be desired as a system of psychotherapy and considerably more research needs to be done to improve it and to make up for some of its deficiencies.

Group REBT and counseling especially have intrinsic disadvantages and limitations when compared to more individualized REBT processes. For example, group members can easily, out of overzealousness and ignorance, mislead other members and at times even present them with harmful directives and views. They can give poor or low-level solutions, for example, continuing to show disturbed people what "practical" methods they can use to make themselves more successful rather than what deeper philosophic changes they can make in their disturbance-creating outlooks.

Group therapy, even when employing an organized and efficient procedure like REBT, has its clear-cut ineffectualities. The best-intentioned members can waste time in irrelevancies, lead the problem-presenter up the garden path, sidetrack and defuse some of the therapist's main points, hold back because they inordinately look for the approval of the therapist or of other group members, bring out their own and others' minor instead of major difficulties, and otherwise get out on various nontherapeutic limbs. Group members can also bombard a presenter with so many and so powerful suggestions that he or she is overwhelmed and partly paralyzed. They can give poor homework assignments or keep presenting so many new problems that old assignments are not sufficiently checked upon. They can allow a member, if the therapist does not actively intervene, to get away with minimal participation and hence make little change in his or her disordered behavior. They can become overly frustrated and hostile and can irrationally condemn participants for their symptoms or for their continuing resistance to giving up these symptoms.

Group REBT, consequently, is hardly a panacea for all ills, nor is it suitable for all individuals who come for help. Some clients are not ready for it and preferably should have some individual REBT before they enter a group. Others—such as compulsive talkers or hypomanic individuals—may benefit from group work but are too disruptive to the group (and require too much monitoring). Hence, it is best to have them work on their problems in other modes of treatment. We firmly believe that the great majority of disturbed clients can benefit as much, and probably more, from group therapy than from individual treatment alone, but *the majority* hardly means *all*.

ETHICAL CONSIDERATIONS

REBT poses ethical problems for people when therapists or members of a group confuse its views on people *being guilty* of unethical and immoral acts and their *feeling guilty* or self-downing about such acts. REBT tries to teach clients that many human acts—such as those that needlessly harm others—are distinctly wrong, unethical, or immoral but that the people who perform these acts are not to be labeled or condemned as *rotten or damnable persons*. It largely takes the Christian position of accepting the sinner but not the sin: it shows clients how to fully or unconditionally accept themselves with their antisocial or self-defeating behavior but not to accept that behavior and to try to do their best to change it. If people wrongly believe that REBT condones immoral acts, rather than fully accepts the humanity and fallibility of those who perform such acts, they can lead others astray and misinterpret one of the main principles of REBT.

Ethics are an exceptionally important part of group therapy because when a member joins a group the assumption is that he or she will be able to open up fully to the other members, reveal things that may be hidden from all others, and receive not only the attention but the cooperation of the group when doing so. Group therapy to a large extent depends on a high degree of confidentiality and trust among the members. If this is lacking, little effective therapy will take place, and considerable harm may be done to some of the participants.

Group therapy also implies that the person joining a group has some definite responsibility to other members not merely to avoid harming them but to do his or her best to help them. If people join a group only to learn about themselves and to help themselves and if they have virtually no interest in the other group members and make no effort to encourage them to bring up problems and to help them solve some of these problems, they are taking a one-sided and essentially irresponsible attitude toward the group. The leader and other members are to bring this to their attention (in a nondamning and non-hostile way) and ask them to "shape up or ship out": make some real effort to help others as well as themselves or else go into individual therapy, where they can be as self-centered as they want and still ethically participate.

GROUP PROTOCOL

Following is an excerpt from a fairly typical session of group REBT. The main presenter is David, a 28-year-old school social worker, who is not only anxious with his clients but has great trouble discussing his cases in group supervision sessions because he is afraid of being criticized and scorned by his chief supervisor and other members of the supervision group. During the first 10 minutes of the present session he tells the group about his problems, and several members and the therapist question him to try to pinpoint what he is most anxious about and under what conditions his anxiety is at its worst. The session continues:*

1.   DAVID: When I hear the criticism of my supervisor and supervision group, I take it to its illogical extremes—which is, I don't listen to it any longer. I withdraw. I turn off emotionally.

2.   THERAPIST: Because "I don't know everything I *should* know about what they're asking me? I can't answer them *perfectly* well"?

3.   DAVID: Yes.

4.   MARY: [a 33-year-old housewife]: But isn't that because your worth as a person is being involved there?

5.   DAVID: Maybe.

6.   JOHN: [a 45-year-old psychiatrist]: Let's get back to more specific examples of when you feel hurt and small. In your description you mentioned feelings of incompetency. Let's assume that you do act incompetently. Let's assume that it's really dyed-in-the-wool incompetence. How does the *feeling* of incompetence come about?

7.   DAVID: I suppose that what you're trying to get me to say is that in order to be competent, I must be competent 100% of the time.

8.   MARY: I suppose you want me to say: "I have a feeling that you think we're all trying to program you."

---

*The responses are numbered because they are discussed individually in the following section.

9.   DAVID: I guess . . . I know by the book what the rational answer is, and I can give you the rational answer. But it's obviously not the way I am behaving at the moment I turn off.

10.   THERAPIST: Well, let me ask, When you give the rational answer, do you believe it's *true*? Or do you believe you just give it because you read it in one of my books?

11.   DAVID: I believe that that's probably what I know. I think I do know what's going on. But I'm not very successful at working at it, at feeling that the criticism of me that the supervision group is making is not really all *that* important.

12.   JOAN: [a 28-year-old artist]: Oh, when you do see what's going on, when you feel put down by criticism, how do you work at it? Or do you work at it?

13.   DAVID: I say to myself, "I am being defensive. I am closing myself off." I'm feeling put down by the situation or by people.

14.   THERAPIST: O.K. So you see you have a symptom, a poor way of reacting to the situation or to people. Now, that could be negative. For you say to yourself, "Oh shit! I'm defensive. What a louse I am for being defensive!" What else do you say? For I got the feeling before, when you talked about the supervision group's criticizing you, that (a) you were putting yourself down for being criticized, and then (b) you were putting yourself down again for being defensive after they criticized you. Now, what do you do to stop putting yourself down for both *a* and *b*?

15.   DAVID: Well, I typically say, "I am here in order to get feedback on my cases and how I am doing with them." And, "It is not reasonable for me to behave defensively to the feedback that I am getting."

16.   THERAPIST: I still hear you describing that "I'm idiotically doing something." But I don't hear you attacking what you're telling yourself to make yourself defensive about their criticisms of you.

17.   JOHN: When you were answering that, you could give the rational answer, and that's probably what's going on; it seemed to me that it's just not clear to you what's really going on. You're in a fog. How could you find out more precisely what really is going on?

18.   DAVID: I don't know. How could I find out? Oh, I could act as if that's what's going on and challenge it. How, at the moment I am upset, do I know what's going on? I don't know.

19.   JOAN: Why can't you ask yourself, "Why am I upset?"

20.   THERAPIST: Or, better, "What am I doing to upset myself?"

21.   MARY: Maybe . . . It's very difficult if the only thing you want to do is to stop the feeling. One suggestion is that you'd better prolong the feeling of shame about their criticism and examine your thinking and your feelings about having the shame, rather than just concentrate on stopping feeling ashamed.

22.   THERAPIST: Or rather than concentrating on "Oh, shit! I'm having this terrible, this idiotic feeling!"

23.   MARY: Right!

24.   DAVID: Or hating myself for having it.

25.   JOHN: Right!

26.   DAVID: Well, I'm more likely to hate myself for having the feeling of not being able to take the criticism and for turning off.

27.   THERAPIST: Right. But that isn't the solution. That's psychoanalytical-type insight: "Oh, shit! I'm doing it!" But it's not rational emotive behavior therapy.

28.   ROSE: [a 37-year-old teacher]: To get back to what Mary said, I see you, for example, imagining this "put-down" situation, and lying on your bed with the tape recorder going, and letting it run in a stream-of-consciousness kind of way. Perhaps just talking out all these kinds of things that come into your head (about what your feelings are like when in that situation, getting more criticism from your supervision group) will help you get much more in touch with the kinds of things that are exaggerating and escalating your feelings of being put down, your feelings about yourself and so on.

29.   DAVID: Let me ask you a question, Rose. Do you feel, from the description I gave, that I wasn't in touch with my feelings?

30.   ROSE: Yes, I felt so. I felt, as you said before, that you really wanted to cry and squelched the feeling. But if you did feel like crying and cried, what was it going to get for you?

31.   DAVID: Well, I suppose that if I did cry and people heard me cry, all those people are going to feel very sorry for having done this to me—criticized me.

32.   THERAPIST: And change their behavior if they hear me cry and moan!

33.   DAVID: Yes—and change their behavior.

34.   JOAN: David, you say you want feedback from your supervision group. But you also said that you feel that some of what you get is really not feedback but a putdown. And I'm wondering if what you're calling putdown is, in fact, feedback that you can't accept—suggesting that you're really not looking for feedback, but you're looking for approval for what you're doing. And when you don't get it, you call it a putdown.

35.   DAVID: Yes, I think you've got a well-taken point there. It occurs to me that negative feedback or constructive criticism, which is what I'm probably getting, is somehow tied in my head with loss of love or loss or approval.

36.   THERAPIST: And with horror at this loss. But suppose Joan is right and that you always are going for positive feedback, for approval, and saying, "It's horrible not to get it!" Then what's the next step? Which I don't think you're taking!

37.   DAVID: I could ask myself, "Why is it horrible?"

38.   THERAPIST: Do you *do* that? I haven't got any indication, so far today, that you got to that step. You say, "Yes, I'm wrong for feeling it's horrible to be criticized." Or, "Yes, I'm wrong for feeling defensive." I get that. But do you ever say, "*Why* is it horrible to not be approved?"

39.   DAVID: If I do it, it's very superficial.

40.	JOAN:	And seldom, I guess!

40.   JOAN: And seldom, I guess!

41.   JOHN: I think further, though, before you ever ask that question, I think it's important to find out whether you are thinking that.

42.   THERAPIST: But he did seem meaningfully to agree with Joan that he is thinking that.

43.   JOHN: He's thinking that, but what exactly is going on inside him? Whether he's thinking that or whether he's thinking in some other terms.

44.   DAVID: My strategy is to behave so that people will respond to me in a sort of, uh, positive, loving kind of way.

45.   JOAN: Instead of really facing the fact that "I do think it's terrible if they don't. And shit!—I'd better give up that belief!" You immediately jump back to point A, the Activating event, and say, "How can I change A, so that they'll approve of me?" So you're really skipping over B, your Belief system, which is creating your turned-off escape from feeling at point C.

46.   JOHN: I still think you're very unclear about the nature of that Belief at B. For you to spell out that Belief more specifically would be the thing.

47.   DAVID: I don't know how to do it. What do you want me to do?

48.   JOHN: For example, when you're feeling hurt or feel like crying, have you sat down and tried to figure out what's going on in your head—what kind of feelings are happening?

49.   MARY: David, I've got a feeling that you're saying one thing and feeling something else right now. You're just looking exasperated.

50.   DAVID: I feel kind of frustrated. I—I really made touch with what Joan said.

51.   THERAPIST: But you're not making touch with what John said. John is telling you exactly what he would like you to do and then you say, "I don't know what you want me to do."

52.   DAVID: I can't see concretely what to do.

53.   THERAPIST: But he's being concrete. Except, John, you may be lousing David up with the word *feeling*. Forget about that word! Let me repeat what John said. Let's suppose you feel very hurt. Now I think it's fairly clear what you frequently do to avoid feeling that way. You said it a couple of minutes ago: "I immediately try to change my behavior and change that behavior so I won't feel hurt."

54.   DAVID: Yes, that's what I usually do. I turn right off and feel practically nothing.

55.   THERAPIST: Now, instead of letting yourself just do that and keep doing that self-defeatingly and never get to the source of your problem or how to solve it, John is telling you, (1) "Stay with your feelings," and (2) "Look exactly for what you're doing, what you're saying to yourself, to create the hurt. Take the responsibility for hurting yourself. And look precisely for your Beliefs, at B, which lead you to create it. Don't just infer what these Beliefs are. Because that's what you're doing; you're inferring it from the book. "Well, I guess I must be saying this and this to myself when I feel hurt and withdraw." But John is saying: "Don't guess. Look for what you are

actually believing, actually saying to yourself. There's something precise there, and it may not be the sentence we're using or those you read in the book."

56.   JOE: [a 50-year-old accountant]: There are two reasons for prolonging the feeling of hurt that you're trying to avoid having: (1) so that you can see more precisely what you're thinking to create it, and (2) so that you can challenge your idea that you can't tolerate this feeling. So it seems that a major suggestion for the first step is for you to prolong the feeling—so that you can use it to examine the feeling itself and to check the idea that you can't stand it.

57.   THERAPIST: Yes, stay with it. And then do what John is suggesting—which is, first, "What am I doing to create it?" and then also, "Why can't I tolerate it?" For that is another thing you're probably saying to yourself: "I can't tolerate the feeling of hurt. I must get rid of it immediately!" But we'd like to see that you're saying that. You're just inferring it. And you don't really see what is going on in your head just before you have the feeling and attempt to squelch it. Most people, when they at first infer what they're saying to themselves, later manage to see it as clear as a bell—as I say in one of my books. But you somehow manage to skip seeing it clearly. And you say, "Well, I guess I'm saying that." Then you don't get on to the next step: "Well, if I am saying that, why the hell do I have to believe what I'm saying?" You're not contradicting your belief because you're not really admitting what you're saying. Now, is that clear?

58.   DAVID: Yes.

59.   THERAPIST: But why wasn't it clear before? John said it pretty well. Why wasn't it clear when he said it?

59a.   DAVID: I don't think he said it that clearly. It has to be clearer, for me to get it, than he put it. When you're saying to me, it's very clear, very specific, very concrete. I understand it. It's very direct.

60.   JOAN: And he also said it more vigorously. Was it the vigor?

61.   DAVID: No, I don't think so.

62.   JOHN: He was more direct, though. Is that it?

63.   DAVID: I think it was the directness. That's what I respond to. [To John]: I had a feeling that you wanted me to say something, but I wasn't sure what you wanted me to say.

64.   JOAN: So you started debating with yourself, "What'll I say? What'll I say?" Is that right?

65.   DAVID: Yes. I wasn't able to zero in on John's wavelength because I wasn't sure of where he was going.

66.   JOHN: Do you find it difficult to think that I'm simply inquiring, just asking—rather than having some previously conceived idea that you've got to come up with?

67.   THERAPIST: But you do have a preconceived idea. That's horseshit, to pretend that you don't!

68.   JOHN: Oh, I do, but . . .

69. THERAPIST: Yeah! So he says to himself, "He's inquiring, when he knows fuck-
ing well what the answer is! So why is he inquiring in that fashion?"
So—you're giving him an extra problem!

70. JOHN: To an extent. But specifically, I suspect he's thinking something
along the lines we reached with him.

71. DAVID: But, John . . .

72. JOHN: But the exact nature, that I don't know.

73. DAVID: I realize that it would be better if you could evoke this from me. But
if I can't go with you, perhaps the next best thing is to be more direct
and tell me what you think I am doing.

74. THERAPIST: You'd better take a flyer and say, "Isn't it *x*? Isn't it *y*? Isn't it *z*?"

75. DAVID: Yes.

76. THERAPIST: You're doing it too nondirectively. "What is it?" That sometimes
works. But with confused people, it often does more harm than good.

77. DAVID: Yes, I think it does in my case.

78. MARY: We seem to be coming to the end of the session. Why don't we give
David some homework?

79. THERAPIST: Yes. What would you suggest for yourself, David?

80. DAVID: Well, you all suggested, which I think is good, that when I begin to
feel hurt, that I prolong that feeling rather than moving to my
defensive kind of comfortable avoidance.

81. MARY: Stay with your feeling and. . .?

82. DAVID: Try really to experience or come in touch with what in fact I am saying to myself to cause these feelings. And to challenge those statements.
And also to challenge the statement that I can't stand the feeling.

83. MARY: Well spoken!

84. JOHN: Yes, let me emphasize that maybe the first few times exploring it or
investigating it can be the prime thing to do before you get in there
and start questioning it too much. I find you really have to do it two
or three times before you really discover all the crap that's going on
in your head, before you really ferret out all those meanings you
believe that accompany your feelings.

85. JOE: On the other hand, he might be able to start on one of them, see
clearly what his meaning is, and knock it down before he starts on
the other meanings. Even if he doesn't discover all of his horseshit,
if he hits on one irrational idea and knocks it down, it may help him
later discover the others.

86. THERAPIST: Right! Let's not be perfectionistic! And also, I want to emphasize
what you said before, David. At one time you were in touch with
your feelings—you cried, whined, et cetera—and you found out that
it didn't lead you to the thoughts behind these feelings; and this
release of feeling did lead you to other, pernicious things, like feeling
very sorry for yourself, feeling depressed, and being unable to do
anything. The trouble with your kind of instruction, John, is that
when some people emphasize getting in touch with their feelings in
the manner that you recommend, they do it much too well and mull

around in the juices of their own goddamned negative feelings! So it's an interaction thing, the best way of doing it: letting yourself feel the feeling and looking pretty quickly for the self-defeating and irrational ideas beyond your feelings, and then, as we especially emphasize in REBT, disputing, challenging, and changing these self-defeating feelings.

87.   JOHN: I am only suggesting that Dave *find out* what's going on, since that's the first step to *changing* feelings.

88.   MARY: But they interact, they go together. I agree that we should not try to get David to be too perfectionistic—so that he first has to find all that's going on, then find all his thoughts behind his feelings, and then contradict all these defeating things. It's a little utopian!

89.   THERAPIST: Yes, and I don't think that David works this perfectionistic way. I don't think that many people work that way.

90.   JOE: And working that way may not be necessary to produce change in David.

91.   MARY: Right!

92.   JOHN: Maybe, on the other hand, though, he could use . . . Oh, when your turning off happens, David, you could investigate your thoughts more than once and not assume that you have found them all the first time you do so.

93.   THERAPIST: Oh, yes. Once you start working on it, as several of the group members are saying, you can later work on another aspect of your thinking, and then another aspect, and then still another aspect. You do not have to do it all at once, the first time. Is that clear, David?

94.   DAVID: Fine, I'll try that.

DISCUSSION OF PROTOCOL

Many of the main aspects of REBT group work are illustrated in the excerpt from this session. Let me make the following points in this connection:

Response 4: Mary brings up the possibility that David's real problem is his worth as an individual; that is, his downing of *himself*, his *total being*, if he fails in a single major aspect of his life, such as in the eyes of his supervision group. She does this not merely because David has already shown, in previous sessions or earlier in this one, that he is overconcerned about his worth as a person but because, on *theoretical* grounds, REBT holds that this is a basic problem of *most* humans. They not only rate their *performances* (which is often good and happiness-producing) but rate *themselves* (which is illegitimate and shame-producing). REBT constantly fights against this *self*-rating tendency; and as a member of an REBT group and consequently one of its practitioners, Mary raises the issue of self-rating and asks David if this is not one of his fundamental problems.

Response 9: David says, "I know by the book what the rational answer is," because he (and the other group members) read such recommended books as *A Guide to Rational Living* (Ellis & Harper, 1997), *Reason and Emotion in Psychotherapy* (Ellis, 1994c), and *A Guide to Personal Happiness* (Ellis & Becker, 1982). Bibliotherapy is a strong part of REBT, and it is frequently found that it aids the therapeutic process appreciably. But one of the main purposes of individual and group REBT sessions is to make sure that the client actually *thinks through* rather than *passively parrots* some of the rational ideas he partly gets through the reading.

Response 12: Joan rightly emphasizes that David's "knowing" that "the criticism of me that the supervision group is making is not really all that important" will do him little good unless he consistently works at applying this knowledge whenever he feels shame in his gut or acts defensively to run away frrom this shame. In REBT the client is not only shown, to use a superstition model, that he magically and unrealistically believes that viewing a black cat can hurt him, but he is also shown that he had better work and work to *dis*believe that superstition before he can expect to become unaffected by the thought of seeing a black cat. Unless he *actively proves to himself*, many times, that his seeing a black cat cannot possibly harm him, he is not likely to think that it will merely because he "knows" that he is superstitious about black cats.

Response 14: The therapist is not only active in REBT group work but is frequently the most active, meaning the most actively *teaching*, member of the group. He encourages other members to use the REBT system to help therapize the individuals bringing up concrete problems; but he also supplements what these group members say, particularly if they omit important aspects of an issue. Here he brings up the point that clients not only feel inadequate and worthless because they condemn themselves (rather than their poor performances) but also that, once they *recognize* the self-downing feelings, they frequently denigrate themselves again for *having* such negative feelings. He tries to encourage David to see that he is damning himself *twice*, for the original criticism he receives from his supervision group and for his feeling depressed about the criticism.

Response 16: The therapist emphasizes the main cognitive aspect of REBT: the client's *attacking* his own irrational ideas about others' criticizing him, once he has *seen* and *understood* that he has these ideas. This is one of the main differences between REBT and many other "insight" therapies. The latter may clearly reveal to the client what he is thinking to create his "emotional" disturbances, but they rarely try to persuade him, as REBT does, to directly and vigorously attack, challenge, or dispute these ideas. REBT teaches him a logicoempirical method (i.e., the basic method of science) of *disputing* his unrealistic and dysfunctional hypotheses about people and the world. It teaches most clients to be scientific about *themselves* and their own lives—to be flexible, undogmatic, and antiabsolutistic, which is the essence of the scientific method. Without this kind of active disputation and scientific thinking, at first done by the therapist and then taught to the clients to do for themselves (for the rest of their lives), REBT simply wouldn't be REBT (Ellis, 1962, 1963, 1994c, 1996a, 1996b).

Response 20: The therapist (and other group members) remind David that he is not merely *getting* upset or *being made* upset by external people or events. He is specifically *doing* something *himself* to bring on his feelings of disturbance (or his defenses against these feelings). In REBT each client is urged to take *full responsibility* for his dysfunctional feelings and never to hold that *others* made him have such feelings. He is taught to say, "I made myself angry" or "I upset myself," rather than "It made me angry" or "You upset me." REBT theory and practice says to the Davids of the world: "Since you are doing something to upset yourself and since you can almost invariably change what you are doing, let's get you to find out exactly what you are doing (including what you are telling yourself) so that you can many times undo it. The so-called why of your upsetness is rather meaningless unless it concretely includes what you are doing to make yourself upset."

Response 27: When the therapist says that David has psychoanalytical-type insight, he means that he has, at most, only the first of three insights that are stressed in REBT. Insight No. 1 is the client's realization that he has some kind of symptom and that it is psychologically caused, that is, connected with some antecedent process (such as his innate and acquired tendencies to condemn himself when he makes some "serious" error). Insight No. 2 is his realization that, no matter how, when, and where his basic dysfunctional ideas arose (how and why he originally started blaming himself for his mistakes), he now actively carries on this self-defeating process. This *continuation* or *here-and-nowness* of the dysfunctional philosophy is really the issue, rather than its supposed (and often unrevealable) origin. Insight No. 3 is his realization that because he very vigorously still holds onto his fundamental irrational ideas (and may even have a strong biological tendency to keep believing in them), nothing short of persistent *work and practice* at disbelieving them is likely to change them significantly. The therapist, in this response, is really urging David to acknowledge the importance of Insights No. 2 and 3, now that he seems to have Insight No. 1 (Ellis, 1963, 1985c, 1994c, 1996a).

Response 36: A little more explicitly than the other members of the group, the therapist emphasizes the *horror* that David feels whenever he gets negative feedback or criticism. This, again, is the essence of REBT: to show the client not merely that he thinks that something, such as criticism of himself by others, is bad but that it is *awful, horrible, or terrible*. For when a human being evaluates something as bad, inconvenient, unfortunate, or disadvantageous, he normally stays within the realm of reality, for these are empirically *provable* assessments. Thus, David may be able to show how it would truly be unpleasant or inconvenient to him if he kept getting negative feedback from his supervision group and thus was shown to be a fairly inadequate therapist. But he cannot (nor can anyone else) possibly show that such an unpleasantness or inconvenience is truly *awful or horrible*. Why? Because *awful* usually means *totally bad* or *more than* unfortunate. And it means that because David's poor therapeutic behavior is disadvantageous, he *absolutely shouldn't* or *mustn't* behave in the manner and is a *rotten person* if he does (Ellis, 1987a; Ellis & Becker, 1982).

But of course nothing in reality can be *more than* unfortunate. Absolutistic "shouldn'ts" and "mustn'ts" are magical fictions, categorical absolutes, that have no true existence. And David, *as a person*, cannot be entirely rotten, even though some or much of his behavior may be poor and ineffectual. So REBT, through the therapist and the group members, tries to keep teaching David to give up these absolutistic, demonological *awfuls*, *shouldn'ts*, and *rotten person* concepts and to live thoroughly in reality (which can be disadvantageous enough, without his dreaming up imaginary *horrors* to add to its disadvantages) (Ellis, 1985c, 1994c, 1995a, 1996a; Ellis & Abrams, 1994).

Response 45: Joan tries to get David back to the essential ABCs of REBT. According to rational emotive behavior theory, David experiences an Activating event at point A, his being responded to negatively by members of his supervision group. Immediately, at point C, his emotional Consequence, he reacts with feelings of anxiety or depression and then with a defense against these feelings, numbness or avoidance of the "traumatizing" situation at A. He tends to believe wrongly, as most disturbed individuals do, that A causes C—that the Activating events cause him to feel anxious or to retreat defensively. However, B, his Belief system, is the real issue. At B he first has a set of Rational Beliefs (RBs): "How unfortunate for them to be so critical of me! I wish I were a better therapist and they criticized me less! How annoying to be found out like this!" If he stayed rigorously with these Beliefs and did not magically add to them, he would feel healthily, sorry, sad, frustrated, and irritated and would usually be motivated to get even more feedback from his supervision group, at point A, and to change the therapeutic behavior that is encouraging them to criticize him.

But being human (and innately and by training predisposed to think magically and demonologically), David goes on to a very important set of Irrational Beliefs (IBs): "Isn't it *horrible* that they are so critical of me! I *have to be* a better therapist and be criticized less! I'm a *thorough ass and rotten person* if they keep seeing me in this negative light!" These highly self-defeating, unvalidatable, unfalsifiable Beliefs cause him to feel anxious and depressed and to make him numbly run away from facing his critics.

If he sticks with the REBT framework, he will force himself, no matter how hard it is for him to do so, to acknowledge his painful feelings at C, to see clearly the irrational Beliefs (IBs) with which he is creating them, and to Dispute them at D. His Disputing follows the logical, empirical, and pragmatic methods of challenging any hypothesis: "*Why* is it horrible that the members of my supervision group are so critical of me? *Where is the evidence* that I *have to be* a better therapist and be criticized less? How does their seeing me negatively *prove* that I am truly a thorough ass and a rotten person? What kind of results will I get if I keep believing that I *absolutely must not* be criticized?" In using REBT Disputing, David also gives up his dogmatic *musts* and looks for (as science flexibly does) alternative theories and solutions to solve his problem (Dryden & Ellis, 1986; Ellis, 1962, 1973, 1985b, 1985c, 1987, 1994c, 1996a, 1996b).

If David will persist at this kind of rational emotive behavioral attack on his irrational Beliefs, he will almost always tend to end up with E—an Effective New Philosophy. E is the logical, realistic, and pragmatic answer to D (Disputing). For example: "Well, it really is too bad that my supervision group sees me as being so ineffectual as a therapist, but that's all it is, too bad! Now, in order to improve this bad position that I'm in, why don't I heed their suggestions, change some of my procedures, become a more effective therapist, and gain more approval from them? In fact, whether *they* approve of me or not, why don't I use their criticism to help me as a therapist so that I can better enjoy myself and help others in that capacity?" If he comes to this kind of conclusion, David will almost always find that his feelings of anxiety and depression will vanish and that he will not have to drive himself into defensive numbness.

Therefore, Joan (and then John) try to help David to see the ABCs of his disturbance and to work through them at D (Disputing) until he arrives at E (Effective New Philosophy).

Response 53: The therapist, attempting to clarify what John has been saying to David, tries to get him to stay with his feelings of anxiety instead of immediately retreating from them and then to look specifically for his ideas, his Irrational Beliefs (IBs), with which he creates such feelings. But instead of vaguely *inferring* what these Beliefs are (which he can do on the basis of REBT theory), he endorses John's point that David had better concretely *search for* these Beliefs.

Response 56: Joe, who has been silent up to this point, comes in to reinforce what John, the therapist, and others are saying to David. In REBT, all the group members are encouraged to be therapists to any one member who raises a problem. The theory says that the more of this kind of thing that occurs, the more likely is the problem-presenting member to be helped. Moreover, by helping talk him out of his difficulties, the other group members (most of whom have similar philosophic problems of downing themselves when they make errors and are socially criticized) are likely to talk themselves out of their own basic Irrational Beliefs (Bard, 1980; Ellis, 1962, 1985c, 1992c).

Response 63: If David is right, and it was directness rather than more democratic or Socratic questioning that he responded to, this is an important point that is often overlooked in therapy. It is conventionally assumed, especially by psychoanalytical or person-centered therapists (Freud, 1965; Rogers,

1961), that the client will be most benefited if he comes to basic insights about himself largely on his own, or with a minimum of therapist teaching. But REBT theory says that this is all very well with some clients but that others are so confused and befuddled when they come to therapy that direct teaching is likely to help them more than any kind of nondirective reflection of feeling (Ellis, 1962, 1971a, 1973, 1985c, 1994a, 1995a, 1996a, 1996b; Ellis & Abrahms, 1978; Ellis & Harper, 1997).

In this particular instance, John's somewhat objective and nondirective questioning of David mainly influenced David to say to himself, "I wonder what 'right' answer he wants me to give? What is it he wants? What is it he wants?" This helped him to create greater anxiety and to be *less* likely to give the "right" answer. When the therapist and other group members, however, more directly gave David the "right" answer and then asked if it was correct in his case, he was more able to handle this answer, to reflect on it, and to make it his own. Even though the therapist largely restated John's original points, David felt much more comfortable with this restatement and was able to use it. Direct teaching, in his case, paid off better than more "democratic" indirectness. John, a psychiatrist, was so "psychological" that he wasn't sufficiently direct!

Response 76: The more David is asked about why he did not respond to John but did respond to the therapist's restatement of what John said, the more it appears that he is one of those confused people who can use considerable therapeutic direction and that with him, as with many such people, open-ended questioning can do more harm than good. Perhaps John's line of questioning would have eventually paid off if the other group members were not present to interfere with it. But perhaps it would have only continued to help David become more confused. Anyway, the therapist, seeing what was happening, did not hesitate to intervene and try to help David in another way. And his active intervention seems to have paid off, at least in this particular instance. In other instances it is possible that it would have been more disruptive than helpful. But in general it is found that highly directive and didactic presentations of REBT material within a group session, especially to confused clients, frequently produces excellent results and sometimes produces them when other less directive techniques do not help the client.

Response 78: In REBT, in vivo or activity homework assignments are frequently given because it is held that clients not only talk themselves but act themselves into disordered behavior; hence, it is highly valuable for them to act in a less disordered way before they become truly habituated, in thought and feeling as well as in behavior, to that new and healthier way of life. Typically, clients who are nonassertive are given homework assignments of approaching members of the other sex, trying for new jobs, or otherwise acting more assertively. And clients who are hostile and avoidant are given assignments of deliberately jumping into hostility-creating situations (such as visiting hated relatives) and training themselves how to think and feel less hostilely while they are doing so.

In David's case he is given the assignment of staying with his uncomfortable (anxiety-inciting) feelings, to challenge his Irrational Beliefs (IBs) that he *can't stand* these feelings, and to find his other basic self-defeating Beliefs, such as the idea that he is a horrible person if he continues to draw negative criticism from his supervision group and to actively Dispute these Beliefs until he gives them up. Urged on by the group to these assignments, David largely carried them out during the next few weeks and seemed to benefit considerably in terms of being able, first, to keep in touch with his feelings of anxiety and, second, to minimize these feelings. Two months after the session that is reported here he was able to report back to the group that he had become one of the most open individuals in his supervision group and that he had no difficulty facing this supervision group's criticism of his therapy sessions.

Response 86: The therapist points out that although it is advisable for David to get in touch with his feelings of hurt about criticism, being *too much* in touch with such feelings, as he used to be, has its own distinct disadvantages and is not to be recommended. The *reason* for getting in touch with one's feelings, in REBT, is not merely to acknowledge them and to feel them but to *change* them when they are self-defeating. Moreover, REBT does not assume that if clients *merely* reveal and express their feelings they automatically will improve. It hypothesizes, instead, that a truly therapeutic understanding of one's feelings includes the understanding of the philosophies that one is employing to create them *and* a radical changing of these philosophies when they consistently lead to anxiety, depression, and hostility.

Response 88: Just as REBT combats human perfectionism in general and shows how it is the root of much evil, it combats perfectionism in therapy itself. The goal of REBT is not to have the clients *perfectly* understand or change themselves, because they will always remain quite fallible humans and will have difficulties and problems of one sort or another. Its goal is to have them reduce much of their *needless* emotional pain and suffering but not to become truly unemotional or even devoid of healthy negative emotions, such as sorrow, regret, and extreme annoyance, when faced with truly obnoxious Activating events. REBT mainly teaches human tolerance, including tolerance of imperfect therapeutic results!

Troubled humans can decide to work persistently at changing and acting against their irrational beliefs, or they can get help in doing so from straighter-thinking therapists or friends or from books, lectures, demonstrations, tape recordings, and other sources (Ellis, 1993a, 1996a). They can help themselves in a large-scale group or class; they can also work with an individual therapist or group leader. If they choose a regular small-scale group process and if they pick a therapy group that follows rational emotive behavioral or cognitive-behavioral principles, they will avail themselves of a multifaceted, comprehensive therapeutic procedure that has been shown to be effective in a large number of research studies and clinical presentations. It is hypothesized that REBT group treatment is more likely to help people find a quicker, deeper, and more lasting solution to their emotional problems than other contemporary methods of psychotherapy (Ellis, 1973, 1982b, 1992c; Shostrom, Ellis, & Greenwald, 1976).

8

Rational Emotive Behavioral Marathons and Intensives

We and our associates at the Institute for Rational Emotive Behavior Therapy in New York City have been experimenting for 20 years with various types of encounter groups in order to develop a procedure that would accomplish two main goals: first, to provide maximum encountering experiences for all the group members and, second, to include a good measure of cognitive and action-oriented group psychotherapy that is designed not only to help the participants *feel* better but also to *get* better. We have participated during this time in several hundred marathon groups and intensives. We have deliberately used a variety of techniques, ranging from the usual REBT procedures to many of the highly experiential or expressive methods that are commonly employed in basic encounter and marathon groups (Bach, 1966; Ellis, 1969; Otto, 1968; Perls, 1969; Schutz, 1967.

We have devised and have often successfully used a procedure that we call a Rational Emotive Behavioral Marathon. This procedure is more highly structured than the usual basic encounter, and it is deliberately weighted more on the verbal than on the nonverbal side.

LENGTH OF MARATHONS

REBT marathons may take from 10 to 14 hours. A marathon group usually consists of 12 to 18 people and can be run by one leader or two co-leaders. Institute marathons are led only by professional therapists who have been solidly trained in individual and group REBT and who have also had special marathon training.

Parts of this chapter were adapted from Albert Ellis, "A Weekend of Rational Encounter," in Arthur Burton (Ed.), *Encounter* (pp. 112–127), San Francisco: Jossey-Bass, 1969. Used by permission.

OPENING PROCEDURES

A typical rational emotive behavioral marathon begins with the leader welcoming the participants, explaining to them that everything that goes on in the group will be strictly confidential and is to be subsequently discussed only with other group members. All participants are then asked to introduce themselves and to answer the questions "Why are you here? How do you feel at this moment about being here?" All members are given a maximum of 5 minutes to present themselves. They are allowed to take as little time as they want and to run down before 5 minutes are up.

The group members are then asked the following one or two questions: (1) "What are you bothering yourself about most right now, either (a) in this group situation or (b) in your outside life?" (1) "What are you most ashamed of at present? Be as honest as you can be." While individuals are responding to these questions, other group members are permitted briefly to query them, to find out how they feel and what is going on inside them. The leader then says to the group, "*Look* for something right now that touches you emotionally (positively or negatively). Feel it. Report your feeling to the group." Several of the members may volunteer to express their feelings at this point, or all of them may be called upon.

SOME SUBSEQUENT PROCEDURES

A number of regular and special experiential exercises are used throughout the REBT marathon. For example, the group leader may say, "Think of something risky you can do at this moment. Do it." Again, volunteers can be allowed to respond, or all group members can be asked to do something risky. If some remain silent, they can be asked: "Why didn't you think or do something risky after the other members did so?" (The group leader explains, at some point during the early stages of the marathon or at this particular point, that members are allowed to do anything they like in the group as long as it is not physically harmful to themselves or others. Breaking the furniture or jumping out of the window, for example, is not allowed; taking off one's clothes or calling someone names is permitted.)

The leader may say, "With what member of this group would you like to have a love or affectionate experience? Ask this person if he or she will cooperate with you in having this kind of experience. If he or she consents, engage in it as much as you can do, right now. If both of you feel that you would like to have or to continue this love experience outside the room, you may leave the group for a maximum of 5 minutes and have it in one of the other rooms in the building. Be sure, however, to return after 5 minutes are up." The leader then sees that (1) individuals having love or affectionate experiences in the room are asked about what they felt during the experience; (2) individuals who do not choose to have love experiences with anyone are asked why they did not choose to do so; (3) individuals who choose to go out of the room for 5 minutes to have their love experiences are asked, when they return to the room, to describe in detail exactly what they did and what they felt while doing it. In one way or another, all the members of the group are induced either to have warm experiences with at least one other member or to report why they do not desire to have them.

REBT PROCEDURES

The leader says, "Pick out someone in the group who you think might well be able to use some help with one of his or her basic problems. Sit in the center of the group with him or her and try to help with these problems." All or most of the members are encouraged to work with at least one other member about his or her problems. Then the other members of the group, after watching and listening for a while, are encouraged to join in to help the individual whom the selector is trying to help. By the time this procedure is instituted, virtually all the members have had sufficient opportunity—usually over a period of 5 or 6 hours—to express themselves, to engage in some nonverbal (especially affectionate) behavior, and to show what some of their problem areas are. They are therefore presumably ready for more detailed examination of their main problems; and this technique intimately involves at least two members at a time in the problem-solving process; encourages the members, whether they like it or not, to go into more details about their thoughts, feelings, and behavior than they previously may have done; and actively gets around to the REBT aspect of the marathon, with the therapist beginning to supervise the actual attempts of the members to help each other.

This problem-solving and cognitive restructuring part of the marathon is usually repeated several times. Thus, Jim and Jane sit in the center of the group and Jane helps Jim with his problem, let us say, of making himself severely depressed when he is socially rejected. Jane tries to show Jim what his Irrational Beliefs (IB's) are that lead to his depressed feelings, and to help him Dispute these IB's. The leader of the marathon group, who is well trained in REBT, supervises Jane and helps her work with Jim. The leader also encourages other members to help Jane and assist Jim to think more rationally. This part of the marathon resembles the work done in regular REBT group therapy and largely consists of cognitive restructuring. All the members of the marathon group are taught some of the main principles of the ABCDE's of REBT and all or most of them are given a chance to use these principles with other group members and also to apply them to one of their own emotional and/or behavioral problems. As the marathon continues, the members usually become considerably more adept at using the ABCDE's of REBT under the watchful supervising eye of the leader, who in turn tends to become a better REBT teacher.

CLOSING PROCEDURES

After the marathon has reached its two-thirds point, a modified version of Fritz Perls' "hot seat" exercise is given; the usual version, where everyone is encouraged to take the "hot seat" and also forced to comment on everyone who takes the seat, is usually too time-consuming and inefficient. In the REBT version all participants are encouraged (but not forced) to sit in the hot seat in the center of the room and all the others are encouraged (but not forced) to tell them—*briefly!*—their positive and negative thoughts and feelings about them, particularly in regard to how they have behaved in the marathon. The person in the hot seat is not allowed to answer or rebut these comments. But at the end of the exercise anyone who cares to reply is briefly allowed to do so.

In the closing hours of the rational emotive behavioral encounter marathon the group and the leader usually tend to smoke out anyone who has not as yet brought up any problem for detailed discussion. Such individuals are directly asked why they have not said too much about themselves previously and are induced to look for a major problem and to discuss it openly.

In the closing hours of the marathon there can be round-robins on these questions: (1) "What are a few of the most important experiences you have had during the marathon and the most important things you have learned about yourself?" (2) "In thinking about your marathon experience, what are some of the things that you did not say to the group or to individuals in the group when you had the chance to do so previously? Say these things now."

For the final half-hour or so of the marathon the leader selects one member of the group at a time to sit in the center of the room while the leader says to the rest of the group: "Anyone who can think of a suitable homework assignment to give X that might help her solve some of the problems raised here or to live more happily and creatively in the future, suggest this kind of an assignment right now. Let X, if necessary, take notes about these assignments so as not to forget them."

After the REBT marathon encounter has ended, a date may be set for 6 to 10 weeks ahead, at which time the group members are invited to return to the original setting for about 4 hours to discuss what they think they got from the original marathon, what changes may have been effected in their lives as a result of it, how they carried out (or failed to carry out) the homework assignments that were given them, and other questions of this sort.

REBT INTENSIVES

Therapeutic lectures, classes, and sermons have been given for many centuries by Confucius, Epictetus, Mary Baker Eddy, Emile Coué, Dale Carnegie, Normal Vincent Peale, and other teachers and preachers. After the experiential movement got going in the 1960s, Werner Erhard and a number of his imitators started in the 1970s to combine emotive-evocative exercises with impassioned lectures and to give weekend Intensives. These include lectures, experiential exercises, and emotional sharing and are usually given to groups of 50 to 200 people.

I (AE) had a series of planning sessions with several of our therapists at the Institute for Rational-Emotive Therapy in New York in 1983 and we devised a 9-hour REBT Intensive. I, Ray DiGiuseppe, Diana Richman, Janet Wolfe, and a number of Fellows and Associate Fellows of the institute have been giving these Intensives every year in New York and other major cities and have found them to be quite effective. In fact, a study that we did of self-ratings of participants before they took the Intensive and 2 months after they took it showed significant improvement in their healthy Beliefs (Ellis, Sichel, Leaf, et al., 1989). Personal communications by participants who were new to REBT and by those who also had some REBT sessions before taking the Intensive also bear out this finding.

The REBT Intensive commonly used by the institute usually has six major sections, each of which takes about 1 1/4 hours: (1) "The ABCs of REBT and Disputing of Irrational Beliefs," (2) "Perfectionism and Unconditional Self-Acceptance," (3) "Dealing with Anger and Rage," (4) "Dealing with the Dire Need for Approval and Love Slobbism," (5) "Dealing with Low Frustration Tolerance," and (6) "Goal Setting and Homework."

Each section starts with a strong, evocative lecture on the REBT approach to understanding and handling a major aspect of emotional disturbance, followed by an experiential exercise that all the participants are encouraged to perform. Then there is a 15-minute period for the sharing of thoughts and feelings about the lecture and about participation in the exercise. By the end of the 9-hour Intensive almost all the participants have been drawn into the exercises and the sharing of their feelings. Many of them report dramatic personal experiences in the course of the Intensive, as well as later changes in their lives.

The Intensive has a number of cognitive advantages for the participants, including learning the general principles of REBT; learning to take responsibility for many of their emotional and personality problems; modeling themselves after other Intensive participants who begin opening themselves up; seeing their own problems, of which they were previously unaware; and seeing how many other people are suffering from similar problems.

A good deal of cognitive restructing is included in every Intensive. Each lecture shows that Irrational Beliefs are quite different from Rational Beliefs and lead to unhealthy feelings and behaviors. Several of the sections show participants how to dispute and change their iBs and how to reach Effective New Philosophies (E's). Methods of reframing and of REBT referenting (cost-benefit analysis) are explained and illustrated. When the participants give unrealistic and illogical answers during some of the exercises, the leader of the Intensive briefly and sometimes humorously responds to them and shows them and the rest of the participants what more practical solutions would be. Participants are encouraged to ask questions and briefly raise personal problems; and these are answered by the leader in terms of REBT philosophies. Some illustrative disputing of the dysfunctional Beliefs of several participants is done. Several people are shown how to specifically question their own iBs, to come up with alternative RB's, and to take for homework assignments the steady and vigorous repetition of their newly arrived at Effective Philosophies.

Emotively, the Intensive participants receive forceful presentations of REBT and engage in some of its dramatic-evocative exercises, such as its famous shame-attacking exercise. They are encouraged to take verbal and activity risks, participate in the singing of rational humorous songs, and urged to be adventure-seeking and pleasure-seeking.

Behaviorally, participants are given active-directive instructions, are encouraged to take on goal-seeking and homework assignments, and are given practice in carrying out REBT thinking, encountering, and skill training. The Institute for Rational Emotive Behavior Therapy in New York also offers a series of follow-up talks and workshops on various aspects of REBT that are open to any Intensive participants who want to take part in them. If some individuals realize, in the course of the Intensive, that they have ongoing personality problems, the Institute also offers regular sessions of individual and group therapy that they can arrange to take. As usual, the Institute also distributes a good many pamphlets, books, audio- and videocassettes, and other self-help materials that Intensive participants can use for continuing homework assignments.

As is also true of individuals who have effective REBT Marathon experiences, those who benefit from REBT Intensives may experience a cognitive and emotional "high" for a few weeks following their participation but may easily fall back later to their former lower levels of functioning. This has been found in participants of all kinds of marathons and intensives. Therefore, follow-up procedures and materials had better be available for participants who are willing to use important aspects of REBT on a continuing basis.

9

Teaching the Principles of Unconditional Self-Acceptance in a Structured Group Setting

In this chapter we will describe an 8-week psychoeducational group that I (WD) run, in which I teach group members the REBT principles of unconditional self-acceptance. In the chapter we will do the following:

1. Briefly review the REBT concept of ego disturbance.
2. Present the REBT principles of unconditional self-acceptance.
3. Outline the steps of a self-acceptance group, some of the exercises that can be used at each step and discuss briefly the context in which I run these groups.

REBT AND EGO DISTURBANCE

REBT therapists can, in our view, be seen as psychological educators in that they teach their clients (a) the basic REBT view of disturbance and (b) how to identify, challenge, and change the Irrational Beliefs that underpin their psychological problems. Because this chapter concerns a structured group approach to teaching clients unconditional self-acceptance, we will briefly review the REBT concept of ego disturbance before presenting in the next section the REBT concept of unconditional self-acceptance.

Adapted from Windy Dryden (1996), "Teaching the Principles of Unconditional Self-Acceptance in a Structured, Group Setting." In R. Bayne, I. Horton, & J. Bimrose (Eds.), *New directions in counselling*. London: Routledge. Used by permission.

Ego Disturbance

REBT theory distinguishes between two major types of psychological disturbance: ego disturbance and discomfort disturbance (Dryden, 1994a). Ego disturbance stems from irrational beliefs related to a person's "self," whereas
discomfort disturbance stems from irrational beliefs related to that individual's
personal domain unconnected to his "self" but centrally concerned with his
sense of comfort.

Ego disturbance results when a person makes a demand on himself, others,
or the world; and when that demand is not met, the person puts himself down
in some way. The following themes are usually involved in ego disturbance:

- failing to achieve an important target or goal
- acting incompetently (in public or private)
- not living up to one's standards
- breaking one's ethical code
- being criticized
- being ridiculed
- not being accepted, approved, appreciated, or loved by significant others

Although irrational ego Beliefs are found in a variety of emotional disturbances, we are not saying that such beliefs completely account for the emotions listed below. Rather, we are saying that these beliefs are often found when
clients report these emotional experiences.

In the following examples of ego disturbance, you will note that each of
these Irrational Beliefs contains two elements. First, there is a demanding
Belief, which often takes the form of a "must," "absolutely should," "have to,"
or "got to"; second, there is a self-downing Belief, which takes the form of a
global negative evaluation of one's total "self." REBT theory states that self-
downing Beliefs tend to be derived from musturbatory beliefs.

Depression

"Because I have failed the test, as I absolutely should not have done, I am a
failure."

"Since my partner has rejected me, as he absolutely should not have done,
this proves that I am no good."

Anxiety

"If I fail at my upcoming test, which I must not do, I would be a failure."

"If he rejects me, as I think he will soon but which he must not do, I would
be no good."

Guilt
"I have hurt the feelings of my parents, which I absolutely should not have done, and therefore am a bad person."

"I failed to help a good friend of mine. The fact that I did not do what I absolutely should have done proves that I am a rotten person."

Shame
"I have acted foolishly in front of my peers, which I absolutely should not have done, and this makes me an inadequate person."

"I have been having sexual feelings toward my sister, which I absolutely should not have, and the fact that I have these feelings makes me a shameful person."

Hurt
"My ex-boyfriend is going out with my best friend, which absolutely should not happen. Since it is happening, this proves that I am unlovable."

Anger
"You absolutely should not have criticized me in the way that you did. Your criticism reminds me that I am a failure."

Jealousy
"If my wife looks at another man, which she must not do, it means that she finds him more attractive, which must not happen and proves that I am worthless."

Envy
"My friend is making better progress than I am in our respective careers. I must have what he has; and because I don't, this makes me less worthy than I would be if I had what he has."

UNCONDITIONAL SELF-ACCEPTANCE (USA)

As we showed in the section above, ego disturbance occurs when a person makes a global negative evaluation of her total self, which in turn tends to be based on the existence of a musturbatory belief. REBT theory states that the healthy alternative to ego disturbance is rooted in a set of beliefs based on the concept of unconditional self-acceptance. In this section we will outline 10 principles that underpin this concept.

1. Human beings cannot legitimately be given a single global rating.
In the previous section we gave several examples of the ways in which people put themselves down (e.g., "I am a failure," "I am a bad person," etc.). Each

of these examples involves the person giving himself or herself a single global rating. Indeed, the concept of self-esteem frequently advocated by the majority of counselors and psychotherapists is based on this same principle. Low self-esteem involves the assignment of a single negative global rating to a person, and high self-esteem involves the assignment of a single positive global rating to the person.

REBT theory argues that it is not possible to give a person a single global rating whether negative or positive. This is best shown if we define clearly the terms *self* and *esteem*. First, let's take the term *self*. Paul Hauck (1991) has provided a very simple but profound definition of the self. He says that the self is "every conceivable thing about you that can be rated" (p. 33). This means that all your thoughts, images, feelings, behaviors, and bodily parts are part of your self, and all these different aspects that belong to you from the beginning of your life to the moment just before your death have to be included in your self. Now let's consider the term *esteem*. This term is derived from the verb *to estimate*, which means to give something a rating, judgment, or estimation. The question then arises: Can we give the self a single *legitimate* rating, estimation, or judgment that completely accounts for its complexity? The answer is clearly no. As Hauck notes, it is possible to rate different aspects of one's self, but a person is far too complex to warrant a single legitimate global rating.

Even if it were possible to give a person a single global rating—a task that would involve a team of objective judges and a computer so powerful that it could analyze the millions upon millions of data produced by that person—as soon as that global judgment was made, it would become immediately redundant because the person would continue to produce more data. In other words, a person is an ongoing, ever-changing process and thus defies the ascription of a single static global judgment (Ellis & Harper, 1994c, 1996a; Ellis & Harper, 1961a, 1997).

To summarize, it is not possible, in any legitimate sense, to give one's self a single global rating because (a) you are too complex to merit such an evaluation and (b) you are an ongoing ever-changing process that defies being statically rated.

By contrast, the concept of unconditional self-acceptance does not involve any such rating or evaluation. Rather, accepting yourself involves acknowledging that you are a complex, ongoing, ever-changing process that defies being rated by yourself or by others. However, and this is a crucial point, unconditional self-acceptance does allow you to rate different aspects of yourself. Indeed, it encourages this type of evaluation because doing so allows you to focus on your negative aspects and do something to improve them without self-blame. Conversely, if you focus on your negative aspects from the standpoint of self-esteem, then you are less likely to change them because you are sidetracked by giving your self a global negative rating for having these aspects. It is difficult to change anything about yourself while you are beating yourself over the head for having those aspects in the first place.

2. Human beings are essentially fallible.

REBT theory holds that if human beings have an essence it is probably that we are essentially fallible. As Maxie Maultsby (1984) has put it, humans have an incurable error-making tendency. I would add that we frequently make more serious mistakes than we are prepared to accept and that we often keep repeating the same errors. Why do we do this? As Paul Hauck (1991) has put it, we keep repeating our errors out of stupidity or ignorance or because we are psychologically disturbed. Albert Ellis (1994c) has noted that humans find it very easy to disturb themselves and difficult to undisturb themselves. Self-acceptance, then, means acknowledging that our essence is fallibility and that we are not perfectible.

3. All humans are equal in humanity but unequal in their different aspects

This principle follows from the two listed above. If the essence of humanity is fallibility, then all humans are equal in their humanity; and because human beings cannot be rated, it follows that no human is worthier than any other. This principle reveals REBT as one of the most, if not the most, humanistic of all psychotherapies. However, this principle of parity among humans does not deny that there is a great deal of variation among human beings with respect to their different aspects. Thus, Adolf Hitler may be equal in humanity to Mother Teresa, but in terms of their compassion toward human beings, the latter far outscores the former.

4. The rational use of the concept of human worth.

From the principles discussed thus far, you will see that the concept of human worth is problematic because it rests on the assignment of a single global rating (worth) to a process (the self) that defies such a simple rating. However, a number of clients want to retain the idea of human worth even though it has inherent problems. The main problem with the concept of human worth is that people normally make their worth contingent on variables that change (e.g., "I am worthwhile if I do well in my exams," which implies that if I do not do well then I am not worthwhile). Even if a person fulfills the conditions of worth at any given moment, she is still vulnerable to emotional disturbance if those conditions are not continually met.

The only way that a person can apply the concept of human worth in a rational manner is to make her worth contingent on one of two constants. First, she can say that she is worthwhile because she is human, and that will work. Second, she can say that she is worthwhile as long as she is alive. This will also work and can be even applied by people who believe in an afterlife ("I am worthwhile as long as I am alive in this life or any future life that I may have"). The difficulty with this concept, as Ellis (1972) has shown, is that someone can just as easily say: "I am worthless because I am alive" or "I am worthless because I am human." For this reason, many REBT therapists discourage their clients from using the concept of human worth.

5. Unconditional self-acceptance avoids errors of overgeneralization.
When people apply the concept of conditional self-esteem, they constantly make errors of overgeneralization or what might be called part-whole errors. In the part-whole error, a person infers that he has failed to achieve a certain goal (which represents a part of the person), evaluates this failure negatively, and then concludes that he is a failure (which is the whole of the person). In other words, he rates the whole of himself on the basis of his rating of a part of himself. Applying the concept of unconditional self-acceptance to this example, the person would still infer that he has failed to achieve his goal and would still evaluate this failure negatively. However, his conclusion, that his failure proves that he is a fallible human being, would be perfectly logical

6. Unconditional self-acceptance is based on flexible, preferential philosophy.
Earlier in this chapter we pointed out that self-downing beliefs tend to be derived from rigid, musturbatory beliefs, or in Albert Ellis's memorable phrase, "Shouldhood leads to shithood. You're rarely a shit without a should." What follows from this is that unconditional self-acceptance beliefs are derived from flexible, preferential beliefs. For example, if you believe that you're inadequate because you acted in a socially inappropriate manner, then this self-downing belief tends to stem from the rigid belief "I must not behave inappropriately in a social context." A self-accepting alternative belief would involve your accepting yourself as a fallible human being who is not inadequate. This belief in turn would tend to stem from the flexible belief "I would prefer not to act in a socially inappropriate manner, but there's no reason why I absolutely must not do so."

7. Unconditional self-acceptance promotes constructive action, not resignation.
If we can accept ourselves as fallible human beings with all that this means, paradoxically we have a much better chance of minimizing our errors and psychological problems than if we condemn ourselves for having them in the first place. Such acceptance, then, does not imply resignation, as many people think. Rather, it promotes our constructive efforts to learn from our errors and minimizes our tendency to disturb ourselves. Self-acceptance does this because, as shown above, it is based on a flexible philosophy of desire, in this case a desire to live as happily as possible. This desire motivates us to take constructive action. Conversely, resignation is based on the idea that there is nothing we can do to improve aspects of ourselves, so there is no point in trying. This, then, is the antithesis of self-acceptance.

8. Unconditional self-acceptance is a habit that can be acquired (but never perfectly, nor for all time).
Behavior therapists often construe self-defeating behavior as bad habits that can be broken. Many clients resonate to the idea that self-downing is a bad habit that can be broken. If you want to use the idea of self-downing and unconditional self-acceptance as habits, you can do so but with the following

caveats. Be careful to stress that the "habit" of self-downing can be broken but never perfectly and not in a once-and-for-all manner. Similarly, stress that unconditional self-acceptance can be acquired but, again, never perfectly nor for all time. Emphasize that it is the very nature of fallible human beings to go back to self-downing under stress even though your client may have worked very hard to break this habit. In doing so you are helping your client to accept herself for her lack of self-acceptance!

9. Internalizing the philosophy of unconditional self-acceptance is difficult and involves hard work.

Understanding the concept of unconditional self-acceptance is not that difficult. Internalizing a philosophy of unconditional self-acceptance so that it makes a positive difference to the way we think, feel, and act most certainly is difficult. Here it is useful to help clients view the acquisition of unconditional self-acceptance as similar to the acquisition of any new skill that has to be learned against the background of a well-ingrained habit that has been well practiced and is now in place (e.g., golf or tennis). As such, acquiring self-acceptance will involve your clients in a lot of hard work, work that has to be done even though the clients will experience feelings and tendencies to act that are consistent with their more thoroughly ingrained philosophy of self-downing. This means that clients will have to tolerate a period of "feeling all wrong" as they strive to internalize a philosophy that makes perfect sense but is not yet believed. Such conviction comes from repeatedly challenging self-downing beliefs and acting in a way that is consistent with a self-accepting beliefs.

10. Unconditional self-acceptance requires force and energy.

The hard work that we mentioned above can be done in two ways. First, it can be done with force and energy; for example, clients can challenge their self-downing beliefs with a great deal of force and throw themselves into acting in ways that are consistent with their newly acquired self-accepting beliefs. Second, this work can be done in a weak, "namby-pamby" fashion. Because people tend to hold their self-downing beliefs quite rigidly, the latter way of working to acquire a philosophy of self-acceptance will just not work. Thus, it is important to help clients understand the importance of meeting strength with strength or fighting fire with fire. Thus, the more clients use force and energy as they strive to accept themselves, the better their results will be.

RUNNING SELF-ACCEPTANCE GROUPS

We will begin this section by providing a brief outline of the basic assumption that underpins self-acceptance groups. Then we will describe the context in which I (WD) run these groups before providing a session-by-session account of a typical self-acceptance group.

Basic Assumption

Self-acceptance groups are based on the idea that the philosophy of unconditional self-acceptance can be taught in a structured, educational manner and can be understood by group members in a short time. Although internalizing this philosophy is a long and arduous endeavor that takes far more time than the 8-week period over which the group is run, it is possible in this short period to help group members take the first steps in integrating this philosophy into their belief system.

The Context

The context in which a therapy group is run has a decided impact on how it is established and how much impact it has on the well-being of its members. As one colleague complained, "How can you run a group when every week the chairs are different?" To which I (WD) replied that where I work the chairs are the same every week, but the group membership is different. For I (WD) used to work one morning a week in a private hospital setting where two types of groups were offered: open groups, in which people come and go and every week the size and membership of the group is different, and closed groups, in which the same group of clients meets every week for a time-limited period. The self-acceptance groups to be described here are, in our experience, best run as a closed group. If they are run as an open group, we would have to introduce the same ideas every week and group cohesion would be lost. A closed group means that clients are taken through the same ideas at the same time and are introduced to the same techniques at the same time, which means that they can help one another in a way that they couldn't if the group were open.

One issue that does need to be addressed if you work in a private hospital is clients' appointments with their consultant psychiatrists. Unless you inform consultants of the times that you run your self-acceptance group and elicit their agreement that they will not schedule appointments during this time, then the group will be disrupted by clients coming back from or going out to see their consultants.

Forming the Group

Before forming the group, you need to make decisions about the size of the group, how often it is to meet and for how long each session. In a private hospital there is the additional constraint that many clients, once they have become "day patients," do not attend for long periods unless they can afford the high fees or their insurance coverage permits long-term attendance. Consequently, my (WD) practice was to run a self-acceptance group weekly for 1½ hours over an 8-week period. I found that a group of between seven and nine clients works best (allowing for one dropout per group).

Because my attendance at the hospital was limited, I did not have time to interview all the people who wish to join the group. I thus left the selection of group members to one of the full-time workers at the hospital who knows the nature of the group and the type of clients who will benefit most from it. These were people whose problems were mainly ego-related and who had previous exposure to REBT or cognitive therapy and agreed with the idea that dysfunctional beliefs are at the core of psychological disturbance. In addition, group members had to commit to weekly attendance over the life of the group and be prepared to put into practice what they learn form the group, which in practice meant the regular completion of homework assignments.

Session-by-Session Outline of a Self-Acceptance Group

Session 1

1. *Introductions.* The members of the group and I introduce ourselves to one another.

2. *Clarifying the preconditions for attendance.* Here I stress that the group is for people whose problems have to do with negative attitudes toward the self and that weekly attendance is expected from all. I also explain the usual rule of confidentiality for group members and elicit members' willingness to comply with this rule.

3. *Who wants high self-esteem?* I normally begin a self-acceptance group by asking members who among them would like to have high self-esteem (or feel better about themselves). Virtually everyone raises his hand. I then ask each member to indicate what would raise their self-esteem. The kinds of answers I get include

- doing well at work
- being a better mother
- being loved
- living up to my principles
- doing voluntary work

4. *Teaching the principles of unconditional self-acceptance.* Before I deal with the responses to the question "What would raise your self-esteem?" I spend most of the first session teaching the 10 principles of unconditional self-acceptance outlined in the first half of this chapter. After teaching each point I pause for questions and observations from group members.

5. *Another look at self-esteem.* After I have finished teaching the 10 principles of unconditional self-acceptance, I ask the group members to reconsider their answers to my previous question, "What would raise your self-esteem?" I help them to see that their responses do not serve to raise their self-esteem but are desirable things to have or achieve in their own right. I show them that self-esteem is contingent upon doing well at work, being loved, and so on; and if they were to do poorly at work later or lose the love of a significant person, for example, their self-esteem would plummet. Helping group members to understand that the concept of self-esteem is the cause of their problems and not the solution is very liberating for most.

6. *Homework.* Virtually all the members in my self-acceptance groups have been exposed to REBT or cognitive-behavior therapy and therefore are familiar with the important role that homework assignments have in the therapeutic process. It is beyond the scope of this chapter for us to deal with cases where group members do not do their homework assignments or modify them in some way; for this I refer the interested reader to Dryden (1995b).

The first homework assignment that I suggest group members carry out before the second group session is to read chapters 1 and 3 of Paul Hauck's (1991) book on unconditional self-acceptance entitled *Hold Your Head Up High* (or *Overcoming the Rating Game* in the American edition). Chapter 1 outlines the problems that occur when people do not accept themselves, and chapter 3 presents the principles of unconditional self-acceptance. As such, these chapters serve as a reminder of the material covered in the first session. I suggest that, while reading the material, group members make a note of points they disagree with or are unsure of for discussion the following week.

Session 2

1. *Reviewing homework.* It is an important principle of REBT that if you set a homework assignment then you review it the following session. So at the beginning of this session (and all subsequent sessions) it is important to review what the group members did for homework. In doing so, I correct any misconceptions that group members display in their reading of the chapters in Hauck's (1991) book.

2. *Goal setting.* At this point the group members are ready to consider what they can achieve from the group and what they can't. I point out that my role is to teach them both the principles of unconditional self-acceptance and some techniques to help them begin to internalize this philosophy. What I can do is to help them begin the journey toward self-acceptance. In 8 weeks I cannot help them to complete this journey. Given this limitation, I ask them to set suitable goals for the group. "What," I ask, "would they have achieved by the end of the eight weeks that would show them that they had begun the long and arduous journey toward self-acceptance?" I encourage members to divide

into smaller groups and to make their goals as realistic and specific as possible. I then ask one group member to make a written note of everybody's goals, which I then photocopy and distribute at the end of the session so that everybody has a copy of the goals of each member.

3. *Dealing with a specific example of the target problem.* I then ask group members to choose a specific example of a situation in which they considered themselves to be worthless, inadequate, bad, and so on. I then ask each member in turn to talk about the experience briefly to the rest of the group. After the person has finished relating the experience, I use the ABC framework of REBT to help her assess it (where *A* stands for the actual or inferred activating event, *B* for her musturbatory and self-downing beliefs, and *C* for her major disturbed negative emotion and/or self-defeating behavior).

4. *Homework.* For homework, I ask each group member to use the ABC framework to analyze another example of "low self-esteem."

Session 3

1. *Reviewing homework.* At the beginning of the session, I check each person's ABC assessment and offer corrective feedback where relevant.

2. *Teaching disputing of irrational ego beliefs.* A central task of group members in a self-acceptance group is to learn how to dispute their musturbatory and self-downing irrational beliefs. Thus, I devote the bulk of this session to teaching this core skill. As DiGiuseppe (1991) has shown, disputing involves group members asking themselves three different types of questions of their irrational ego beliefs:

- Are they consistent with reality?
- Are they logical?
- Do they yield healthy results?

As we showed in the first half of this chapter, the answer to these questions is no when they are applied to self-downing beliefs (see Dryden [1994a] for a full discussion of why musturbatory beliefs are also inconsistent with reality and illogical and yield unhealthy results for the individual concerned).

Disputing also involves helping group members to construct preferential and self-accepting beliefs as healthy alternatives to their irrational ego beliefs. Therefore, I spend a good deal of the third session helping group members to construct rational ego beliefs.

3. *Homework: identifying and disputing irrational ego beliefs in specific situations.* Armed with their new skill of disputing irrational ego beliefs and constructing alternative rational ego beliefs, group members are now ready to put this new skill into practice in their everyday lives before the next session. This forms the basis for the homework assignment for that week.

Session 4

1. *Reviewing homework.* I begin the fourth group session by reviewing the previous week's homework assignment and offering corrective feedback as before.

2. *Teaching the portfolio method.* As mentioned above, disputing irrational beliefs is a core client skill in REBT in general and in self-acceptance groups in particular. As I have recently shown (Dryden, 1995a), the purpose of disputing in the present context is to help group members understand why their irrational ego beliefs are irrational and why their alternative rational ego beliefs are rational. Once group members have understood this point, they need additional help to enable them to integrate this understanding into their belief system so that it influences for the better the way they think and feel about themselves and the way they act in the world. Helping them to develop a portfolio of arguments in favor of their rational ego beliefs and against their irrational ego beliefs is the cognitive technique that I use to initiate this integration process.

Having introduced the idea of the portfolio, I suggest that group members spend about 20 minutes in the session developing their own portfolio of arguments. Then I ask them to work in two small groups, reviewing one another's arguments and suggesting additional arguments. During this time I act as consultant, listening to the small group discussion, offering feedback on the arguments developed, and being available as a troubleshooter if either of the groups get stuck.

3. *Homework.* For homework I suggest that group members review and add to the arguments they have developed for their portfolio. I also suggest that they make a particular note of any arguments about which they have reservations or doubts or do not find persuasive.

Session 5

1. *Reviewing homework.* I begin the fifth session by reviewing the previous week's homework, paying particular attention to arguments that group members have doubts or reservations about or do not find persuasive. I initiate a group discussion on these arguments and intervene to correct misconceptions or to provide additional explanations to help dispel these doubts and to make their rational arguments more persuasive.

2. *Teaching the zigzag technique.* As noted above, it is common for people to respond to their own arguments developed in favor of a self-accepting philosophy with what might be called irrational rebuttals, that is, arguments that cast doubt on the concept of unconditional self-acceptance and in fact advocate a return to the philosophy of self-downing. The zigzag technique formalizes this debate between the irrational and rational "parts" of the person and gives the

person practice at defending her rational ego belief against her own irrational attack. This technique helps group members to integrate their rational ego beliefs into their belief system.

In the zigzag technique, the group member begins by writing down a rational ego belief and rating her degree of conviction in this belief on a 0–100 rating scale. Then she responds to this belief with an irrational argument, which she then rebuts. The group member continues in this vein until she has responded to all of her attacks and can think of no more. She then rerates her degree of conviction in her rational ego belief, which is usually increased if the person used the technique properly.

Once I have taught the group members the rudiments of this technique, I ask them to carry out the technique on their own in the session. I stress the importance of keeping to the point, as it is easy for the person to get sidetracked when using this technique. As group members do this task, I go from person to person ensuring that they are doing it correctly and, in particular, keep the focus of the debate on their target rational ego belief (see Dryden [1995a] for an extended discussion of the zigzag technique).

3. *Teaching tape-recorded disputing.* Tape-recorded disputing is similar to the zigzag method in that group members put the dialogue between their rational and irrational ego beliefs on tape. In addition to emphasizing once again that it is important to keep to the point while using this method, it is useful to stress that group members respond to their irrational attacks with force and energy. It should be explained that because people often hold their irrational ego beliefs very strongly, weak rational responses will have little lasting effect on irrational attacks. It is useful to give the group members some examples so that they can discriminate between weak and forceful disputing (see Dryden [1995a] for an extended discussion of tape-recorded disputing).

4. *Homework.* Tape-recorded disputing is a good homework assignment to set at this point, but it is important to establish first that group members all have access to tape recorders. If not, suitable arrangements should be made for them to gain such access. In addition, I usually suggest that group members read and note any objections to chapter 4 of Paul Hauck's (1991) book, which considers the importance of behavioral methods in the development of unconditional self-acceptance. This will be the focus of the next two group sessions.

Session 6

1. *Reviewing homework.* In checking group members' tapes it is important to pay particular attention to their ability to stay focused on the target beliefs and to the tone they used during disputing, and suitable feedback should be given accordingly on these two points. As with other reading material, particular emphasis should be given to group members' reservations about the place of behavioral methods of developing unconditional self-acceptance.

2. *Providing a rationale for the conjoint use of cognitive and behavioral methods in real-life settings.* REBT theory states that behavioral methods have a central role to play in the therapeutic change process. Unless group members act on their rational ego beliefs, the benefits they will derive from the group will ultimately be minimal. However, the power of behavioral methods is best harnessed when they are used conjointly with cognitive methods designed to give group members the opportunity to practice their rational ego beliefs in a real-life setting.

3. *Negotiating behavioral-cognitive tasks.* After you have provided group members with a rationale for the conjoint use of behavioral and cognitive techniques, it is important to encourage them to agree to set one or two behavioral-cognitive tasks that they can implement as homework assignments before the next group session. These tasks should preferably be related to group members' goals.

4. *Teaching rational-emotive imagery.* Rational-emotive imagery (REI) is an evocative technique designed to give group members practice in strengthening their rational ego beliefs in the face of negative activating events (A's). In self-acceptance groups I suggest the use of REI as preparation for the implementation of the behavioral-cognitive techniques discussed above. Once group members have set a behavioral-cognitive technique, I ask them to imagine a worst-case scenario that constitutes the A in an ABC episode and have them identify and get in touch with an ego-related, disturbed negative emotion (e.g., hurt). Then, while they are still imagining the same negative A, I ask them to change their emotion to a self-accepting, healthy negative emotion. As I have noted elsewhere (Dryden, 1995a), group members achieve this by changing their irrational ego beliefs to rational ego beliefs (see Dryden [1995a] for a fuller discussion of REI).

5. *Homework.* For homework, I suggest that group members practice REI three times a day for a few days before implementing their behavioral-cognitive tasks.

Session 7

1. *Reviewing homework.* In checking group members' use of REI, you need to make sure that they did, in fact, change their irrational ego beliefs to their rational alternatives rather than change the negative activating event to something more positive. In reviewing their behavioral-cognitive tasks, you need to ensure (a) that they actually faced the situation they wanted to confront or acted in the manner planned and (b) that they practiced thinking rationally while doing so.

2. *Agreeing on other behavioral-cognitive tasks.* If members were successful in implementing their behavioral-cognitive assignment, then it is important to capitalize on this success by negotiating two additional behavioral tasks. Encourage group members to choose tasks that are challenging but not overwhelming for them. However, if any group member struggled with their ini-

tial behavioral-cognitive task, then you will have to be less adventurous in the next such assignment you negotiate with that person.

3. *Explaining and agreeing on shame-attacking exercises.* Shame-attacking exercises involve group members acting in a so-called shameful manner and accepting themselves as they do so. They should attract attention to themselves without alarming others, breaking the law, or getting themselves into trouble at work. Examples of good shame-attacking exercises are as follows:

- wearing different colored shoes
- asking to see a three-piece suite in a sweet shop
- singing off-key in public
- asking for directions to a road one is on

I suggest that group members do at least one shame-attacking exercise before the last group session.

4. *Homework.* The last set of homework assignments is as described above. In addition, I ask group members to come to the last session prepared to talk about what they have achieved from the group and to give feedback about their experience of being in the group.

Session 8

1. *Reviewing homework.* For the last time, I check on group members' homework assignments and give corrective feedback as usual. Group members are usually keen to learn about one another's shame-attacking exercises, and this generates a sense of fun that, in my opinion, is quite suitable to the ending of a group of this educational nature.

2. *The self-acceptance quiz.* In the spirit of fun and to assess what group members have learned, I then ask them to complete in writing a short written quiz (see Figure 9.1).

Why not take the quiz yourself to see what you have learned from this chapter?

3. *Evaluating progress and eliciting feedback on the group.* I then ask group members to relate what progress they have made toward unconditional self-acceptance and whether or not they have achieved their goals. I also ask them to give feedback on the group experience, my way of running it, and how it might be improved. Because all group members are involved in other groups in the hospital and many are also in individual psychotherapy, it has not been possible for me to carry out formal research into the effectiveness of self-acceptance groups.

4. *Helping group members to maintain and extend their gains.* The final task that I ask group members to do is to develop a list of ways that they can maintain and extend the gains that they have made from participating in the group (see Dryden [1995a, 1995b] for a fuller discussion of these two points). I stress to them that they have taken the first few steps along the road to self-acceptance

Give reasons for each answer.

1. Having the love of a significant other makes you a more worthwhile person.
   True or false?

2. If someone you admire is better than you at an important activity, he or she is a better person than you.
   True or false?

3. If you fail at something really important, you are not a failure but a fallible human being.
   True or false?

4. You can give a human being a single global rating that completely accounts for them.
   True or false?

5. Someone who rapes a small child is wicked through and through.
   True or false?

6. Mother Teresa has more worth than Adolf Hitler.
   True or false?

FIGURE 9.1 Unconditional self-acceptance quiz.

and that how far they go along this road will be largely dependent on the amount of work that they are prepared to do on themselves using the tools that I have taught them during the group. On this point, I wish them well and we say our good-byes.

It is likely that brief psychoeducational group interventions will become increasingly popular within the managed care climate that is beginning to dominate mental health delivery systems. As this chapter shows, with its emphasis on teaching clients the nature of good mental health and what to do to achieve it, REBT is in a good position to make a very useful contribution to the development of such interventions.

10

The Rational Emotive Behavioral Approach to Sex Therapy

It is exceptionally difficult to present the rational emotive behavioral approach to sex counseling and therapy within a brief chapter. This approach has a comprehensiveness that goes beyond the techniques usually employed by sex therapists attached to other schools, such as those used by psychoanalysts, behavior therapists, Reichian and bioenergetic practitioners, or Masters-and-Johnson-schooled therapists. It not only includes many of the main methods utilized by these other schools, but it does so on theoretical rather than mere practical grounds, as part and parcel of an integrated theory of psychotherapy. It avoids some of the popular methods of sex counseling, such as psychoanalytic and Reichian procedures, because it considers them nontherapeutic or harmful.

We shall not, therefore, try to state everything that goes on—and that does not go on—in the REBT treatment of sex problems in this chapter. Several other books and articles are devoted to this subject (Ellis, 1958b, 1960, 1976f, 1979b). We shall try to mention briefly various aspects of rational emotive behavior therapy (REBT) that significantly overlap with various other kinds of sex therapies and shall emphasize those aspects that seem rather unique to REBT and to allied cognitive-behavior practices.

From its inception, REBT was vigorously applied to human sex problems, particularly those of impotence and frigidity. Indeed, had I (AE) not done a great deal of sex therapy first, I might never have developed rational emotive behavioral methods because, almost more than any other human psychological problem, sexual malfunctioning practically *requires* (as Masters & Johnson [1970] later found) the effective use of direct teaching, training, and homework

Parts of this chapter were adapted from Albert Ellis, "The Rational-Emotive Approach to Sex Therapy," *The Counseling Psychologist*, 1975, 5(1), 14–22. Used by permission.

assigning methods by an effective therapist. And by experimenting in these respects, especially after I discovered that the "depth-centered" techniques of psychoanalysis frequently harmed rather than helped sexually dysfunctioning people, I probably led myself to give up traditional psychotherapy and develop the REBT approach long before I otherwise would have done.

Anyway, the REBT treatment of sex difficulties uses a comprehensive, inter-locking cognitive-emotive-behavioral approach. Let us outline some of its main elements.

COGNITIVE SEX THERAPY

Information Giving

Like Masters and Johnson (1970), Kaplan (1974), and other therapists, the REBT practitioner teaches most clients with sex anxiety, hostility, or compul-siveness a good amount of corrective information, which, at the start, they usu-ally seem to lack. In accordance with REBT theory, this information serves largely to disabuse them of several dysfunctional ideas—for example, that they *must* have conventional coitus to have successful and enjoyable sex; that all nor-mal men and women desire sex incessantly and can easily get aroused and sat-isfied; that spontaneous arousal by both partners must occur if they have good sex; that loving partners automatically and easily feel aroused by their mates; that adulterous desires are illegitimate and immoral; that sex play, to seem proper, must end up with penile-vaginal copulation; that any knowledgeable individual can easily turn on and give many orgasms to his or her partner (Ellis, 1979b, 1980c).

REBT therapists give as much or more down-to-earth information as any other sex therapists. But they do it not only to provide more knowledge and training procedures to sexually maladjusted individuals but also to try to help them achieve a generally open, experimenting, individualistic, rational attitude toward sex, love, and marriage and to help them surrender self-defeating and couple-sabotaging myths, superstitions, and dogmas (Ellis, 1960, 1979). Finally, REBT therapists also give their clients up-to-date information about safe sex practices and how to get the most out of sex without putting themselves at risk for HIV/AIDS.

Imaging Methods

In line with its emphasis on cognition, REBT employs a good amount of imaging methods in sex therapy. In particular, males and females who have difficulty in feeling aroused or reaching orgasm are shown how to use any kind of fantasy that will work in their individual cases and to do so without any shame or guilt if their fantasy seems "bizarre" or socially disapproved.

The therapist may help them use regular sex fantasies, various kinds of "pornographic" images, romantic fantasies, focusing on their own or their partner's sensations and responses, or fantasies mutually verbalized with their partners. When advisable, written or pictorial materials may be recommended as fantasy aids.

A special kind of imaging that has powerful cognitive, emotive, and behavioral elements included in it remains in the special province of REBT: rational-emotive imagery (REI), originally developed by Maxie C. Maultsby, Jr. (1971) and incorporated as one of the main techniques of REBT (Ellis, 1993a). I (AE) employed REI effectively with Sally, whose case I presented in an article, "The Treatment of Sex and Love Problems in Women" (Ellis, 1974b). Sally came to see me because she only occasionally achieved a climax, even when her lovers massaged her clitoral region for 15 or 20 minutes and at the time she came for therapy had started to feel completely turned off to sex, so that virtually nothing aroused her. As I explained the REI procedure to her, in the course of her second session:

"Close your eyes, right now, and fantasize just as vividly as you can, having sex relations with your lover. Can you do that?"

"Yes."

"All right. Continue in your imagination, having sex with him. But picture, quite vividly, that little or nothing happens. You do not get in the least aroused, the whole thing proves a complete bust, and he starts feeling quite irritable and disappointed in you because you keep failing. In fact, he wonders and makes overt remarks about your continually failing, and he indicates that he begins to suspect you are just a dud, sexually, and that you will not likely ever satisfy any man in that respect. Picture these scenes just as dramatically as you can. See it as really happening!"

"I can see it. I can clearly see it now."

"Fine. How do you feel? How do you honestly feel, right in your gut, as you envision this kind of sexual failure?"

"Awful! Depressed!"

"Right. You normally feel that way when you think of this kind of thing happening. Now, change the feeling in your gut to a feeling of *only* disappointment and frustration. Keep the same fantasy in your head, exactly the same picture, but *only* feel sorry, disappointed, and frustrated. *Not* awful, not depressed, *only* disappointed. Can you do that?"

"I see I have great trouble feeling that way. I find it hard!"

"I know. But I know you can do it. You do have the power to change your feelings—if only for a short time. So try some more. Feel *only* disappointed and frustrated. See if you can do that."

(After a pause): "All right. I guess I can do it."

"Do what?"

"Feel *just* disappointed. It keeps running back into depression. But I can feel it, at least for a while."

"Good. I knew you could. Now, what did you do to make yourself feel that way?"

"Let me see. I guess I kept thinking, 'It isn't the end of the world. I really would *like* to feel much more aroused and to please Henry. But I don't *have* to.'"

"Yes. Anything else?"

"Yes, I guess: 'I won't be a rotten person, even if I *never* get very sexy again. It only is one of my traits, sexiness, and doesn't constitute *me*. If I lose that, I still very much have the *rest* of me.'"

"Fine. You could continue to think exactly that if you want to feel disappointed but *not* depressed. For you *don't* become a rotten person if you lose your sexiness. There *is* much more to you than that. And you *can* enjoy yourself and even have a good love relationship going if you never feel very sexy again."

"Yes. I see now that I can."

"Right! Now, if you will practice this rational-emotive imagery technique every day for the next few weeks, if you really keep practicing it, it will become more and more a part of you. You'll see, more clearly than you ever did, that you have a *choice* of what you think when you envision sex failure, that you can *choose* to feel sorry and disappointed—or awful and depressed. And you will get *used* to feeling the former and not the latter until it becomes almost an automatic part of your thinking and feeling. Up to now, you have really vigorously practiced the opposite—*making yourself* feel depressed whenever you think, as you often do, of not becoming aroused or orgasmic. Now you can *make yourself* feel differently, until you 'naturally' keep feeling that way. So every day, for the next few weeks, practice this kind of rational-emotive imagery that we have just done, until it becomes 'second nature.' Will you do that?"

"Yes, I will," said Sally.

And she did practice it steadily for the next few weeks and reported that when she had sex with her lover and began to feel depressed at the thought of failing, she quickly and almost automatically started making herself feel sorry and disappointed instead. After a few weeks, she even had trouble feeling depressed! And she then, much more easily and better than before, proved capable of practicing intense sexual imaging of an exciting nature and of arousing herself considerably and coming to orgasm.

Antiawfulizing and Antiabsolutizing

Rational-emotive imagery, as just demonstrated, usually constitutes an antiawfulizing and antiabsolutizing technique because it helps sexually malfunctioning individuals, imaginatively, emotively, and behaviorally, to *practice* thinking and acting differently and, notably, to change their awfulizing, antiempirical philosophies of life. The main premise of REBT holds that humans mainly feel disturbed and act dysfunctionally, in sex-love and other areas, when they change almost any desire, preference, or wish into an absolutistic, perfectionistic *should, ought, must,* command, or *demandingness* (Ellis, 1962, 1972b, 1973, 1980d, 1994c; Ellis & Harper, 1961b, 1997; Hauck, 1973, 1991; Knaus, 1974; Young, 1974). REBT especially sees *mast*urbation as good and harmless but *must*urbation as pernicious and disturbance-creating. It consequently teaches people to look for their irrational *must's* and vigorously and persistently dispute them and change them back to *it would be better's.*

In REBT we teach most people with sexual problems the ABCs of emotional disturbance, and we help them acquire cognitive (as well as emotive and behavioral) tools to change these ABCs significantly. We deal, as does Helen Kaplan (1974), not only with the client's specific sex problems but usually, as well, with his or her general tendencies to create emotional disturbance in nonsexual areas of life.

I (AE) will now illustrate REBT procedures with a summary of my treating a 29-year-old male with a fairly typical case of impotence. Although he had succeeded sexually with his ex-wife, to whom he remained married for 4 years, he had not regularly achieved a good degree of erection with other females, either before or after his marriage, except with prostitutes or "low level," "whorish" women who looked to him like hookers. He had explored his presumed Oedipal feelings toward his mother (who had kept criticizing him sexually since his early childhood) and its supposed connection with his impotence in the course of a 5-year period of psychoanalysis. But he had only become more impotent during that time.

I quickly showed this client that although his inability to get aroused may have at first partly stemmed from his fear of sex and his horror of having it with a "nice woman," who may have symbolized a mother figure to him, its continuing and main cause probably had little to do with the dysfunctional idea that he would be a sinner if he succeeded sexually with any mother surrogate but had other philosophic sources. At point C, his behavioral Consequence (or neurotic symptom), was that he failed to have an erection with "nice women." And as an additional emotional Consequence, he felt exceptionally ashamed of his failing. At point A, his Activating experience or Activating event, he received permission from a "good woman" to have sex with her, and he got into bed and attempted to have it. Because, in REBT terms, C follows A but does not really create or *cause* it (as assumed in psychoanalysis and several other therapeutic systems), the thing to look for and change consists of B—this individual's Belief system. What, in other words, did he irrationally keep believing or telling himself at B?

As in many cases like this, I first start with the client's *second* C: his shame *about* his impotence. In this REBT model, A (his Activating experience) represented his sexual failure, and C (his emotional Consequence) represented his feelings of shame, depression, and self-downing *about* A. B (his Belief System) included two parts: a Rational Belief (RB) and an Irrational Belief (IB). His Rational Belief (as he soon agreed) was obvious: "I would very much like to succeed sexually with all types of females, including 'nice women,' and since I have just failed with this present one, I find that unpleasant and inconvenient. How said that I failed! I wish I had succeeded instead. Now let me see what I can do the next time I go to bed with her, so that I can get aroused and enjoy myself and please her sexually."

This set of Rational Beliefs, if he only stayed with them, would tend to produce in the client (at C) healthy feelings of sorrow, regret, frustration, and annoyance about his impotence at A. Thus he would feel healthily sad, sorry, and frustrated about his impotence. But because we (he and I) knew that he felt unhealthily, ashamed and self-downing about it (at C), we strongly suspected that he had Irrational Beliefs, at B, in addition to his rational Beliefs. And, looking for these Irrational Beliefs (IBs), we soon found that he kept telling himself: "How *awful* that I am impotent! I *can't stand* having such symptoms! I *must* not act that way; and what a *worm*, what a *complete slob* I am if I am as impotent as that!" He then, after having these profound beliefs, felt ashamed and self-downing at C.

Because this client wished to minimize or eliminate his unhealthy feelings at C, I helped him go to D—disputing his irrational Beliefs. To do this, I showed him how to ask himself four main questions: (1) "What makes it *awful* (or *terrible* or *horrible*) if I am impotent?" (2) "Why can't I *stand* having such symptoms?" (3) "Show me the evidence that I *must* not have them." (4) "If I do behave impotently, how do I become a *worm* or a *complete slob* for behaving that way?"

He then began to answer himself, at point E (his Effective New Philosophy):

1. "Nothing makes it *awful* (or *terrible* or *horrible*) if I am impotent. It is *inconvenient* and *frustrating*. But that doesn't amount to *awful* or *horrible*! *Awfulness* means 100% inconvenience. And that hardly exists. *Horror* stems from my believing that things *shouldn't* work out inconveniently. But if they do, they do! Tough! No matter how inconvenient or disadvantageous it is to be impotent, it never can be *more than* that."

2. "I can, again, *stand* impotence, though I of course need never *like* it. I can also *stand* having any symptoms that I do have. And I'd better not make myself *ashamed* of my impotence, only *distressed* about having it."

3. "I can't find *any* evidence supporting the proposition that I *must* not be impotent. It would be highly *desirable* to act potently, but that hardly means that I *must*. I will hardly die if I remain impotent. More important, I can have sex pleasure, distinctly satisfy my partner, and have many kinds of nonsexual joy in life, even if I stay sexually impotent forever."

4. "My impotence definitely doesn't make me a *worm*, or a *complete slob*; but at worst, a *person with a handicap*. Having a *poor trait* never makes me a *bad person*. I can fully accept myself and keep determined to lead as happy a life as I can lead, even though I have important deficiencies, such as sexual impotence."

By helping this client go through his A-B-C-D-E's in this fashion, I first helped him to accept himself *with* his impotence and to feel unashamed of having it. Once he began to feel better in this respect, he could work more adequately on the impotence itself. In this respect, his ABCs went as follows: Activating experience (A): "This 'nice woman' wants me to have sex with her." Rational Belief (RB): "Wouldn't it be unfortunate if I failed with her, especially in view of the fact that I have failed in these circumstances before." Irrational Belief (IB): "It would be *terrible* if I failed! I *have* to succeed, or else I prove myself a thorough weakling instead of a man!"Behavioral Consequence (C): Lack of adequate erection. Disputing of irrational Beliefs (D): "How is everything *terrible* if I fail? What evidence exists that I *have* to succeed? How does it prove, if I fail, that I am a thorough weakling instead of a man?" Effect of Disputing (E): "Nothing is really *terrible* if I fail. Things still remain unfortunate, handicapping, and inconvenient. But nothing more! There is no evidence that I *have* to succeed, though it obviously would be high desirable if I did. I don't *have* to succeed. I don't *have* to do anything! If I fail, I clearly am not a Failure, a Weakling, or a Non-man. I still am a human, a man, who presently fails and who may well succeed in the future. Even if I never get fully sexually potent, I don't become a *bad* person. Only my behavior, not my essence, is bad or weak."

As he kept going through these ABCs, my client grew more and more potent. After the third session he had intercourse with a "nice woman" and succeeded reasonably well. Immediately thereafter, he assertively picked up another "good woman" on a bus and spent a "wonderful weekend" in bed with her. Thereafter he had virtually no sex problems, no matter what kind of a partner he selected. He also, at first spontaneously and then with my help, began to tackle his feelings of inadequacy at his job, accountancy, and after several more months improved in that respect. As I find common, his sex problems were overcome much more quickly and thoroughly than his general feelings of worthlessness. But the mastering of the former helped him go on to the latter.

I used several of the other techniques mentioned in this chapter with this client, particularly that of helping him imagine "nice women" as "sexy" and that of getting him to question and challenge all his guilt feelings about sex. However, doing his ABCs about his shame about impotence and about his impotence itself proved most useful.

Removing Sex Guilt

As just noted, my impotent client found it quite helpful to rid himself of his feelings of guilt. In treating people with sex problems, the technique of shame and guilt reduction is often valuable. As I have shown in several books (Ellis, 1958b, 1960, 1976, 1979b), even in today's relatively enlightened age millions of people still make themselves needlessly ashamed or guilty about some of their sex acts. Although other therapies—such as Gestalt therapy (Perls, 1969), client-centered therapy (Rogers, 1961), and Reichian therapy (Reich, 1942)—tackle this problem in their own ways, REBT specializes in the minimization of shame and guilt.

When, for example, people feel guilty (at point C) about what they have done sexually (at point A), the REBT therapist immediately looks for their Beliefs (at point B). In the sexual area they have usually convinced themselves of two major Beliefs: (1) this sex act that I have done is definitely wrong; and (2) because of its wrongness, I *should* not have done it and must consider myself a lousy person for doing so. Normally, Belief No. 1 may be rational because people obviously can and do commit many wrong, mistaken, foolish, or unethical sex acts (such as compulsive peeping or rape). However, this Belief may actually be unhealthy. Such acts, for example, as masturbation, noncoital sex play leading to orgasm, and frequent sex fantasizing have often been labeled as "wrong" or "wicked" when no evidence exists for their foolishness or immorality. Consequently, people frequently make themselves ashamed of or guilt about perfectly harmless, even beneficial sex acts. And in REBT we help them question the "erroneousness" of such acts, just as we would get them to ask themselves whether various nonsexual acts (such as primarily devoting oneself to one's own life rather than following one's parents' rules) truly are wrong.

Second, and most important, REBT teaches people that even when they commit an indubitably wrong, self-defeating, or antisocial act, they had better not go on to Belief No. 2: "Therefore, I am a lousy person!" According to REBT, no lousy people exist—only those who do rotten things (Ellis, 1972b, 1973, 1994c). We had better feel highly *responsible* for but not self-downing about our poor behaviors. REBT therapists show people how to feel guilty about their wrong and antisocial acts, and to feel remorse and regret about doing them—but not to feel guilty and deprecating about *themselves* for these poor *actions*. They thereby help sexually troubled clients to free themselves of senseless guilt and to achieve maximum satisfaction (Ellis, 1973, 1976f, 1979b, 1988, 1994c).

Supplementary Psychoeducative Procedures

As an integral part of its program of cognitive restructuring, REBT employs a great deal of bibliotherapy and recorded therapy. Following as it does the educational model, it uses all kinds of audiovisual modalities, including pamphlets, books, recordings, films, talks, workshops, and computer programs, such as those starred in the reference list of this book.

Clients frequently record their own sex therapy sessions on a cassette recorder and listen to the recordings several times in between sessions. They fill out REBT self-help reports (Sichel & Ellis, 1984) about their therapeutic progress and use the report forms to help them with their ABCs of REBT. They participate in live workshops, lectures, and seminars at the Institute. They have motto cards and games available to help them acquire REBT teachings. Sex therapy at the Institute consists not only of regular therapy sessions but of large- and small-group educative procedures and various supplementary psychoeducational methods.

EMOTIVE SEX THERAPY

Although REBT's most unique and best-known procedures tend to lie in the cognitive area, it also includes a considerable amount of emotive-dramatic–evocative methods. Let me exposit a few of these in connection with REBT sex therapy.

Unconditional Acceptance by the Therapist

REBT is rivaled only by Rogerian therapy (Rogers, 1961) in its unconditional acceptance of the client by the therapist. True to REBT principles, the therapist accepts people with sex problems no matter how foolishly or antisocially they behave (Ellis, 1973). Group REBT (where a good deal of sex therapy is often done) also specializes in teaching all the members of the group to accept (though not necessarily to like) the others members and to help show these others that they have a perfect right to accept themselves in spite of their sometimes execrable conduct. REBT practitioners, in addition to giving clients with sex problems unconditional acceptance, go beyond Rogerian methods by actively teaching them how to give it to themselves *whether or not* others favor them (Ellis, 1962, 1972b, 1973, 1974b, 1976a, 1994c; Ellis & Becker, 1982; Ellis & Harper, 1997; Hauck, 1991; Mills, 1993).

Shame-Attacking Exercises

According to REBT, shame or self-downing constitutes the most important part of many human disturbances. Clients, therefore, frequently are given shame-attacking exercises of a sexual or nonsexual nature so that they thereby can prove to themselves that their world will not come to an end if they actually perform so-called shameful, foolish, or ridiculous acts and even do so publicly. When performing such "shameful" acts, either in the course of individual or group REBT sessions, they do not do anything that would lead to real trouble or self-defeatism, such as behaviors that would encourage them to get fired or jailed. But they are encouraged to perform nonharmful "shameful" behaviors such as wearing sexy or ridiculous clothing; wearing conspicuous buttons, including those that may have antipuritanical views emblazoned in large letters; starting discussions of sex topics in social groups; talking intimately to strangers about some of the details of their love and sex lives; and pushing themselves to perform supposedly "far-out" sex acts with some of their regular partners.

We find that these kinds of shame-attacking exercises frequently help inhibited, unassertive, uptight individuals attain good results, sometimes in a short period of time. This is especially true because in the course of REBT individual or group therapy, we not only encourage such exercises as emotive procedures to be acted upon rather than merely talked about, but we *then* follow them up with antiawfulizing discussions that show how they may be socially "wrong" but not really "shameful." Just as we give our cognitive procedures an emotive vector, we give these emotive procedures a cognitive vector; and the two sides nicely tend to interact with and reinforce each other.

Risk-Taking Exercises

Along with shame-attacking, REBT therapists specialize in the use of risk-taking exercises. Humans, in sex-love as well as in other areas of their lives, stubbornly refuse to take risks because they often *define* them as *horribly* or *awfully* dangerous when they actually involve little danger. Their most fearful risks involve acting foolishly in the eyes of others. Sexually, they frequently define various sex acts as "risky" or "dangerous" and avoid them like the plague. In REBT we often persuade, encourage, and urge our clients to do emotive risk-taking acts.

In both our individual and group therapy sessions we give our sexually troubled clients risk-taking exercises. For example: "Go to a dance, singles bar, or other social gathering and talk to at least five members of the other sex and try to make a date with at least one of them." "Take the risk of asking your regular partner to engage in a sex act that you feel afraid he or she would like to perform or would criticize you for asking him or her to perform." "Pick a person for whom you feel you have a special liking and ask that person to go on a date with you or do something else that you would normally feel afraid to ask this person to do." However, in this aspect of the REBT approach to sex therapy, as in all others, we strongly encourage our clients to practice safe sex. Although we wish them to take healthy risks, we certainly do not want them to expose themselves to situations where they could develop HIV/AIDS.

Rational-Emotive Imagery

As noted above in the section on imaging methods, we frequently employ rational-emotive imagery (REI) with our sex therapy clients because it not only involves cognitive elements but important emotive factors as well. We therefore use it with REBT clients who have sexual and nonsexual problems.

Nonverbal Exercises

Many REBT clients have difficulty doing nonverbal activities (far more, some-times, than they have with verbal activities), so we frequently give them non-verbal exercises. We may have them express their feelings to each other, as they mill around the room slowly. One of them may stand within a circle while the other members of the group show nonverbally how they feel toward him or her or do various kinds of hand-holding, face massaging, or back rubbing exer-cises. We may encourage them to behave foolishly in a nonverbal manner.

We use most of the nonverbal procedures nonsexually for general loosen-ing-up processes. But some of them have clear-cut sexual meaning or impli-cations. Thus, we sometimes have two males and two females respond to each other physically to see if they bring out any hangups about homosexual feel-ings when doing so. Or we may have males and females caress each other to see what problems they reveal in the course of this kind of exercise.

Emotive Verbalizations

According to the theory of REBT, people create their own emotional upsets largely by strong beliefs and *vigorously* help disturb themselves by holding *vehe-ment* negative philosophies. Thus, men or women who have trouble achieving an orgasm may very *powerfully* feel convinced that they *must* achieve it, *can't* obtain it easily, and are *worthless* if orgasm remains unachieved. If these indi-viduals only *mildly* contradict such beliefs, they may still mainly hold them and remain emotionally upset by them. Consequently, in REBT we not only attempt to help people to see their disturbance-creating ideas but to contra-dict and dispute these in a highly emotive manner.

Thus, when we ask an impotent male why it would be *awful or horrible* if he remained unarousable with his favorite partner, and he finally answers, in a rather namby-pamby way, "Well, I guess it wouldn't," we frequently say to him, *"But I think it really would!"* Or we say: "You don't convince me one bit, by that tone of voice, that you think it wouldn't be awful. Now let me hear you say, much more vigorously, 'No matter how many times I fail sexually with my partner, I can still find it highly inconvenient but *not* awful!'" And we show him how to repeat this statement strongly until he starts to truly believe it.

In other instances, REBT sex therapists help clients to powerfully convince themselves that they can succeed sexually, that they *have* a right to enjoy them-selves in bed, that their parents and early teachers often held very *wrong* views about sex, and that masturbation and various other kinds of "shameful" acts really are thoroughly unshameful and *good*. We not only, in REBT, encourage clients to actively work and practice against their self-sabotaging sex views and in favor of saner, health-creating views but to keep doing so with much strength and forcefulness.

Emotive Feedback

In REBT individual and group sessions we frequently give emotive feedback to clients. If a woman has a desperate need for love and keeps sabotaging her sex-love relations because she exudes this need, the therapist or one of the group members may say to her: "Look, if I went on a date with you and I saw how you keep acting—thoroughly obsessed with how much I care for you and not really, because of your obsession, giving a shit about me—I'd say to myself: 'Who needs this? She may have lots of brains and good looks but she obviously won't be a good partner. Screw it! I think I'll look for someone who shows much more interest in *me*.' " Or to a male, the therapist or a group member may say: "If I went with you and you asked me to have sex with you in the manner you just indicated you used with your woman friend, I'd feel very turned off. I'd feel that you only cared for my tits and ass and hardly a fig for me as a human. So even though I might feel attracted to you, I'd run!"

This kind of emotive feedback, when used in REBT, shows the client how *others* will likely react and how he or she may change to bring about more favorable reactions. The therapist and group members employ it educatively and correctively, not just expressively.

BEHAVIORAL SEX THERAPY

As indicated above, REBT utilizes a great deal of behavior therapy. Its theory states that humans rarely change and keep disbelieving a strong self-defeating belief until they act against it. Consequently, REBT therapists have pioneered in giving activity, in vivo homework assignments, to sexually malfunctioning clients. Because REBT behavioral therapy overlaps significantly with the techniques of Masters and Johnson (1970), Masters, Johnson, and Kolodny (1982), and of other behavior therapists (Leiblum & Rosen, 1989), I shall only briefly mention some of its main methods here.

Activity Homework Assignments

REBT favors in vivo desensitization in many instances. Thus, sexually malfunctioning clients are encouraged to have more sex activities instead of their common avoidance of such acts, to have sex with a partner without at first attempting any kind of penile-vaginal intercourse (Masters and Johnson [1970] call this technique the *sensate focus*), to work on overcoming their hostility or avoidance while remaining with an unsatisfactory partner instead of copping out and running away from sex with that individual, to practice certain activities over and over until they acquire adeptness at them, and to practice sexually arousing fantasies (Ellis, 1976f, 1979b, 1985c).

Operant Conditioning

REBT often employs operant conditioning or self-management techniques. Thus, clients are taught to reinforce their having sex with their mates and to penalize (but *not to damn*) themselves when they avoid sex. Or they are shown how to reinforce so-called shameful but harmless activities and how to use self-management principles to minimize or stop their dysfunctional sex compulsions. Following the procedures of behavior-oriented therapists, they frequently are supervised in making sex-love contracts with their mates and monitored in carrying out these contracts (Heiman & LoPiccolo, 1988; Leiblum & Rosen, 1989; Wolpe, 1990; Zilbergeld, 1992).

REBT also specializes in the use of operant conditioning techniques to reinforce cognitive and emotive changes. If, for example, clients agree to antiawfulize or to dispute some of their irrational ideas about how horrible things would be if they failed sexually and if they did not persistently carry out these cognitive homework assignments, we show them how to reward and penalize themselves so as to increase the probability of their performing their assignments. We find that operant conditioning techniques, when voluntarily accepted by clients, serve as one of the best methods of backing up the kind of homework assignments originally invented by Hertzberg (1945), Salter (1949), and other active-directive therapists a good many years ago and now incorporated as routine REBT procedures.

Assertion Training

Assertion training procedures, used especially with shy and unassertive individuals, now constitute one of the most common behavior therapy procedures (Alberti & Emmons, 1995; Lange & Jakubowski, 1976; Lazarus, 1989; Wolpe, 1990). Such procedures have existed as an integral part of REBT since its beginnings. For example, in the first edition of *The Intelligent Woman's Guide to Dating and Mating* (Ellis, 1979a), I (AE) included a pioneering chapter, "How to Become Assertive without Being Aggressive," showing women how to train themselves to overcome their usual passivity and to help themselves to act as assertively as males frequently do in sex-love affairs.

Because women in our culture are often trained to be "femininely" passive, REBT practitioners often help female clients, through a series of graduated homework assignments, to pick up attractive males in public places (such as dances, singles gatherings, or bars), to phone their men friends instead of passively waiting for the men to call, to make sexual overtures when they wish to do so, to ask their partners to engage in sex–love practices that they particularly enjoy, and to do many other "unfeminine" things they truly would like to do (Ellis, 1974b; Wolfe, 1980, 1992; Wolfe & Naimark, 1991). As Patricia Jakubowski-Spector (1973) has shown in an incisive article, "Facilitating the

Growth of Women through Assertive Training," REBT techniques, along with the usual kind of behavioral assertive training, can immensely help females in our society. At the same time, of course, this same combination is used by REBT therapists to enable a large number of overly passive, unassertive males to succeed much better in their sex-love relations.

SUMMARY

In this brief presentation of the REBT approach to sex therapy we have necessarily skimmed over some of the main details of this comprehensive cognitive-emotive-behavioral practice. The main things we would like to note, in summary, are the following: REBT *consciously and on theoretical grounds* employs many of the methods used by other well-known therapies. It holds that humans simultaneously and transactionally think, emote, and behave and that when what we call their emotions or behavior are disordered, we had better also seriously take into account their thinking, imagining, and evaluating. It especially stresses the desirability of profound cognitive or philosophic change if people want to modify their sexual and nonsexual malfunctioning elegantly and permanently. But it never neglects changing beliefs through altering emotions and actions (Ellis, 1957, 1994c; Ellis & Velten, 1992). As a general system of psychotherapy, REBT envisions most serious sex problems within a framework of prevailing emotional upsetness and strives for reduced *general* disturbability along with correcting specific *sexual* malfunctioning. It recognizes, however, that *some* sex problems require concrete informational and training procedures, without the individual's having to receive extensive or intensive psychotherapy, and it tries to remain practical, hard-headed, and efficient as well as philosophically depth-centered.

11

The Use of Hypnosis with REBT

WHY REBT IS EFFECTIVE WITH HYPNOSIS

Rational emotive behavior therapy (REBT) is often used in conjunction with hypnosis and has been shown to work effectively in several controlled outcome studies (Golden, 1982; Reardon & Tosi, 1977; Reardon, Tosi, & Gwynne, 1977; Stanton, 1977, 1989; Tosi & Marzella, 1977; Tosi & Reardon, 1976; Tosi & Murphy, 1995). There are several reasons why REBT and hypnosis can be effectively combined:

1. Many authorities have held that therapeutic hypnosis itself largely works through suggestion and mainly consists of giving clients strong positive statements and inducing them to internalize and act on these self-statements. REBT particularly teaches people how to dispute and challenge their negative self-statements (Ellis, 1962, 1971a, 1973; Ellis & Whiteley, 1979). But it also stresses (as do other forms of cognitive-behavior therapy) the use of repeated and powerful positive or functional coping statements (J. Beck, 1995; Burns, 1980; Dryden, 1984c; Dryden & Ellis, 1986; Dryden & Trower, 1986; Ellis, 1988, 1994c, 1996a; Ellis & Abrahms, 1978; Ellis & Becker, 1982; Ellis & Grieger, 1977; Ellis & Harper, 1975; Grieger & Boyd, 1980; Grieger & Grieger, 1982; Walen, DiGiuseppe, & Dryden, 1992; Wessler & Wessler, 1980).

2. Autohypnosis and regular hypnosis assume that humans upset themselves with ideas, images, and other cognitions and that they can be taught and trained

Parts of this chapter were adapted from Albert Ellis, "Anxiety about Anxiety: The Use of Hypnosis with Rational-Emotive Therapy," in E. Thomas Dowd & James M. Healy (Eds.), *Case Studies in Hypnotherapy* (pp. 3–11), New York: Guilford Press, 1986; and from Albert Ellis, "Rational-Emotive Therapy and Hypnosis," in J. W. Rhue, S. J. Lynn, & I. Kirsch (Eds.), *Handbook of Clinical Hypnosis* (pp. 173–186). Washington, DC: American Psychological Association, 1993. Used by permission.

to change these cognitions and thereby significantly change their feelings and actions (Araoz, 1983; Ellis, 1962, 1993b; Golden et al., 1987). REBT strongly posits and implements this same assumption.

3. Hypnosis and REBT are both highly active-directive methods and differ significantly from many other passive and nondirective therapies, such as psychoanalytic and person-centered therapies.

4. REBT and hypnosis both emphasize homework assignments and in vivo desensitization and frequently urge clients to do the things they are afraid of and to work against their feelings of low frustration tolerance and their self-defeating addictions.

Because some of the basic theories and practices of hypnotherapy and REBT significantly overlap, I (AE) have combined REBT with hypnosis since the early 1950s; one of my first published papers on RET was "Hypnotherapy with Borderline Psychotics" (expanded version, Ellis, 1962). At first I had several sessions with clients with whom I used hypnosis so that they could be trained to go into a moderate or fairly light trance. I noticed, however, that a number of clients who achieved only light trance states—states of deep relaxation but hardly hypnosis—did just as well or better with the REBT I taught them as did clients who achieved deep or "true" hypnotic trances.

I therefore created a new hypnotic method that saved me and my clients hours of therapy time. Using this method, I put the clients in what is usually a light hypnotic (or deeply relaxed) state, employing a modified version of Jacobsen's (1938) progressive relaxation technique, which takes only about 10 minutes to effect. I follow this with 10 minutes of REBT instruction, designed to show the clients that they have a few specific Irrational Beliefs (IBs) with which they are creating some major problem (e.g., anxiety, depression, rage, or self-downing) and that if they keep actively and strongly disputing these IBs (as I have previously taught them to do in several nonhypnotic sessions) they will change their beliefs and thereby also appreciably change their self-defeating feelings and behaviors that stem from and help reinforce these IBs.

The unique feature of this REBT hypnotic procedure is that I often use it only once, for a single session, to work on a client's main presenting problem. I record both the 10 minutes of hypnotic-relaxation induction plus the following 10 minutes of REBT instruction on a C-60 cassette and give the cassette to the clients to keep listening to every day, at least once a day, for the next 30 to 60 days. Using this method, I see the clients for only a single 20-minute hypnotic session, but they get 15, 30, or more hours of recorded REBT hypnotic therapy at their own home or office for the next month or two. If they actually use this time as I direct them to do, they often develop deeper and deeper trance states, even though during the original live session they develop only a very light trance or, as many of them report, no real trance state at all.

To illustrate the use of this method, let me (AE) report the case of a 33-year-old personality disordered female who had a 20-year history of being severely anxious about her school, work, love, and sex performances. She became classically anxious about her anxiety, had a severe case of phrenophobia (fear of going crazy), and was sure that she would end up as a bag lady without any friends, lovers, or money. Actually, she was quite attractive, could have 10 to 15 orgasms a week when she felt secure with a love partner (which was rare), and made a large salary as a sales manager.

I had 13 sessions with this severely anxious woman, and at times she used the main message of REBT—that you largely feel the way you think—and notably decreased her feelings of terror about failing in love, sex, and business. But a few weeks later she would fall back again almost to zero and make herself exceptionally upset, especially about her anxiety itself. After hearing that one of her friends was helped to stop smoking by hypnotherapy, she asked me if I used it along with REBT, and I said that I sometimes did but that I often did not encourage clients to resort to it because they thought of it as a form of magic and used it *instead* of working at the REBT. I agreed, however, to try it with her and used it once. Here is a transcript of my first and only hypnotic session with her.

TRANSCRIPT OF REBT HYPNOTIC SESSION

First loosen your toes and then tense them up. Just tense your toes. Now relax them. Relax, relax. Now I'm going to put you through a series of relaxation exercises like the one you just did with your toes but emphasizing the second part—focusing on physical relaxation. I want you to relax your toes and only focus on relaxing them. Think about your toes and focus on relaxing them. Relax them, relax them, relax them. Then relax the rest of the muscles of your feet—all your sole, instep, heel, and ankle muscles. Let all your feet muscles sink into a nice, easy, free, relaxed state. Relax the soles of your feet, your ankles, your heels, your whole feet. Just relax, relax, relax, relax.

Then relax the calves of your legs, let both calves relax—easy, free, warm, nice, and relaxed. Then relax your knees, let your knee muscles go—nice, free, flexible, warm, relaxed, Then your thighs: relax your thigh muscles, focus on those thigh muscles, and relax, relax, relax them. Relax them, relax them, relax them. Now your hips, let your middle region, your hips, relax, relax, relax. And now go back to your toes again and let your toes, your feet, lower legs, your calves, your knees, your thighs, and your hips relax, relax, all of them relax. Let the whole lower part of your body relax, relax, relax, relax, relax. Now your stomach muscles. Think of your stomach muscles, focus on your stomach muscles, relax all those stomach muscles, relax them, let them go easy, nice, warm, flexible, and free.

And now your chest muscles. Breathe easily—in and out, in and out, let go, relax your chest muscles, let your whole chest, as well as your stomach, your legs and your feet, relax, relax, relax, relax.

Now your shoulder muscles. Let go your shoulder muscles and relax them. Let them sink, sink, sink into themselves. Let them sink, sink, sink into any sofa, bed, or chair that you are resting on. Just let them go. Let them relax. And now your upper arm muscles, let them go—easy, warm, free, relaxed. And your elbows—let your elbow muscles relax, relax, relax. And your forearm muscles—let them go, let them go. Warm, free, easy, relaxed. And let your wrist muscles relax. Easy, free, relaxed, flexible, warm. And the muscles of your fingers and your hand. Let them go—flexible, free, nice, warm, easy, relaxed.

Now your whole body's sinking into a totally nice relaxed state from the tip of your toes to your neck. Your shoulders and your arms are getting more and more and more relaxed. Now focus on your neck muscles. Let them go. Let those neck muscles, which are sometimes tense, relax, relax, relax. And now your jaw muscles. Let your mouth hang slightly open. Let your jaw muscles relax, relax, relax. And you can even relax your cheek muscles. You can let them go a little, let them get flabby and relaxed, more than they normally are. And the muscles of your mouth, your lips—relax, relax them, relax them, relax them.

And now the top of your head, your scalp muscles—wrinkle your scalp a little and let the muscles relax, relax, relax. And especially your eye muscles, which are now tense. Let your eyes relax, relax. Easy, free, and flexible. You now *want* to let your eyes close into a nice, relaxed, easy state. And you focus on letting your eyes relax, relax. And they're closing. Easy and free, warm and relaxed. They're getting tired. They *want* to relax and you *want* them to relax. Along with your whole body, you especially want to let your eyes relax, let go. They're closing, getting tired, tired, and more and more relaxed. And now your eyes are closing and becoming more and more relaxed. You really *feel* the relaxation in your eye muscles. They're closing, closing—becoming more and more relaxed. You *want* to go, you *want* to let yourself go and feel fully calm and relaxed. You *want* to sink into a totally, totally relaxed state.

Your eyes are getting heavier and heavier and you want to let yourself sink, you're trying to let yourself sink, into a deeper, deeper, relaxed state. You want to let your whole body, especially your eyes, go *deeper*, and *deeper*, and *deeper*, into a totally free, warm, nice, flexible, relaxed state. And now you're letting yourself go *deeper, deeper, deeper, deeper*. You want to fully relax and get your body out of your way and to go *deep, deep, down deeper, down deeper*, into a fully, fully, fully free and easy relaxed state. You're only listening to the sound of my voice, that's all you're focusing on, that's all you want to hear—the sound of my voice, that's all you're focusing on, that's all you want to hear—the sound of my voice. And you're going to do what I tell you to do because you *want* to, you *want* to do it. You *want* to stay in this relaxed state and be fully aware of my voice and do what I ask you to do because you *want* to do it, you *want* to be relaxed. You *want* to rid yourself of your anxiety and you *know* that this will help you relax and listen, relax and listen, go into a fully free and relaxed state.

You're only focusing on my voice, and you're going to listen carefully to what I'm telling you. You're going to remember everything I tell you. And after you awake from this relaxed, hypnotic state, you're going to feel very good. Because you're going to remember everything and use what you hear—use it for *you*. Use it to put away all your anxiety and all your anxiety *about* your anxiety. You're going to remember what I tell you and use it every day. Whenever you feel anxious about anything, you're going to remember what I'm telling you now, in this relaxed state, and you're going to fully focus on it, concentrate on it very well, and do exactly what we're talking about—relax and get rid of your anxiety, relax and get rid of your anxiety.

Whenever you get anxious about anything, you're going to realize that the main reason you're anxious is because you are saying to yourself, telling yourself, "I *must* succeed! I *must* succeed! I *must* do this, or I *must* not do that!" You will clearly see and fully accept that your anxiety mainly comes from your self-statements. It doesn't come from without. It doesn't come from other people. *You* make yourself anxious, by demanding that something *must* go well or *must* not exist. It's *your* demand that makes you anxious. It's almost always you and your self-talk; and therefore *you* control it and *you* can change it.

You're going to realize, "*I* make myself anxious. I don't *have* to keep making myself anxious, if I give up my demands, my must's, my should's, my ought's. If I really *accept* what is, *accept* things the way they are when I can't change them, then I won't be anxious. I can always make myself unanxious and less tense by giving up my must's, by relaxing—by wanting and wishing for things but not *needing*, not *insisting*, not *demanding*, not *must*urbating about them."

You're going to keep telling yourself, "I can *ask* for things, I can *wish*. But I do not *need* what I want, I never *need* what I want! There is nothing I *absolutely must* have; and there is nothing I *must* avoid, including my anxiety. I'd *like* to get rid of this anxiety. I *can* get rid of it. I'm *going* to get rid of it. But if I tell myself, 'I *must* not be anxious! I *must* not be anxious! I *must* be unanxious!' then I'll be anxious.

"Depression won't kill me. Anxiety won't kill me. Lack of sex won't kill me. There are lots of unpleasant things in the world that I don't like, but I can *stand* them, I don't *have* to get rid of them. If I'm anxious, I'm anxious—too damn bad! Because *I* control my emotional destiny—as long as I don't feel that I *have* to do anything, that I *have to* succeed at anything. That's what destroys me—the idea that I *have* to be sexy or I have to succeed at sex. Or that I *have* to get rid of my anxiety."

In your regular life, after listening to this tape regularly, you're going to think and to keep thinking these things. Whenever you're anxious, you'll look at what you're doing to *make* yourself anxious, and you'll give up your demands and your must's. You'll dispute your ideas that "I *must* do well! I *must* get people to like me! They *must* not criticize me! It's terrible when they criticize me!" You'll keep asking yourself, "Why *must* I do well? Why do I *have* to be a great sex partner? It would be *nice* if people liked me, but they don't *have* to. I do not *need* their approval. If they criticize me, if they blame me, or they think I'm too sexy or too little sexy, too damn bad! I do not *need* their approval. I'd *like* it, but I don't *need* it. I'd also *like* to be unanxious but there's no reason why I *must* be. Yes, there's no reason why I *must* be. It's just *preferable*. None of these things I fail at are going to kill me.

"And when I die, as I eventually will, so I die! Death is not horrible. It's a state of *no* feeling. It's exactly the same state as I was in before I was conceived. I won't feel *anything*. So I certainly need not be afraid of that!

"And even if I get very anxious and go crazy, that too isn't terrible. If I tell myself, 'I *must* not go crazy! I *must* not go crazy!' then I'll make myself crazy! But even if I'm crazy, so I'm crazy! I can *live* with it even if I'm in a mental hospital. I can *live* and not depress myself about it. *Nothing* is terrible—even when people don't like me, even when I'm acting stupidly, even when I'm very anxious! *Nothing* is terrible! I *can* stand it! It's only a pain in the ass!"

Now this is what you're going to think in your everyday life. Whenever you get anxious about anything, you're going to see what you're anxious about, you're going to realize that you are demanding something, saying "It *must* be so! I *must* get well! I *must* not do the wrong thing! I *must* not be anxious!" And you're going to stop and say, "You know—I don't need that nonsense. If these things happen, they happen. It's not the end of the world! I'd *like* to be unanxious, I'd *like* to get along with people, I'd *like* to have god sex. But if I don't, I *don't*! Tough! It's not the end of everything. I can always be a happy human *in spite of* failures and hassles. If I don't *demand*, if I don't insist, if I don't say, 'I must, I must!' Must's are crazy. My *desires* are all right. But, again, I don't *need* what I *want*!"

Now this is what you're going to keep working at in your everyday life. You're going to keep using your head, your thinking ability, to focus, to concentrate on ridding yourself of your anxiety—just as you're listening and concentrating right now. Your concentration will get better and better. You're going to be more and more in control of your thoughts and your feelings. You will keep realizing that *you* create your anxiety, *you* make yourself upset, and *you* don't have to, you never have to keep doing so. You can give your anxiety up. You can change. You can always relax, and relax, and relax, and not take *anyone*, not take *anything* too seriously.

This is what you're going to remember and work at when you get out of this relaxed state. This idea is what you're going to take with you all day, every day: "*I* control me. I don't *have* to upset myself about anything. If I do upset myself, too bad. I may feel upset for a while but it won't ruin my life or kill me. And I can be anxious without putting myself down, without saying, 'I must not be anxious!' At times I will make myself anxious, but I can give up my anxiety if I don't *demand* that I be unanxious."

And you're going to get better and better about thinking this rational way. You'll become more in control of you. Never *totally* in control because nobody ever is totally unanxious. But you'll make yourself much less anxious and able to live with it when you are anxious. And if you live with it, it will go away. If you live with it, it will go away. Nothing is terrible, not even anxiety. That's what you're going to realize and to keep thinking about until you really, really believe it.

Now you feel nice and free and warm and fully relaxed. In a few minutes I'm going to tell you to come out of this relaxed, hypnotic state. You will then have a good day. You will feel fine when you come out of this state. You will experience no ill effects of hypnosis. You will remember everything I just said to you and will keep working at using it. And you will play this tape every day for the next 30 days. You will listen to it every day until you really believe it and follow it. Eventually, you will be able to follow its directions and to think your way out of anxiety and out of anxiety *about* being anxious without the tape.

You will then be able to release yourself from anxiety by yourself. You can always relax and use the antianxiety technique you will learn by listening to the tape. You can always accept yourself *with* your anxiety and can stop telling yourself, "I must not be anxious! I must not be anxious!" Just tell yourself, "I don't *like* anxiety, I'll work to give it up. I'll conquer it. I'll control myself, control my own emotional destiny. I can always relax, make myself feel easy and free and nice, just as I feel now, get away from cares for a while and then feel unanxious. But I can more elegantly accept myself first with my anxiety, stop fighting it desperately, and stop telling myself it's awful to be anxious. Then I can go back to the original anxiety and get rid of it by refusing to awfulize about failing and vigorously disputing my irrational beliefs, 'I must do well! I must not be disapproved.'"

Now you feel good, you feel relaxed, and in a couple of minutes I'm going to count to three, and when I count to three you will awake and feel quite alive, have a good day, and experience no bad effects, no headaches, no physical discomfort! Everything is going to be fine, and you'll have a good day. You will remember all this, and as I said, you will listen to this tape whenever you possibly can, at least once a day. And you will think and act more and more on its message. You'll be able to control yourself and reduce your anxiety appreciably. And when you do feel anxious, you'll live with the anxiety, accept it, and refuse to panic yourself about it. All right, I'm going to count to three, and when I say *three* you'll wake and be fully alive and alert and feel great for the rest of the day. One, two, three!

DISCUSSION

My client used the recording of her hypnotic REBT session once or twice a day for the next 45 days and reported a significant decrease in her anxiety level, especially in her anxiety about her anxiety. She stopped being phrenophobic, convinced herself that if she had a breakdown and went to the mental hospital it would be highly inconvenient but not horrible or shameful, and then hardly thought at all about going crazy. When she did, she was able to feel comfortable within a few minutes by strongly telling herself, "So I'll be crazy! Tough! I'm sure I won't stay that way very long—and if I do, that will just be tougher. But not shameful! No matter how crazy I am, I'll never be a turd for being that way!"

As she began to get over her anxiety about her anxiety, this woman's enormous fears of failure, particularly of sex failure, for a while almost completely disappeared. When, weeks lalter, they reappeared, they were relatively light, and she was almost invariably able to cope successfully with them. She continued in REBT nonhypnotic treatment for 14 months more but had only 18 half-hour sessions during that time. For the past 15 years she has maintained her gains, with occasional moderate setbacks when a love affair ended, and is now happily married and unanxiously highly productive. Once in a while she still listens to the original hypnotic tape and believes that it was quite instrumental in helping her make much greater progress than she had previously made in REBT.

I tend to agree with her, partly because I have used similar taped sessions to good avail with many other clients (although with little or no success with several others). One important question I have not yet resolved is, does the benefit presumably derived from this tape of recorded hypnotic sessions stem from the use of the entire 20-minute tape, including the hypnotic-relaxation instructions, or would equal benefit stem from the client's listening a number of times to the 10 minutes of REBT instruction on the tape even if this were heard apart from the hypnotic section? I have tried to induce several researchers to do a controlled study of this question, but so far no one, to my knowledge, has done so. I still hope that this experiment will be done one day. Until then I shall continue to use this recorded hypnosis–REBT procedure with some amount of faith in the clinical results I have this far achieved with it.

There are several advantages to using REBT hypnotherapy, as against using REBT regularly without hypnosis, including these:

1. Some clients believe, rightly or wrongly, in the power (or the magic) of hypnosis, therefore ask for it, and are likely to be more favorably predisposed toward therapy when they have it.
2. The manner in which REBT hypnotherapy is done, as outlined in this chapter, includes repetition of the therapeutic message many times, because the clients are asked to listen to the original tape for at least a month or two, every single day, to reinforce the REBT methods that are included on it.
3. Usually, only one problem at a time is tackled; and if and when the clients are successful with that problem, other problems are then handled.

4. This manner of doing REBT hypnotherapy includes homework assignments, and these are repeated many times to encourage the clients to do them.

5. Hypnotherapy, in the manner indicated in this chapter, can be mixed with regular individual or group REBT and can be used to supplement non-hypnotic RET.

The disadvantages of using REBT hypnotherapy include the following:

1. Clients tend to use all kinds of hypnotherapy as taking the authoritative suggestions of the hypnotist as their own. REBT generally tends to emphasize *thinking scientifically*, and taking the hypnotist's suggestions (or any kind of suggestion from the therapist) may play down *self*-thinking, which REBT considers to be more profound and more elegant.

2. Hypnotism implies *easy* and *magical* ways of clients' changing themselves, whereas REBT generally emphasizes their working hard at therapy, including giving up their low frustration tolerance and their beliefs in magic. The form of REBT hypnotherapy outlined in this chapter minimally resorts to suggestion, magic, and ease of self-change, but it still may have these meanings to some clients and may thereby help them make only partial progress in eliminating and continuing to overcome their basic disturbances. For these reasons, I (AE) use REBT hypnotherapy only occasionally and often talk clients out of it so that they use regular REBT in a more independent and hardworking fashion. But it adds an emotive quality to some clients' therapy and therefore can be useful in selected cases.

Appendix

How to Maintain and Enhance Your Rational Emotive Behavior Therapy Gains

ALBERT ELLIS, PhD
Institute for Rational-Emotive Therapy
New York City

If you work at using the principles and practices of rational emotive behavior therapy (REBT), you will be able to change your self-defeating thoughts, feelings, and behaviors and to feel much better than when you started therapy. Good! But you will also, at times, fall back—and sometimes far back. No one is perfect and practically all people take one step backward to every two or three steps forward. Why? Because this is the nature of humans: to improve, to stop improving at times, and sometimes to backslide. How can you (imperfectly!) slow down your tendency to fall back? How can you maintain and enhance your therapy goals? Here are some methods that we have tested at the Institute for Rational Emotive Behavior Therapy in New York and that many of our clients have found quite effective.

HOW TO MAINTAIN YOUR IMPROVEMENT

1. When you improve and then fall back to old feelings of anxiety, depression, or self-downing, try to remind yourself and pinpoint exactly what thoughts, feelings, and behaviors you once changed to bring about your improvement. If you

again feel depressed, think back to how you previously used REBT to make yourself undepressed. For example, you may remember that:

a. You stopped telling yourself that you were worthless and that you couldn't ever succeed in getting what you wanted.
b. You did well in a job or in a love affair and proved to yourself that you did have some ability and that you were lovable.
c. You forced yourself to go on interviews instead of avoiding them and thereby helped yourself overcome your anxiety about them.

Remind yourself of thoughts, feelings, and behaviors that you have changed and that you have helped yourself by changing.

2. Keep thinking, thinking, and thinking rational Beliefs (RBs) or coping statements, such as: "It's great to succeed but I can fully accept myself as a person and enjoy life considerably even when I fail!" Don't merely parrot these statements but go over them carefully many times and think them through until you really begin to believe and feel that they are true.

3. Keep seeking for, discovering and disputing and challenging your irrational Beliefs (IBs) with which you are once again upsetting yourself. Take each important irrational Belief—such as "I have to succeed in order to be a worthwhile person!"—and keep asking yourself: "Why is this Belief true?" "Where is the evidence that my worth to myself, and my enjoyment of living, utterly depends on my succeeding at something?" "In what way would I be totally unacceptable as a human if I failed at an important task or test?" "If I keep holding this Belief, what kind of results will I get?"

Keep *forcefully* and *persistently* disputing your irrationally Beliefs whenever you see that you are letting them creep back again. And even when you don't actively hold them, realize that they may arise once more, bring them to your consciousness, and preventively—and *vigorously*—dispute them.

4. Keep risking and doing things that you irrationally fear—such as riding in elevators, socializing, job hunting, or creative writing. Once you have partly overcome one of your irrational fears, keep acting against it on a regular basis. If you feel uncomfortable in forcing yourself to do things that you are unrealistically afraid of doing, don't allow yourself to avoid doing them—and thereby to preserve your discomfort forever! Often, make yourself as *un*comfortable as you can be, in order to eradicate your irrational fears and to become unanxious and comfortable later.

5. Try to clearly see that difference between healthy negative feelings—such as those of sorrow, regret, and frustration, when you do not get some of the important things you want—and unhealthy negative feelings, such as those of depression, anxiety, self-hatred, and self-pity, when you are deprived of desirable goals and plagued with undesirable things. Whenever you feel *over*concerned (panicked) or

unduly miserable (depressed), acknowledge that you are having a statistically normal but a psychologically unhealthy feeling and that you are probably bringing it on yourself with some dogmatic *should, ought,* or *must.* Realize that you are capable of changing your unhealthy (or *must*urbatory) feelings back into healthy (or preferential) ones. Take your depressed feelings and work on them until you *only* feel sorry and regretful. Take your anxious feelings and work on them until you *only* feel concerned and vigilant. Use rational emotive imagery to vividly imagine unpleasant Activating events even before they happen; let yourself feel unhealthily upset (anxious, depressed, enraged, or self-downing) as you imagine them; then work on your feelings to change them to healthy negative emotions (concern, sorrow, annoyance, or regret) as you keep imagining some of the worst things happening. Don't give up until you actually do change your feelings.

6. Avoid self-defeating procrastination. Do unpleasant tasks fast—today! If you still procrastinate, reward yourself with certain things that you enjoy—for example, eating, vacationing, reading, and socializing—only *after* you have performed the tasks that you easily avoid. If this won't work, give yourself a severe penalty—such as talking to a boring person for 2 hours or burning a $100 bill—every time that you procrastinate.

7. Show yourself that it is an absorbing *challenge* and something of an *adventure* to maintain your emotional health and to keep yourself reasonably happy no matter what kind of misfortunes assail you. Make the uprooting of your misery one of the most important things in your life—something you are utterly determined to steadily work at achieving. Fully acknowledge that you almost always have some *choice* about how to think, feel, and behave; and throw yourself actively into

making that choice for yourself.

8. Remember—and use—the three main insights of REBT that were first outlined in *Reason and Emotion in Psychotherapy* in 1962:

Insight No. 1: You largely *choose* to disturb yourself about the unpleasant events of your life, although you may be encouraged to do so by external happenings and by social learning. You mainly feel the way you think. When obnoxious and frustrating things happen to you at point A (Activating events), you consciously or unconsciously *select* rational Beliefs (RBs) that lead you to feel sad and regretful, and you also *select* irrational Beliefs (IBs) that lead you to feel anxious, depressed, and self-hating.

Insight No. 2: No matter how or when you acquired your irrational Beliefs and your self-sabotaging habits, you now, in the present, *choose* to maintain them—and that is why you are *now* disturbed. Your past history and your present life conditions importantly *affect* you; but they don't *disturb* you. Your present *philosophy* is the main contributor to your *current* disturbance.

Insight No. 3: There is no magical way for you to change your personality and your strong tendencies to needlessly upset yourself. Basic personality change requires persistent *work and practice*—yes, *work and practice*—to enable you to alter your irrational Beliefs, your unhealthy feelings, and your self-destructive behaviors.

9. Steadily—and unfrantically!—look for personal pleasures and enjoyments—such as reading, entertainment, sports, hobbies, art, science, and other vital absorbing interests. Take as your major life goal not only the achievement of emotional health but also that of real enjoyment. Try to become involved in a long-term purpose, goal, or interest in which you can remain truly absorbed. A good, happy life will give you something

to live *for*, will distract you from many serious woes, and will encourage you to preserve and to improve your mental health.

10. Try to keep in touch with several other people who know something about REBT and who can help go over some of its aspects with you. Tell them about problems that you have difficulty coping with and let them know how you are using REBT to overcome these problems. See if they agree with your solutions and can suggest additional and better kinds of REBT disputing that you can use to work against your irrational Beliefs.

11. Practice using REBT with some of your friends, relatives, and associates who are willing to let you try to help them with it. The more often you use it with others and are able to see what their IBs are and to try to talk them out of these self-defeating ideas, the more you will be able to understand the main principles of REBT and use them with yourself. When you see other people act irrationally and in a disturbed manner, try to figure out—with or without talking to them about it—what their main irrational Beliefs probably are and how these could be actively and vigorously disputed.

12. When you are in REBT individual or group therapy try to tape record many of your sessions and listen to these carefully when you are between sessions so that some of the REBT ideas that you learned in therapy sink in. After therapy has ended, keep these tape recordings and play them back to yourself from time to time, to remind you how to deal with some of your old problems or new ones that may arise.

13. Keep reading REBT writings and listening to REBT audio- and audiovisual cassettes. Included in your instructions sheet, which you were given when you started coming for therapy at the Institute, is a list of some of the main books and

cassettes giving the principles and practices of REBT. Read and listen to several of these—particularly *A Guide to Personal Happiness* (Ellis & Becker); *A Guide to Rational Living* (Ellis & Harper); *Overcoming Procrastination* (Ellis & Knaus); *Overcoming the Rating Game* (Hauck); *A Rational Counseling Primer* (Young); *How to Stubbornly Refuse to Make Yourself Miserable About Anything—Yes Anything!* and *Think Your Way to Happiness* (Dryden & Gordon). Keep going back to the REBT reading and audiovisual material from time to time, to keep reminding yourself of some of the main REBT findings and philosophies.

HOW TO DEAL WITH BACKSLIDING

1. Accept your backsliding as normal— as something that happens to almost all people who at first improve emotionally and who then fall back. See it as part of your human fallibility. Don't make yourself feel ashamed when some of your old symptoms return, and don't think that you have to handle them entirely by yourself and that it is wrong or weak for you to seek some additional sessions of therapy or to talk to your friends about your renewed problems.

2. When you backslide, look at your self-defeating *behavior* as bad and unfortunate, but work very hard at refusing to put *yourself* down for engaging in this behavior. Use the highly important REBT principle of refusing to rate *you*, your *self*, or your *being* but measure only *acts, deeds*, and *traits*. You are always a *person who* acts well or badly—never a *good person* nor a *bad person*. No matter how badly you fall back and bring on your old disturbances again, work at fully accepting yourself *with* this unfortunate or weak behavior—and then try, and keep trying, to change your behavior.

3. Go back to the ABCs of REBT and clearly see what you did to fall back to your old symptoms. At A (Activating Event), you usually experienced some failure or rejection once again. At RB (rational Belief) you probably told yourself that you didn't *like* failing and didn't *want* to be rejected. If you only stayed with these rational Beliefs, you would merely feel sorry, regretful, disappointed, or frustrated. But when you felt disturbed again you probably then went on to some irrational Beliefs (IBs), such as: "I *must* not fail! It's *horrible* when I do!" "I *have to* be accepted, because if I'm not that makes me an *unlovable worthless person!*" Then, after convincing yourself on these IBs, you felt, at C (emotional Consequence), once again depressed and self-downing.

4. When you find your irrational Beliefs by which you are once again disturbing yourself, just as you originally used Disputing (D) to challenge and surrender them, do so again—*immediately* and *persistently*. Thus, you can ask yourself, "Why *must* I not fail? Is it really *horrible* if I do?" And you can answer: "There is no reason why I *must* not fail, though I can think of several reasons why it would be highly undesirable. It's not *horrible* if I do fail— only distinctly *inconvenient*." You can also Dispute your other irrational Beliefs by asking yourself, "Where is it written that I *have* to be accepted? How do I become an *unlovable, worthless person* if I am rejected?" And you can answer: "I never *have to be* accepted, though I would very much *prefer* to be. If I am rejected, that makes me, alas, a *person who* is rejected this time by this individual under these conditions, but it hardly makes me an *unlovable, worthless person* who will always be rejected by anyone for whom I really care."

5. Keep looking for, finding, and actively and vigorously Disputing your irrational Beliefs which you have once again revived and that are now making you feel

anxious or depressed once more. Keep doing this, over and over, until you build intellectual and emotional muscle (just as you would build physical muscle by learning how to exercise and then by *continuing* to exercise).

6. Don't fool yourself into believing that if you merely change your language you will always change your thinking. If you neurotically tell yourself, "I *must* succeed and be approved" and you sanely change this self-statement to, "I *prefer* to succeed and be approved," you may still really be convinced, "But I really *have to* do well and *have got to be* loved." Before you stop your Disputing and before you are satisfied with your answers to it (which in REBT we call E, or an Effective New Philosophy), keep on doing it until you are *really* convinced of your rational answers and until your feelings of disturbance truly disappear. Then do the same thing many, many times—until your new E (Effective New Philosophy) becomes hardened and habitual—which it almost always will if you keep working at arriving at it and re-instituting it.

7. Convincing yourself lightly or "intellectually" of your new Effective New Philosophy or rational Beliefs often won't help very much or persist very long. Do so very *strongly* and *vigorously*, and do so many times. Thus, you can *powerfully* convince yourself, until you really *feel* it: "I do not *need* what I *want*! I never *have to* succeed, no matter how greatly I *wish to* do so!" "I *can* stand being rejected by someone I care for. It won't *kill* me—and I *still* can lead a happy life!" "*No* human is damnable and worthless —including and especially *me*!"

HOW TO GENERALIZE FROM WORKING ON ONE EMOTIONAL PROBLEM TO WORKING ON OTHER PROBLEMS

1. Show yourself that your present emotional problem and the ways in which you bring it on are not unique and that virtually all emotional and behavioral difficulties are created by irrational Beliefs (IBs). Whatever your IBs are, moreover, you can overcome them by strongly and persistently disputing and acting against them.

2. Recognize that you tend to have three major kinds of irrational Beliefs that lead you to disturb yourself and that the emotional and behavioral problems that you want to relieve fall into one of these three categories:

a. "I *must* do well and *have to* be approved by people whom I find important." This IB leads you to feel anxious, depressed, and self-hating; and to avoid doing things at which you may fail and avoiding relationships that may not turn out well.

b. "Other people *must* treat me fairly and nicely!" This IB contributes to your feeling angry, furious, violent, and over-rebellious.

c. "The conditions under which I live *must* be comfortable and free from major hassles!" This IB tends to create your feelings of low frustration tolerance and self-pity; and sometimes those of anger and depression.

3. Recognize that when you employ one of these three absolutistic *musts*—or any of the innumerable variations on them that you can easily slide into—you naturally and commonly derive from them other irrational conclusions, such as:

a. "Because I am not doing as well as I *must*, I am an incompetent worthless individual!" (self-downing).

b. "Since I am not being approved by people whom I find important, as I *have to be*, it's *awful* and *terrible*!" (Awfulizing).

c. "Because others are not treating me as fairly and as nicely as they *absolutely should* treat me, they are *utterly rotten people* and deserve to be damned!" (Damnation).

d. "Since the conditions under which I live are not that comfortable and since my life has several major hassles, as it *must* not have, I can't stand it! My existence is a horror!" (Can't-stand-it-itis).

e. "Because I have failed and got rejected as I *absolutely ought not* have done, I'll *always* fail and *never* get accepted as I *must* be! My life will be hopeless and joyless forever!" (Overgeneralizing).

4. Work at seeing that these irrational Beliefs are part of your *general* repertoire of thoughts and feelings and that you bring them to many different kinds of situations that are against your desires. Realize that in just about all cases where you feel seriously upset and act in a distinctly self-defeating manner you are consciously or unconsciously sneaking in one or more of these IBs. Consequently, if you get rid of them in one area and are still emotionally disturbed about something else, you can always use the same REBT principles to discover your IBs in the new area and to eliminate them there.

5. Repeatedly show yourself that it is almost impossible to disturb yourself and to remain disturbed in *any* way if you abandon your absolutistic, dogmatic *should's*, *ought's*, and *must's* and consistently replace them with flexible and unrigid (though still strong) *desires* and *preferences*.

6. Continue to acknowledge that you can change your irrational Beliefs (IBs) by rigorously (not rigidly!) using flexible scientific methods. With scientific thinking, you can show yourself that your irrational Beliefs are only theories or hypotheses—not facts. You can logically and realistically Dispute them in many ways, such as these:

a. You can show yourself that your IBs are self-defeating—that they interfere with your goals and your happiness. For if you firmly convince yourself, "I *must* succeed at important tasks and *have to* be approved by all the significant people in my life," you will of course at times fail and be disapproved—and thereby tend to

make yourself anxious and depressed instead of sorry and frustrated.

b. Your irrational Beliefs do not conform to reality—and especially do not conform to the facts of human fallibility. If you always *had* to succeed, if the universe commanded that you *must* do so, you obviously *would* always succeed. And of course you often don't! If you invariably *had* to be approved by others, you could never be disapproved. But obviously you frequently are! The universe is clearly not arranged so that you will always get what you demand. So although your desires are often realistic, your godlike commands definitely are not!

c. Your irrational Beliefs are illogical, inconsistent, or contradictory. No matter how much you *want* to succeed and to be approved, it never follows that therefore you *must* do well in these (or any other) respects. No matter how desirable justice or politeness is, it never *has to* exist.

Although the scientific method is not infallible or sacred, it efficiently helps you to discover which of your beliefs are irrational and self-defeating and how to use factual evidence, logical thinking, and practical analysis to minimize them. If you keep using flexible thinking, you will avoid dogma and set up your hypotheses about you, other people, and the world around you so that you always keep them open to change.

7. Try to set up some main goals and purposes in life—goals that you would like very much to reach but that you never tell yourself that you absolutely must attain. Keep checking to see how you are coming along with these goals; at times revise them; see how you feel about achieving them; and keep yourself goal-oriented without *demanding* that you achieve your aims.

8. If you get bogged down and begin to lead a life that seems too miserable or

dull, review the points made in this pamphlet and work at using them. Once again: if you fall back or fail to go forward at the pace you prefer, don't hesitate to return to therapy for some booster sessions or to join one of the Institute's regular therapy groups.

I gratefully acknowledge the contributions of the following people at the Institute for Rational Emotive Behavior Therapy in New York who read this pamphlet when it was in manuscript and who made valuable comments on it: Raymond DiGiuseppe, Mal Holland, Terry Jordan, Leonor Lega, Naomi McCormick, Harriet Mischel, Beverly Pieren, Susan Presby, Karin Schleider, Janet Wolfe, Joe Yankura, and Thea Zeeve. However, I take all responsibility for the views expressed in the pamphlet.

Additional copies of this pamphlet are available at: 10 copies for $2.50; 50 copies for $10.00; 100 copies for $15.00
from the
INSTITUTE FOR RATIONAL EMOTIVE BEHAVIOR THERAPY
45 East 65th Street/New York, N.Y. 10021 - 6593
(212) 535-0822 FAX (212) 249-3582

References

Items preceded by an asterisk include the main books and other materials on rational emotive behavior therapy (REBT). Most of these materials are obtainable from the Institute for Rational Emotive Behavior Therapy, 45 East 65th Street, New York, NY 10021-6593; (212) 535-0822. The institute will continue to make available these and other materials on RET, as well as present talks, seminars, workshops, training practica, and other presentations for professionals and members of the public. Those interested can send for its free list of publications and events.

Ackerman, N. (1958). *The psychodynamics of family life*. New York: Basic Books.

Adler, A. (1927). *Understanding human nature*. New York: Garden City.

Ainslie, G. (1974). Specious reward: A behavioral theory of impulsiveness and impulse control. *Psychological Bulletin*, 82, 463–496.

*Alberti, R. E., & Emmons, M. L. (1995). *Your perfect right* (6th ed.). San Luis Obispo, CA: Impact.

Araoz, D. L. (1983). *Hypnosis and sex therapy*. New York: Brunner/Mazel.

Bach, G. R. (1966). The marathon group: Intensive practice of intimate reaction. *Psychological Reports, 18*, 995–1002.

Bandura, A. (1986). *Social foundations of thought and action: A social cognitive theory*. Englewood Cliffs, NJ: Prentice-Hall.

*Bard, J. (1980). *Rational-emotive therapy in practice*. Champaign, IL: Research Press.

Barrish, H. H., & Barrish, I. J. (1985). *Managing parental anger: The coping parent series*. Leawood: Kansas: Overland Press.

Barrish, I. J., & Barrish, H. H. (1989). *Surviving and enjoying your adolescent*. Kansas City, MO: Westport Publishers.

Bartley, W. W., III. (1984). *The retreat to commitment* (rev. ed.). Peru, IL: Open Court.

Baucom, D. H., & Epstein, N. (1990). *Cognitive-behavioral marital therapy*. New York: Brunner/Mazel.

Beck, A. T. (1976). *Cognitive therapy and the emotional disorders.* New York: International Universities Press.

Beck, A. T., Rush, A. J., Shaw, B. F., & Emery, G. (1979). *Cognitive therapy of depression.* New York: Guilford.

Beck, A. T. (1988). *Love is not enough.* New York: Harper & Row.

Beck, J. S. (1995). *Cognitive therapy: Basics and beyond.* New York: Guilford.

*Bernard, M. E. (Ed.). (1991). *Using rational-emotive therapy effectively: A practitioner's guide.* New York: Plenum.

*Bernard, M. E., & DiGiuseppe, R. (Eds.). (1989). *Inside RET: A critical appraisal of the theory and therapy of Albert Ellis.* San Diego, CA: Academic Press.

*Bernard, M. E., & Wolfe, J. L., (Eds.). (1993). *The RET resource book for practitioners.* New York: Institute for Rational-Emotive Therapy.

Bernheim, H. (1947). *Suggestive therapeutics.* New York: London Book Company. (Original publication, 1886)

Beutler, L. E. (1983). *Eclectic psychotherapy: A systematic approach.* New York: Pergamon.

Bordin, E. S. (1979). The generalizability of the psychoanalytic concept of the working alliance. *Psychotherapy: Theory, Research and Practice, 16,* 252–260.

*Boutin, G. E, & Tosi, D. J. (1983). Modification of irrational ideas and test anxiety through rational stage directed hypnotherapy (RSDH). *Journal of Clinical Psychology, 39,* 382–391.

Bowlby, J. (1988). *Attachment and loss: 3. Loss: Sadness and depression.* New York: Basic Books.

Burns, D. D. (1980). *Feeling good: The new mood therapy.* New York: Morrow.

Comfort, A. (1974). *The joy of sex.* New York: Crown.

Coué, E. (1921). *My method.* New York: Doubleday, Page.

*Crawford, T. (1982, October). *Communication and rational-emotive therapy.* Workshop presented at the Institute for Rational-Emotive Therapy, Los Angeles.

*Crawford, T., & Ellis, A. (1989). A dictionary of rational-emotive feelings and behaviors. *Journal of Rational-Emotive and Cognitive-Behavior Therapy, 7*(1), 3–27.

Danysh, J. (1974). *Stop without quitting.* San Francisco: International Society for General Semantics.

*DiGiuseppe, R. (1991). Comprehensive cognitive disputing in RET. In M. Bernard (Ed.), *Using rational-emotive therapy effectively.* New York: Plenum Press.

*DiGiuseppe, R., Miller, N., & Trexler, L. (1979). A review of rational-emotive psychotherapy outcome studies. In A. Ellis & J. M. Whiteley (Eds.). *Theoretical and empirical foundations of rational-emotive therapy* (pp. 218–236). Monterey, CA: Brooks/Cole.

Dreikurs, R. (1974). *Psychodynamics, psychotherapy and counseling* (rev. ed.). Chicago: Alfred Adler Institute.

*Dryden, W. (1983). Audiotape supervision by mail: A rational-emotive approach. *British Journal of Cognitive Psychotherapy*, *1*(1), 57–64.

Dryden, W. (1984a). *Individual therapy in Britain*. London: Harper & Row.

*Dryden, W. (1984b). Rational-emotive therapy. In W. Dryden (Ed.), *Individual therapy in Britain* (pp. 235–263). London: Harper & Row.

*Dryden, W. (1984c). *Rational-emotive therapy: Fundamentals and innovations*. Beckenham, Kent, England: Croom Helm.

Dryden, W. (1984d). Therapeutic arenas. In W. Dryden (Ed.), *Individual therapy in Britain* (pp. 1–22). London: Harper & Row.

*Dryden, W. (1985a). Challenging but not overwhelming: A compromise in negotiating homework assignments. *British Journal of Cognitive Psychotherapy*, *3*(1), 77–80.

*Dryden, W. (1985b). Marital therapy: The rational-emotive approach. In W. Dryden (Ed.), *Marital therapy in Britain* (Vol. 1, pp. 195–221). London: Harper & Row.

Dryden, W. (1987). Theoretically-consistent eclecticism: Humanizing a computer "addict." In J. C. Norcross (Ed.), *Casebook of eclectic psychotherapy* (pp. 221–237). New York: Brunner/Mazel.

*Dryden, W. (1994a). *Invitation to rational-emotive psychology*. London: Whurr.

*Dryden, W. (1994b). *Progress in rational emotive behavior therapy*. London: Whurr.

*Dryden, W. (1995a). *Brief rational emotive behavior therapy*. London: Wiley.

*Dryden, W. (1995b). *Facilitating client change in rational emotive behavior therapy*. London: Whurr.

*Dryden, W. (1995c). *Preparing for client change in rational emotive behavior therapy*. London: Whurr.

*Dryden, W. (Ed.). (1995d). *Rational emotive behavior therapy: A reader*. London: Sage.

*Dryden, W., & DiGiuseppe, R. (1990). *A primer on rational-emotive therapy*. Champaign, IL: Research Press.

*Dryden, W., & Ellis, A. (1986). Rational-emotive therapy (RET). In W. Dryden & W. Golden (Eds.), *Cognitive-behavioural approaches to psychotherapy* (pp. 129–168). London: Harper & Row.

*Dryden, W., & Ellis, A. (1990). *The essential Albert Ellis*. New York: Springer Publishing Co.

*Dryden, W., & Ellis, A. (1991). *A dialogue with Albert Ellis: Against dogma*. Philadelphia: Open University Press.

*Dryden, W., & Gordon, J. (1991). *Think your way to happiness*. London: Sheldon Press.

*Dryden, W., & Hill, L. K. (Eds.). (1993). *Innovations in rational-emotive therapy*. Newbury Park, CA: Sage.

*Dryden, W., & Neenan, M. (1995). *Dictionary of rational emotive behaviour therapy*. London: Whurr.

*Dryden, W., & Trower, P. (Eds.). (1986). *Rational-emotive therapy: Recent developments in theory and practice*. Bristol, England: Institute for RET (UK).

Duckro, P., Beal, D., & George, C. (1979). Research on the effects of disconfirmed client role expectations in psychotherapy: A critical review. *Psychological Bulletin, 86*, 260–275.

Dunlap, K. (1932). *Habits: Their making and unmaking*. New York: Liveright.

Eisenberg, J. M., & Zingle, H. W. (1975). *Journal of Marriage and Family Counseling*, (1), 81–91.

*Ellis, A. (1957). *How to live with a "neurotic": At home and at work*. New York: Crown; revised ed., Hollywood, CA: Wilshire Books, 1975.

*Ellis, A. (1958a). Rational psychotherapy. *Journal of General Psychology, 59*, 35–49. Reprinted by the Institute for Rational-Emotive Therapy, New York.

*Ellis, A. (1958b). *Sex without guilt*. New York: Lyle Stuart; rev. ed., New York, Lyle Stuart, 1965.

*Ellis, A. (1960). *The art and science of love*. Secaucus, NJ: Lyle Stuart.

*Ellis, A. (1962). *Reason and emotion in psychotherapy*. Secaucus, NJ: Lyle Stuart.

*Ellis, A. (1963). Toward a more precise definition of "emotional" and "intellectual" insight. *Psychological Reports, 13*, 125–126.

*Ellis, A. (1965). *Suppressed: Seven key essays publishers dared not print*. Chicago: New Classics House.

*Ellis, A. (1968). Is psychoanalysis harmful? *Psychiatric Opinion, 5*(1), 16–25. Reprinted by the Institute for Rational-Emotive Therapy, New York.

*Ellis, A. (1969). A weekend of rational encounter. *Rational Living, 4*(2), 1–8.

*Ellis, A. (1971a). *Growth through reason*. North Hollywood, CA: Wilshire Books.

*Ellis, A. (Speaker). (1971b). *How to stubbornly refuse to be ashamed of anything* (Cassette recording). New York: Institute for Rational Emotive Therapy.

*Ellis, A. (1972a). Helping people get better: Rather than merely feel better. *Rational Living, 7*(2), 2–9.

*Ellis, A. (1972b). *Psychotherapy and the value of a human being*. New York: Institute for Rational-Emotive Therapy.

*Ellis, A. (1973). *Humanistic psychotherapy: The rational–emotive approach*. New York: McGraw-Hill.

*Ellis, A. (1974a). *Technique of disputing irrational beliefs (DIBS)*. New York: Institute for Rational Emotive Therapy.

*Ellis, A. (1974b). The treatment of sex and love problems in women. In V. Franks & V. Burtle (Eds.), *Women in therapy* (pp. 284–306). New York: Brunner/Mazel.

*Ellis, A. (1976a). The biological basis of human irrationality. *Journal of Individual Psychology, 32*, 145–168. Reprinted by the Institute for Rational-Emotive Therapy, New York.

*Ellis, A. (Speaker). (1976b). *Conquering low frustration tolerance* (Cassette recording). New York: Institute for Rational-Emotive Therapy.

*Ellis, A. (Speaker). (1976c). *Rational-emotive psychotherapy applied to groups* (Film). Washington, DC: American Association of Counseling and Development.

*Ellis, A. (1976d). RET abolishes most of the human ego. *Psychotherapy, 13*, 343–348. Reprinted by the Institute for Rational-Emotive Therapy, New York.

*Ellis, A. (Speaker). (1976e). *Rational-emotive therapy with individuals and groups* (Videotape). Austin, TX: Audio-Visual Resource Center, University of Texas.

*Ellis, A. (1976f). *Sex and the liberated man*. Secaucus, NJ: Lyle Stuart.

*Ellis, A. (1976g). Techniques of handling anger in marriage. *Journal of Marriage and Family Counseling, 2*, 305–316.

*Ellis, A. (1977a). *Anger: How to live with and without it*. Secaucus, NJ: Citadel Press.

*Ellis, A. (1977b). Fun as psychotherapy. *Rational Living, 12*(1), 2–6.

*Ellis, A. (Speaker). (1977c). *A garland of rational humorous songs* (Cassette recording). New York: Institute for Rational-Emotive Therapy.

*Ellis, A. (1978a). Family therapy: A phenomenological *and* active-directive approach. *Journal of Marriage and Family Counseling, 4*(2), 43–50. Reprinted by the Institute for Rational-Emotive Therapy, New York.

*Ellis, A. (1978b). Personality characteristics of rational-emotive therapists and other kinds of therapists. *Psychotherapy: Theory, Research and Practice, 15*, 329–332.

*Ellis, A. (1979a). Discomfort anxiety: A new cognitive behavioral construct. Part 1. *Rational Living, 14*(2), 3–8.

*Ellis, A. (1979b). *The intelligent woman's guide to dating and mating*. Secaucus, NJ: Lyle Stuart.

*Ellis, A. (1979c). The issue of force and energy in behavioral change. *Journal of Contemporary Psychotherapy, 10*(2), 83–97.

*Ellis, A. (1979d). The practice of rational-emotive therapy. In A. Ellis & J. M. Whiteley (Eds.), *Theoretical and empirical foundations for rational-emotive therapy* (pp. 61–100). Monterey, CA: Brooks/Cole.

*Ellis, A. (1979e). The theory of rational-emotive therapy. In A. Ellis & J. M. Whiteley (Eds.), *Theoretical and empirical foundations of rational-emotive therapy* (pp. 33–60). Monterey, CA: Brooks/Cole.

*Ellis, A. (1980a). Discomfort anxiety: A new cognitive behavioral construct. Part 2. *Rational Living, 15*(1), 25–30.

*Ellis, A. (1980b). Rational-emotive therapy and cognitive behavior therapy: Similarities and differences. *Cognitive Therapy and Research, 4*, 325–340.

*Ellis, A. (1980c). The treatment of erectile dysfunction. In S. R. Leiblum & L. A. Pervin (Eds.), *Principles and practice of sex therapy* (pp. 240–258). New York: Guilford.

*Ellis, A. (1980d). The value of efficiency in psychotherapy. *Psychotherapy: Theory, Research, and Practice, 17*, 414–418.

*Ellis, A. (1981). The use of rational humorous songs in psychotherapy. *Voices, 16*(4), 29–36.

*Ellis, A. (1982a). Intimacy in rational-emotive therapy. In M. Fisher & G. Striker (Eds.), *Intimacy* (pp. 203–217). New York: Plenum.

*Ellis, A. (1982b). Rational-emotive group therapy. In G. M. Gazda (Ed.), *Basic approaches to group psychotherapy and group counseling* (3rd ed.) (pp. 381–412). Springfield, IL: Thomas.

*Ellis, A. (1982c). The treatment of alcohol and drug abuse: A rational-emotive approach. *Rational Living, 17*(2), 15–24.

Ellis, A. (1982d). Rational-emotive family therapy. In A. M. Horne & M. M. Ohlsen (Eds.), *Family counseling and therapy* (pp. 302–328). Itasca, IL: Peacock.

*Ellis, A. (1983a). Failures in rational-emotive therapy. In E. B. Foa & P. M. G. Emmelkamp (Eds.), *Failures in behavior therapy* (pp. 159–171). New York: Wiley.

*Ellis, A. (1983b). The philosophic implications and dangers of some popular behavior therapy techniques. In M. Rosenbaum, C. M. Franks, & Y. Jaffe (Eds.), *Perspectives in behavior therapy in the eighties* (pp. 138–151). New York: Springer Publishing Co.

Ellis, A. (1983c). Rational-emotive therapy (RET) approaches to overcoming resistance. *British Journal of Cognitive Therapy, 1*(1), 28–38.

*Ellis, A. (1985a). Dilemmas in giving warmth or love to clients: An interview with Windy Dryden. In W. Dryden (Ed.), *Therapist's dilemmas* (pp. 5–16). London: Harper & Row.

*Ellis, A. (1985b). Expanding the ABCs of rational-emotive therapy. In M. Mahoney & A. Freeman (Eds.), *Cognition and psychotherapy* (pp. 313–323). New York: Plenum.

*Ellis, A. (1985c). *Overcoming resistance: Rational-emotive therapy with difficult clients.* New York: Springer Publishing Co.

*Ellis, A. (1986). Anxiety about anxiety: The use of hypnosis with rational-emotive therapy. In E. T. Dowd & J. M. Healy (Eds.), *Case studies in hypnotherapy* (pp. 3–11). New York: Guilford.

*Ellis, A. (1987a). A sadly neglected cognitive element in depression. *Cognitive Therapy and Research, 11*, 121–146.

*Ellis, A. (1987b). The use of rational humorous songs in psychotherapy. In W. F. Fry, Jr. & W. A. Salameh (Eds.), *Handbook of humor and psychotherapy* (pp. 265–286). San Diego: Professional Resource Exchange.

*Ellis, A. (1988). *How to stubbornly refuse to make yourself miserable about anything—yes, anything!* Secaucus, NJ: Lyle Stuart.

*Ellis, A. (Speaker). (1989). *Unconditionally accepting yourself and others* (Cassette recording). New York: Institute for Rational-Emotive Therapy.

*Ellis, A. (Speaker). (1990). *Albert Ellis live at the Learning Annex* (2 cassettes). New York: Institute for Rational-Emotive Therapy.

*Ellis, A. (1991a). Are all methods of counseling equally effective? *New York State Journal for Counseling and Development, 6*(2), 9–13.

*Ellis, A. (1991b). *The case against religiosity* (rev. ed.). New York: Institute for Rational-Emotive Therapy.

*Ellis, A. (1991c). *Humanism and psychotherapy: A revolutionary approach.* (rev. ed.). New York: Institute for Rational-Emotive Therapy. (Original work published 1972)

*Ellis, A. (1991d). *Rational-emotive family therapy.* In A. M. Horne & J. L. Passmore (Eds.), *Family counseling and therapy* (2nd ed., pp. 403–434). Itasca, IL: Peacock.

*Ellis, A. (1991e). Using RET effectively: Reflections and interview. In M. E. Bernard (Ed.), *Using rational-emotive therapy effectively* (pp. 1–33). New York: Plenum.

*Ellis, A. (1992a). Brief therapy: The rational-emotive method. In S. H. Budman, M. F. Hoyt, & S. Fiedman (Eds.), *The first session in brief therapy* (pp. 36–58). New York: Guilford.

*Ellis, A. (1992b). Foreword. In P. Hauck, *Overcoming the rating game* (pp. 1–4). Louisville, KY: Westminster/John Knox.

*Ellis, A. (1992c). Group rational-emotive and cognitive-behavioral therapy. *International Journal of Group Therapy, 42*, 63–80.

*Ellis, A. (1993a). The advantages and disadvantages of self-help therapy materials. *Professional Psychology: Research and Practice, 24*, 335–339.

*Ellis, A. (1993b). Fundamentals of rational-emotive therapy for the 1990s. In W. Dryden & L. K. Hill (Eds.), *Innovations in rational-emotive therapy* (pp. 1–32). Newbury Park, CA: Sage.

*Ellis, A. (1993c). General semantics and rational emotive behavior therapy. *Bulletin of General Semantics, 51*, 12–28. Also in P. D. Johnston, D. D. Bourland, Jr., & J. Klein (Eds.), *More E-prime* (pp. 213–240). Concord, CA: International Society for General Semantics.

*Ellis, A. (1993d). Rational emotive imagery: RET version. In M. E. Bernard & J. L. Wolfe (Eds.), *The RET source book for practitioners* (pp. II8–II10). New York: Institute for Rational-Emotive Therapy.

*Ellis, A. (1993e). The rational-emotive therapy (RET) approach to marriage and family therapy. *Family Journal: Counseling and Therapy for Couples and Families, 1*, 292–307.

*Ellis, A. (1993f). Rational-emotive therapy and hypnosis. In J. W. Rhue, S. J. Lynn, & I. Kirsch (Eds.), *Handbook of clinical hypnosis* (pp. 173–186). Washington, DC: American Psychological Association.

*Ellis, A. (1993g). Vigorous RET disputing. In M. E. Bernard & J. L. Wolfe, (Eds.), *The RET resource book for practitioners* (pp. II-7). New York: Institute for Rational-Emotive Therapy.

*Ellis, A. (1994a). My response to "Don't throw the therapeutic baby out with the holy water": Helpful and hurtful elements of religion! *Journal of Psychology and Christianity, 13,* 323–326.

*Ellis, A. (1994b). Rational emotive behavior therapy approaches to obsessive-compulsive disorder (OCD). *Journal of Rational-Emotive and Cognitive-Behavior Therapy, 12,* 121–141.

*Ellis, A. (1994c). *Reason and emotion in psychotherapy* (revised and updated). New York: Birch Lane Press.

*Ellis, A. (1994d). Secular humanism. In F. Wertz (Ed.), *The humanistic movement* (pp. 233–242). Lakeworth, FL: Gardner Press.

*Ellis, A. (1994e). The treatment of borderline personalities with rational emotive behavior therapy. *Journal of Rational-Emotive and Cognitive-Behavior Therapy, 12,* 101–119.

*Ellis, A. (1995a). Rational emotive behavior therapy. In R. Corsini & D. Wedding (Eds.), *Current Psychotherapies* (5th ed., pp. 162–196). Itasca, IL: Peacock.

*Ellis, A. (Speaker). (1995b). *Using rational-emotive behavior therapy techniques to cope with disability* (Cassette recording). Englewood, CO: Sound Images Inc.

*Ellis, A. (1996a). *Better, deeper and more enduring brief therapy.* New York: Brunner/Mazel.

*Ellis, A. (1996b). A social constructionist position for mental health counseling: A response to Jeffrey T. Guterman. *Journal of Mental Health Counseling.*

*Ellis, A., & Abrahms, E. (1978). *Brief psychotherapy in medical and health practice.* New York: Springer Publishing Co.

*Ellis, A., & Abrams, M. (1994). *How to cope with a fatal disease.* New York: Barricade Books.

*Ellis, A., & Becker, I. (1982). *A guide to personal happiness.* North Hollywood, CA: Wilshire.

*Ellis, A., & Bernard, M. E. (Eds.). (1983). *Rational-emotive approaches to the problems of childhood.* New York: Plenum.

*Ellis, A., & Bernard, M. E. (Eds.). (1985). *Clinical applications of rational-emotive therapy.* New York: Plenum.

*Ellis, A., & Grieger, R. (Eds.). (1977). *Handbook of rational-emotive therapy* (Vol. 1). New York: Springer Publishing Co.

*Ellis, A., & Grieger, R. (Eds.). (1986). *Handbook of rational-emotive therapy* (Vol. 2). New York: Springer Publishing Co.

*Ellis, A., & Harper, R. A. (1961a). *A guide to rational living.* Englewood Cliffs, NJ: Prentice Hall.

*Ellis, A., & Harper, R. A. (1961b). *A guide to successful marriage.* North Hollywood, CA: Wilshire Books.

*Ellis, A., & Harper, R. A. (1997). *A guide to rational living.* (3rd ed.) Revised and updated. North Hollywood, CA: Wilshire.

*Ellis, A., & Knaus, W. (1977). *Overcoming procrastination.* New York: New American Library.

*Ellis, A., & Lange, A. (1994). *How to keep people from pushing your buttons*. New York: Carol Publications.

*Ellis, A., McInerney, J. F., DiGiuseppe, R., & Yeager, R. J. (1988). *Rational-emotive therapy with alcoholics and substance abusers*. Needham, MA: Allyn & Bacon.

*Ellis, A., & Robb, H. (1994). Acceptance in rational-emotive therapy. In S. C. Hayes, N. S. Jacobson, V. M. Follette, & M. J. Dougher (Eds.), *Acceptance and change* (pp. 91–102). Reno, NV: Context Press.

*Ellis, A., Sichel, J., Leaf, R. C., & Mass, R. (1989). Countering perfectionism in research on clinical practice: 1. Surveying rationality changes after a single intensive RET intervention. *Journal of Rational-Emotive and Cognitive-Behavior Therapy, 7*, 197–218.

*Ellis, A., Sichel, J. L., Yeager, R. J., DiMattia, D. J., & DiGiuseppe, R. A. (1989). *Rational-emotive couples therapy*. Needham, MA: Allyn & Bacon.

*Ellis, A., & Velten, E. (1992). *When AA doesn't work for you: Rational steps for quitting alcohol*. New York: Barricade Books.

*Ellis, A., & Whiteley, J. M. (1979). *Theoretical and empirical foundations of rational-emotive therapy*. Monterey, CA: Brooks/Cole.

*Ellis, A., Wolfe, J. L., & Moseley, S. (1966). *How to raise an emotionally healthy, happy child*. North Hollywood, CA: Wilshire Books.

*Ellis, A., & Yeager, R. (1989). *Why some therapies don't work: The dangers of transpersonal psychology*. Buffalo, NY: Prometheus.

Emmelkamp, P. M. G., Kuipers, A. C. M., & Eggeraat, J. B. (1978). Cognitive modification versus prolonged exposure in vivo: A comparison with agoraphobics as subjects. *Behavior Research and Therapy, 16*, 33–41.

*Engels, G. I., Garnefski, N., & Diekstra, R. F. W. (1993). Efficacy of rational-emotive therapy: A quantitative analysis. *Journal of Consulting and Clinical Psychology, 61*, 1083–1090.

Epstein, N., Schlesinger, S. E., & Dryden, W. (Eds.). (1988). *Cognitive-behavioral therapy with families*. New York: Brunner/Mazel.

*Eschenroeder, C. (1979). Different therapeutic styles in rational-emotive therapy. *Rational Living, 14*(1), 3–7.

Freud, A. (1937). *The ego and the mechanisms of defense*. London: Hogarth.

Freud, S. (1965). *Standard edition of the complete psychological works of Sigmund Freud*. London: Hogarth.

Golden, W. L (1982). Rational-emotive hypnotherapy. *International Journal of Eclectic Psychotherapy, 1*(2), 47–56.

Golden, W. L., Dowd, E. T., & Friedberg, F. (1987). *Hypnotherapy: A modern approach*. New York: Pergamon.

Goldfried, M. R., & Davison, G. (1994). *Clinical behavior therapy* (2nd ed.). New York: Wiley.

*Grieger, R. M. (Ed.). (1986). *Rational-emotive couples therapy* (Special issue of *Journal of Rational-Emotive Therapy*). New York: Human Sciences Press.

*Grieger, R., & Boyd, J. (1980). *Rational-emotive therapy: A skills-based approach*. New York: Van Nostrand Reinhold.

*Grieger, R., & Grieger, I. (Eds.). (1982). *Cognition and emotional disturbance*. New York: Human Sciences Press.

*Grieger, R. M., & Woods, P. J. (1993). *The rational-emotive therapy companion*. Roanoke, VA: Scholars Press.

Guerney, B. G., Jr. (1977). *Relationship enhancement: Skill training programs for therapy, problem-prevention and enrichment*. San Francisco: Jossey Bass.

*Haaga, D. A., & Davison, G. C. (1989). Outcome studies of rational-emotive therapy. In M. E. Bernard & R. DiGiuseppe (Eds.), *Inside rational-emotive therapy*. (pp. 155–197). San Diego, CA: Academic Press.

*Hajzler, D., & Bernard, M. E. (1991). A review of rational-emotive outcome studies. *School Psychology Quarterly, 6*(1), 27–49.

*Harper, R. A. (1981). Limitations of marriage and family therapy. *Rational Living, 16*(2), 3–6.

Harris, G. F. (Ed.). (1977). *The group treatment of human problems: A social learning approach*. New York: Grune & Stratton.

*Hauck, P. A. (1973). *Overcoming depression*. Philadelphia: Westminster.

*Hauck, P. A. (1974). *Overcoming frustration and anger*. Philadelphia: Westminster.

*Hauck, P. A. (1977). *Marriage is a loving business*. Philadelphia: Westminster.

*Hauck, P. A. (1981). *Overcoming jealousy and possessiveness*. Philadelphia: Westminster.

Hauck, P. A. (1983a). *How to love and be loved*. London: Sheldon Press.

*Hauck, P. A. (1983b). Working with parents. In A. Ellis & M. E. Bernard (Eds.), *Rational-emotive approaches to the problems of childhood* (pp. 333–365). New York: Plenum.

*Hauck, P. A. (1984). *The three faces of love*. Philadelphia: Westminster.

Hauck, P. (1991). *Hold your head up high*. London: Sheldon Press.

Heidegger, M. (1949). *Existence and being*. Chicago: Henry Regnery.

Heiman, J. R., & LoPiccolo, J. (1988). *Becoming orgasmic* (rev. ed.). New York: Prentice-Hall.

Hertzberg, A. (1945). *Active psychotherapy*. New York: Grune & Stratton.

Hollon, S. D., & Beck, A. T. (1994). Cognitive and cognitive-behavioral therapies. In A. E. Bergin & S. L. Garfield (Eds.), *Handbook of psychotherapy and behavior change* (pp. 428–466). New York: Wiley.

Horney, K. (1950). *Neurosis and human growth*. New York: Norton.

*Huber, C. H., & Baruth, L. G. (1989). *Rational-emotive and systems family therapy*. New York: Springer Publishing Co.

Jacobson, E. (1938). *You must relax*. New York: McGraw-Hill.

Jacobson, N. S. (1992). Behavioral couple therapy: A new beginning. *Behavior Therapy, 23*, 491–506.

Jakubowski-Spector, P. (1973). Facilitating the growth of women through assertive training. *Counseling Psychologist, 4*(1), 75–86.

Janis, I. L. (1983). *Short-term counseling.* New Haven, CT: Yale University Press.

Jones, M. C. (1924). A laboratory study of fear: The case of Peter. *Journal of Genetic Psychology, 31,* 308–315.

Kaplan, H. S. (1974). *The new sex therapy.* New York: Brunner/Mazel.

Kelly, G. (1955). *The psychology of personal constructs* (2 vols.). New York: Norton.

Kendall, P. & Hollon, S. (Eds.). (1980). *Assessment strategies for cognitive-behavioral interventions.* New York: Academic Press.

*Knaus, W. J. (1974). *Rational-emotive education.* New York: Institute for Rational–Emotive Therapy.

Korzybski, A. (1933). *Science and sanity.* San Francisco: International Society of General Semantics.

*Lange, A. J. (1979). Cognitive-behavioral group therapy and assertion training. In D. Upper & S. M. Ross (Eds.), *Behavioral group therapy.* Champaign, IL: Research Press.

*Lange, A,. & Jakubowski, P. (1976). *Responsible assertive behavior.* Champaign, IL: Research Press.

Lazarus, A. A. (1984). *In the mind's eye.* New York: Guilford.

Lazarus, A. A. (1985). *Marital myths.* San Luis Obispo, CA: Impact.

Lazarus, A. A. (1989). *The practice of multimodal therapy.* Baltimore: Johns Hopkins.

Lazarus, R. S,. & Folkman, S. (1984). *Stress, appraisal, and coping.* New York: Springer Publishing Co.

Lederer, W. J., & Jackson, D. D. (1968). *The mirages of marriage.* New York: Norton.

Leiblum, S. R., & Rosen, R. C. (1989). *Principles and practice of sex therapy* (2nd ed.). New York: Guilford.

Levant, R. (1978). Family therapy: A client-centered perspective. *Journal of Marriage and Family Counseling, 4*(2), 35–42.

LoPiccolo, J., Stewart, R., & Watkins, B. (1972). Treatment of erectile failure and ejaculatory incompetence with homosexual etiology. *Behavior Therapy, 3,* 1–4.

*Lyons, L. C., & Woods, P. J. (1991). The efficacy of rational-emotive therapy: A quantitative review of the outcome research. *Clinical Psychology Review, 11,* 357–369.

Macaskill, N. D., & Macaskill, A. (1983). Preparing patients for psychotherapy. *British Journal of Clinical and Social Psychiatry, 2,* 80–84.

Mackay, D. (1984). Behavioural psychotherapy. In W. Dryden (Ed.), *Individual therapy in Britain* (pp. 264–294). London: Harper & Row.

Mackay, D. (1985). Marital therapy: The behavioral approach. In W. Dryden (Ed.), *Marital therapy in Britain: Vol. 1. Context and therapeutic approaches* (pp. 222–248). London: Harper & Row.

Mahoney, M. J. (1991). *Human change processes.* New York: Basic Books.

Margolin, G., & Weiss, R. I. (1978). Comparative evaluation of therapeutic components associated with behavioral marital treatments. *Journal of Consulting and Clinical Psychology, 46,* 1476–1486.

Masters, W., & Johnson, V. A. (1970). *Human sexual inadequacy.* Boston: Little, Brown.

Masters, W. H., Johnson, V. E., & Kolodny, R. C. (1982). *Human sexuality.* Boston: Houghton Mifflin.

Maultsby, M. C., Jr. (1971). Rational emotive imagery. *Rational Living, 6*(1), 24–27.

*Maultsby, M. C., Jr. (1984). *Rational behavior therapy.* Englewood Cliffs, NJ: Prentice-Hall.

*McClellan, T. A., & Stieper, D. R. (1973). A structured approach to group marriage counseling. *Rational Living, 8*(2), 12–18.

*McGovern, T. E., & Silverman, M. S. (1984). A review of outcome studies of rational emotive therapy from 1977 to 1982. *Journal of Rational-Emotive Therapy, 2*(1), 7–18.

Meichenbaum, D. (1992). Evolution of cognitive behavior therapy: Origins, tenets, and clinical examples. In J. K. Zeig (Ed.), *The evolution of psychotherapy: The second conference.* (pp. 114–128). New York: Brunner/Mazel.

Meichenbaum, D, Gilmore, J., & Fedoravicius, A. (1971). Group insight versus group desensitization in treating speech anxiety. *Journal of Consulting and Clinical Psychology, 36,* 410–421.

*Miller, R. C., & Berman, J. S. (1983). The efficacy of cognitive behavior therapies: A quantitative review of the research evidence. *Psychological Bulletin, 94,* 39–53.

*Miller, T. (1983). *The unfair advantage.* Manlius, NY: Author.

*Mills, D. (1993). *Overcoming self-esteem.* New York: Institute for Rational-Emotive Therapy.

*Moore, R. H. (1983). Inference as "A" in RET. *British Journal of Cognitive Psychotherapy, 1*(2), 17–23.

Norcross, J. C., & Prochaska, J. O. (1982). A national survey of clinical psychologists: Characteristics and activities. *Clinical Psychologist, 35,* 1–8.

Otto, H. (1968). *Group methods designed to actualize human potential.* Chicago: Achievement Motivation Systems.

Perls, F. (1969). *Gestalt therapy verbatim.* Lafayette, CA: Real People Press.

*Phadke, K. M. (1982). Some innovations in RET theory and practice. *Rational Living, 17*(2), 25–30.

Popper, K. R. (1959). *The logic of scientific discovery.* New York: Harper & Row.

Popper, K. R. (1963). *Conjectures and refutations.* New York: Harper & Row.

*Powell, J. (1976). *Fully human, fully alive.* Niles, IL: Argus.

Prochaska, J. O., & Norcross, J. C. (1983). Contemporary psychotherapists: A national survey of characteristics, practices, orientations, and attitudes. *Psychotherapy: Theory, Research, & Practice, 20,* 161–173.

Raimy, V. (1975). *Misunderstandings of the self.* San Francisco: Jossey-Bass.

Ravid, R. (1969). Effect of group therapy on long term individual therapy. *Dissertation Abstracts International, 30,* 2427B.

*Reardon, J., & Tosi, D. (1977). The effects of rational stage directed imagery on self-concept and reduction of stress in adolescent delinquent males. *Journal of Clinical Psychology, 33,* 1084–1092.

*Reardon, J., Tosi, D., & Gwynne, P. (1977). The treatment of depression through rational stage directed hypnotherapy (RSDH): A case study. *Psychotherapy, 14,* 95–103.

Reich, W. (1942). *The function of the orgasm.* New York: Orgone Institute.

Rogers, C. R. (1961). *On becoming a person.* Boston: Houghton-Mifflin.

Rose, S. D. (1980). *Casebook in group therapy: A behavioral-cognitive approach.* Englewood Cliffs, NJ: Prentice-Hall.

Russell, B. (1950). *The conquest of happiness.* New York: New American Library.

Russell, B. (1965). *The basic writings of Bertrand Russell.* New York: Simon & Schuster.

Russianoff, P. (1981). *Why do I think I am nothing without a man?* New York: Bantam.

*Ruth, W. J. (1992). Irrational thinking in humans: An evolutionary proposal for Ellis' genetic postulate. *Journal of Rational-Emotive and Cognitive-Behavior Therapy, 10,* 3–20.

Sager, C. J. (1976). *Marriage contracts and marital therapy.* New York: Brunner/Mazel.

Salter, A. (1949). *Conditioned reflex therapy.* New York: Creative Age.

Saxon, W. (1980). *The use of rational therapy with emotionally upset parents of handicapped children.* Unpublished manuscript, University of Southern Mississippi.

Schutz, W. (1967). *Joy.* New York: Grove.

Shahan, L. (1981). *Living alone and liking it.* New York: Warner.

*Shostrom, E., Ellis, A., & Greenwald, H. (Speakers). (1976). *Three approaches to group therapy* (Film). Corona Del Mar, CA: Psychological and Educational Films.

*Sichel, J., & Ellis, A. (1984). *RET Self-Help Form.* New York: Institute for Rational-Emotive Therapy.

*Silverman, M. S., McCarthy, M., & McGovern, T. (1992). A review of outcome studies of rational-emotive therapy from 1982–1989. *Journal of Rational-Emotive and Cognitive-Behavior Therapy, 10*(3), 111–186.

*Stanton, H. (1977). The utilization of suggestions derived from rational-emotive therapy. *International Journal of Clinical and Experimental Hypnosis, 25,* 18–26.

*Stanton, H. E. (1989). Hypnosis and rational-emotive therapy: A de-stressing combination. *International Journal of Clinical and Experimental Hypnosis, 37,* 95–99.

Stuart, R. B. (1980). *Helping couples change: A social learning approach to marital therapy.* New York: Guilford.

Tillich, P. (1977). *The courage to be.* New York: Fountain.

*Tosi, D., & Marzella, J. N. (1977). The treatment of guilt through rational stage directed therapy. In J. L. Wolfe & E. Brand (Eds.), *Twenty years of rational therapy* (pp. 234–240). New York: Institute for Rational-Emotive Therapy.

*Tosi, D. J., & Murphy, M. A. (1995). *The effect of cognitive experiential therapy on selected psychobiological and behavioral disorders.* Columbus, OH: Authors.

*Tosi, D,. & Reardon, J. P. (1976). The treatment of guilt through rational stage directed therapy. *Rational Living, 11*(1), 8–11.

Tsoi-Hoshmund, L. (1976). Marital therapy: An integrative behavioral model. *Journal of Marriage and Family Counseling, 2,* 179–192.

Upper, D., & Ross, S. (Eds.). (1979). *Behavioral group therapy, 1979.* Champaign, IL: Research Press.

Upper, D., & Ross, S. (Eds.). (1980). *Behavioral group therapy.* Champaign, IL: Research Press.

Wachtel, P. L. (1994). From eclecticism to synthesis: Toward a more seamless psychotherapeutic integration. *Journal of Psychotherapeutic Integration, 1,* 43–54.

*Walen, S., DiGiuseppe, R., & Dryden, W. (1992). *A practitioner's guide to rational-emotive therapy* (2nd ed.). New York: Oxford University Press.

*Walen, S. R., DiGiuseppe, R., & Wessler, R. L. (1980). *A practitioner's guide to rational-emotive therapy.* New York: Oxford.

*Warren, R., Deffenbacher, J., & Brading, P. (1976). Rational-emotive therapy and the reduction of test anxiety in elementary school students. *Rational Living, 11*(2), 28–29.

Watson, J. B., & Rayner, R. (1920). Conditioned emotional reactions. *Journal of Experimental Psychology, 3,* 1–14.

*Wessler, R. A., & Wessler, R. L. (1980). *The principles and practice of rational-emotive therapy.* San Francisco, CA: Jossey-Bass.

Wessler, R. L. (1984). Alternative conceptions of rational-emotive therapy: Toward a philosophically neutral psychotherapy. In M. A. Reda & M. J. Mahoney (Eds.), *Cognitive psychotherapies: Recent developments in theory, research and practice* (pp. 65–79). Cambridge, MA: Ballinger.

*Wessler, R. L., & Ellis, A. (1980). Supervision in rational-emotive therapy. In A. K. Hess (Ed.), *Psychotherapy supervision* (pp. 181–191). New York: Wiley.

*Wolfe, J. L. (Speaker). (1980). *Woman—assert yourself* (Cassette recording). New York: Institute for Rational-Emotive Therapy.

*Wolfe, J. L. (1992). *What to do when he has a headache.* New York: Hyperion.

*Wolfe, J. L., & Naimark, H. (1991). Psychological messages and social context: Strategies for increasing RET's effectiveness with women. In M. Bernard (Ed.), *Using rational-emotive therapy effectively.* New York: Plenum.

Wolpe, J. (1990). *The practice of behavior therapy* (4th ed.). Needham Heights, MA: Allyn and Bacon.

*Woods, P. J., & Ellis, A. (1996). Supervision in rational emotive behavior therapy. In C. E. Watkins Jr. (Ed.), *Handbook of psychotherapy supervision*. New York: Wiley.

Yankura, J., & Dryden, W. (1990). *Doing RET: Albert Ellis in action*. New York: Springer Publishing Co.

*Yankura, J., & Dryden, W. (1994). *Albert Ellis*. Thousand Oaks, CA: Sage.

*Young, H. S. (1974). *A rational counseling primer*. New York: Institute for Rational-Emotive Therapy.

*Young, H. S. (1975). Rational thinkers and robots. *Rational Living, 10*(2), 29–31.

*Young, H. S. (1984). The work of Howard S. Young [special issue]. *British Journal of Cognitive Psychotherapy, 2*(2), 1–101.

Zilbergeld, B. (1992). *The new male sexuality*. New York: Bantam.

Index